ISLAND STRIPERS

ISLAND STRIPERS

A Fisherman's Guide to Block Island

Capt. AL ANDERSON

Copyright © 2012 by Capt. AL ANDERSON.

Indexed by Ryan Cortes

Front cover artwork by Paul Osimo

Library of Congress Control Number:		2012912143
ISBN:	Hardcover	978-1-4771-3886-1
	Softcover	978-1-4771-3885-4
	Ebook	978-1-4771-3887-8

All rights reserved. No part of this book may be reproduced or transmitted in any form or by any means, electronic or mechanical, including photocopying, recording, or by any information storage and retrieval system, without permission in writing from the copyright owner.

This book was printed in the United States of America.

To order additional copies of this book, contact:
Xlibris Corporation
1-888-795-4274
www.Xlibris.com
Orders@Xlibris.com
100233

CONTENTS

Several Testimonials..7
Dedication 9
Acknowledgements 15
Introduction 17

I: THE ISLAND

Birth of an Island 23
The Manisseans..35
Explorers and Colonists 40
Recent Island History 46

II: THE STRIPER ECOSYSTEM

Striped Bass Biological Profile..59
Some Striper Problems..71
State of the Striper...84
The American Eel..91

III: TACKLING ISLAND STRIPERS

Wired for Action..107
Wire Line Demystified...118
To Fish a Rip..122
Spring Standard: Sand Eels and Umbrellas.........................131
Little Shooters 137
Dance a Jig..141

IV: "CONDITIONING" ISLAND BASS

Island Tides and Currents..149
Island Striper Weather Q&A 160
The Forage Factor..164

V: ISLAND STRIPER STRUCTURES

Dark Waters: Hank Allen on the Island Surf 173
BI by Fly: Chris Willi Speaks 182
North Rip Primer 194
North Rip Riot 200
North Rip after Dark 208
Parachuting the Ledge 221
After Dark at the SW Corner 226
Some Island Striper Haunts 236

VI: FISH TAGGING

Why Tag Fish? 245
Catch a Tagged Striper? 256
Some Tagging Agencies 268
What's Been Learned: Tale of the Tag 288

VII: SOME TRANSITIONS

2011: Year of the Record Breakers 313
Giving Something Back 325
Some Unexpected Tagging Results 340
A Metamorphosis 348
Glossary 369
Index 375
Selected References 383

SEVERAL TESTIMONIALS

"*Island Stripers* is loaded with intriguing scientific facts and angling insight that will help readers catch more striped bass from the Block and beyond".

Kevin Blinkoff, Editor,
On The Water

"Rich in Island and striper history, *Island Stripers* explains in intricate detail all you need to know about catching Block Island stripers, with valuable insights that apply wherever stripers swim".

Fred Golofaro, Senior Editor,
The Fisherman Magazine

"*Island Stripers*" is a must read for anyone who loves striped bass and wants to learn the secrets of fishing off Block Island.

William Sisson, Editor,
Soundings

"I never thought I would be so interested reading the biology and history of the striper and its forage, the eel! *Island Stripers* educates and entertains and should be read by anyone who has fished for these magnificent fish".

Dave Morel, Publisher
Salt Water Sportsman | Sport Fishing

"It took a "Jersey boy" to write the definitive book on Block Island stripers!"

Al Ristori
Saltwater editor, the Star-Ledger, Newark, NJ
Regional editor, Salt Water Sportsman
Conservation editor, The Fisherman

DEDICATION

He who has gone, so we but cherish his memory, abides with us, more potent, nay, more present than the living man.

—Antoine de Saint-Exupery

Robert Pond (1917-2009)

Robert A. Pond, noted outdoor writer, conservationist, and fishing tackle businessman, passed away on December 26, 2009, in Attleboro, Massachusetts, at age ninety-two. He was born and raised in New Rochelle, New York, and graduated from Syracuse University Forestry College, an education he credited for shaping his lifelong personal commitment to striped bass conservation. Pond started Stripers Unlimited, the first organization devoted to protecting striped bass, in 1965.

Bob was also known within East Coast saltwater fishing circles as "Mr. Striped Bass" for his selfless efforts to save the striped bass from potential extinction. The striped bass was—and remains—the East Coast's premier saltwater game fish species. In the face of declining numbers of striped bass in the late 1970s, Pond mobilized Stripers Unlimited membership to apply significant and highly organized pressure to the various state and federal agencies tasked with safeguarding our beloved striper stocks. The end result of this concerted conservation effort was the passage of the emergency Atlantic Striped Bass Act of 1984, a piece of legislation sponsored by the late Senator John Chaffee of Rhode Island.

Bob Pond
(image courtesy of Greg Metcalf)

Home from World War II after working as a munitions inspector for the British and United States governments, Bob Pond focused on striped bass fishing, especially in the hard-charging waters of the Cape Cod Canal. In 1945, he began developing his famous wooden Atom plug, testing it in the canal. Right after the war, wood was a scarce commodity—one of the reasons he would eventually turn to plastic injection molding to mass-produce his lure designs. Years back, he explained to me the difficulty in creating a watertight seal between the two molded halves of his hollow plugs—since any water intrusion would deaden the lure's uncannily lifelike swimming action. Several months later, he'd found a way to fuse plastic pellets to create his legendary Striper Swiper poppers and swimmers.

In his sales travels up and down the coast, he identified a desire among striper fishermen to fish other states and joined the effort to develop what became, and remains, the Massachusetts Striped Bass Association's (MSBA's) popular Tri-State Tournaments.

In the late 1960s, I fished alongside Bob through various Tri-State Tournaments, learning in the process a variety of new techniques he'd developed to tempt stripers. On a visit to southern Maine, I was introduced to successful spinner-and-worm trolling in the Saco River. While there, I greatly improved my technique of spin-casting Upperman jigs for school-size fish, tagging many in the process. I think of my experiences with him every time I receive an ALS tag recapture from Biddeford Pool, the Saco River proper, or other select areas of coastal Maine. Decades later, the Tri-State tradition continues as a multi-event honor-system catch-and-release tournament.

I had the good fortune to visit Bob at his South Attleboro plant numerous times during my graduate-school years at URI. I joined Stripers Unlimited in 1965; Pond urged me to begin tagging stripers for the American Littoral Society, which at that time was the only fish tagging program open to sport fishermen. Bob Pond—years ahead of his time—impressed upon me early in my career the magnitude of the striper's value to the angling community. These forty-six years later, I'm still tagging striped bass and feel compelled to provide tag-recapture data in hope that through doing, we can enhance our collective understanding of this finned resource we so love.

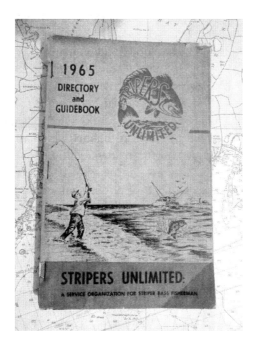

1965 SU Directory and Guidebook

On several occasions, 1966 through the early 1970s, Bob joined me in my nineteen-foot Aquasport skiff, casting his Atom 40 swimmers shoreward into Block Island's whitewater (during those years, the island hosted immense numbers of summertime stripers and blues just outside the surf line). Field-testing his day-glow orange prototypes revealed these hot-colored plugs were veritable bluefish magnets. (These brighter-finish offerings were subsequently marketed primarily as bluefish plugs.)

At one point, while I was pursuing my doctorate in URI's Zoology Department, Bob provided me with several scales removed from an eighty-pound Chesapeake Bay striped bass an SU member had purchased from New York's Fulton Fish market and asked that I attempt to age the massive fish. Using a microscope, I identified thirty-two distinct growth rings (annuli)—similar to the growth rings on a cut tree trunk—and what I believed were two to three indistinct rings. Evidence suggested this female striped bass was approximately thirty-four years old. There are, for what it's worth, records of striped bass in excess of one hundred pounds—those estimated forty-year-old specimens caught in Massachusetts trap nets around the turn of the (nineteenth to twentieth) century.

In the early seventies, using income from Atom, Pond began a series of research trips to Maryland's striped bass spawning rivers, inviting fisheries scientists and state hatchery personnel to aid him in his research. It was on these trips that he began to see serious deformities in spawning population stripers and put out a call for federal funds to further study the problem. Pond's tireless advocacy on behalf of the striped bass resulted in passage of the Emergency Striped Bass Study of 1979 (a subset of the 1965 Anadromous Fish Conservation Act) that allocated $4.7 million to study an array of problem signs within Chesapeake striper populations over a three-year period. Pond was instrumental in the passage of the Atlantic Striped Bass Act of 1984, the legislation that created the Moratorium; and, by extension, Bob Pond was a major figure in the eventual resurgence of the Chesapeake Bay—origin striper stock during the 1990s. At Pond's side through all these efforts was his dear friend—later, wife—Avis Boyd. Tragically, on December 29, 2009—just three days after Bob's death—Avis passed away.

Bob and Avis, MD Striper Hatchery

To this day, I credit Bob Pond with sparking—and supporting—my own career-long commitment to striped bass research, the bulk of it through forty-plus years of intensive tagging efforts. This book is dedicated to the legacy of Mr. Pond's visionary ideals, his genuine and contagious commitment to sound science and sound striped bass conservation.

ACKNOWLEDGEMENTS

Were it not for the nearly half-century of help by friends and clients focused on catching and tagging stripers, along with my 40 plus years of successful chartering the Island's waters, coupled to my interest in fisheries biology and concern for the future of striped bass, this effort would not have been possible.

Second, there were many individuals along the way who assisted my efforts, both with the literature and fieldwork, as well as catching those fish destined to be marked for science. Suffice it to say your name is in the book, as a way of saying thank you for your help, and includes: Maria Casas, URI GSO, William Poly, CalAcademy, Ted Durbin, URI GSO, Zach Harvey, Free Lance Writer & Editor, Jeff Dement, ALS, Joyce Downey, URI GSO, Jay Waller, Sr., PAL, Chris & Jessica Willi, BI Fishworks, William H. Krueger, URI, Nick Bellantoni, UCONN, John Waldman, QC, Cathy Hadad & Sheila Godby, Capt. Segull, Brad Burns, SF, Linda Stehlik, NMFS, Hank & Nelma Allen, Robert Burger, PG, Vincent Minchillo, Capt. Ron Murphy, Capt. Greg Metcalf, Capt. Paul Osimo, Tom Richardson, Boating Local.com, Tom Migdalski, Al Ristori, Don Smith, Steve Tombs, and last, but not least, my wife Daryl Anderson . . . .

Third, thanks to the support of several publications, with permission to use portions of my authored articles, I will forever be grateful.

Last, but not least, thanks to all the striped bass that helped make this effort possible. May they ever reign as "Champions of our Coastal Game Fish."

INTRODUCTION

*Nature, when she adds difficulties,
engages brains.*

—Ralph Waldo Emerson

If you're an ardent, longtime striped bass fisherman like me, you've likely observed that more and more pieces of the striped bass puzzle have recently fallen into place. Lifelong questions are now being answered by information from not only scientific journals but also from my own personal endeavors as well. For example, when and where do the first early-season striped bass that arrive in New England waters, and in particular Block Island, come from? Are there summertime island resident stripers, and if so, when do they depart and why? Did island anglers have a particularly successful striper season, and if so, how did it compare with those two or three decades ago? Do striped bass have memory, and if so, what evidence is there for it? Why do so many early-season island stripers carry abundant fish lice?

Do statements by other striped bass book authors still hold true, now that our scientific knowledge has grown? Is it true that striped bass were once a freshwater fish but then evolved into a saltwater one? Does the act of spawning in freshwater support that contention? Do striped bass have closely related cousins that swim in other oceans of the world? If so, do they also spawn in freshwater?

What evidence do we have, if any, that striped bass evolved as a saltwater (marine) fish? Why do some do just fine today living in freshwater impoundments?

The folded and faulted rocks that once formed our eastern shores are so ancient their history is not fully deciphered, but many of us know them as "old-worn-down mountains," in contrast to the "rugged mountains" of the West. Did our mountains contribute to an abundance of freshwater estuaries in our mid-Atlantic area, and could this be where our stripers developed a change of spawning habitat for maturation purposes, more widely understood today?

The marks of the last wave of glacial ice are fresh and clear, scattershot across the island. But then what has occurred in the last twelve thousand years since the glacial ice retreated remains less clear. Did glaciers form Block Island, as well as other New England striper outposts both east and west, and if so, are these islands composed of similar elements?

Would you believe Block Island was initially formed geologically about twenty-two thousand years ago, a mere fraction of the geological time scale, but was considerably larger than it is today? What has caused it to change so much? Why are Block Island's tides and currents so different from those of the mainland?

Rod-and-reel fishing for striped bass at the island really didn't get started until the mid-1950s, but recent evidence confirms island natives were catching and consuming striped bass well over 3,500 years ago. By what means were they caught?

Unlike other coastal species, why and how are striped bass equipped to become nocturnal feeders? How do they locate a live eel in depths of sixty feet or more in the pitch-black darkness of night? How is it possible their "strike-zone" can increase up to tenfold after darkness?

Why have a number of record-breaking stripers recently come from Block Island waters? Is this unusual, or have other New England areas been historically rich in large size fish as well? If changes have occurred, what were the causes?

Why are there such an abundance of "rips" between Montauk Point, New York and Block Island? Why do rips attract feeding fish like striped bass, particularly at night? Why have live eels become expensive bait for stripers? Is there an evolutionary connection between striped bass and the depleted menhaden stocks? Who or what has caused their decline? What—if anything—is being done to address this issue?

Why have there been such wild swings in the abundance of this regions most popular game fish? Haven't government agencies been charged with control of this and other valuable and popular marine resources? What reasons, if any, caused these changes?

Although I arguably had the best nighttime charter fishing enterprises at Block Island in the 1970s and eighties, I still continue my fishing there today. Back then I had only few answers to most of these intriguing questions, but I feel my long-term experience has allowed me to continue giving something back. Who was responsible for getting my striper tagging started? How has it progressed since then? What's been learned from it?

All these years later, I can—I hope—answer these questions and many more with some confidence, thanks to evidence both recent and previously ignored. Added to the evidence accumulated by the American Littoral Societies tagging program, more pieces to the striper behavior puzzle are coming together. At the same time, additional questions are percolating to the surface—their answers perhaps the work of future authors with future research in hand. For me, it's been a long-term, exciting, fun-filled, and satisfying adventure. As you march through the pages ahead, I'm confident you'll come out the other side with even more questions than answers. Such is the nature of a life in pursuit of our striper.

I
THE ISLAND

BIRTH OF AN ISLAND

*If we could telescope into a single year,
the time since our planet was formed,
the recorded history of man would comprise
only the final seconds of the final day.*

—Man and History, Hammond, 1971

Approaching Block Island from Point Judith, on your way to tangle with a few stripers, either from a boat or from the beach, the first of it you'll see is a majestic headland called—appropriately enough—Clay Head. The most prominent point on the island's north end, these bluffs were used by island fishermen years ago—myself included—to line up ranges for favored fishing spots. Composed of glacial deposits, they range in age from hundreds of thousands to over millions of years old. At close range, these light-colored exposed cliffs of sand, gravel, and clay take on the appearance of a slice of marble cake, with swirls of darker-colored elements coursing through the lighter colored clay. What you see are unstable sedimentary deposits delivered from the nearby mainland and elsewhere. They were brought to the surface long ago by the terminus of a once-mile-high glacier and are presently being exposed by both storms and accompanying surf action they create. A recent U.S. Geological Survey report named Clay Head, Block Island, the fastest-eroding New England shoreline, thanks to its inherently unstable composition. Soon after Hurricane Bob (1991), one could see the scars from wave action that rose over thirty-five feet above sea level, gouging considerable material away.

Clay Head; wave scars

The most recent glacial period lasted about thirty thousand years, ending about twenty-two thousand years ago. As that receded, it deposited materials that today make up Cape Cod, Martha's Vineyard, the Elizabeth Islands, Block Island, and Long Island.

If, by some magical force, you could stand on what is now called Beacon Hill about twenty thousand years ago, you would be deep in a coniferous/deciduous forest; immediately to your north would be a mile-high, receding glacier. The edge of the Atlantic Ocean would be about sixty-five miles south of your position; to the west would be a river whose estuarine zone, come springtime, undoubtedly hosted spawning striped bass. That river coursed through Block Channel and later became known as the Connecticut River. Fast forwarding, the island then was simply two large hills and did not connect until about six thousand years ago. As sea levels began rising prior to that time, the proglacial freshwater lake between the mainland and those two hills was replaced by rising seawater washing into it. Over time, those two hills connected and Block Island, as we know it today, took shape.

Early Formation

Allow me to take you on a magic carpet ride back into time, starting with the earth's formation over 4.5 billion years ago. By four million years ago, the earth had cooled enough that the outer surface hardened into a crust, and oceans began to form. The crust began separating into two types: oceanic crust and continental crust. Continental crust is lighter than oceanic crust and, because of gravity, stands up higher on the earth's surface than its oceanic counterpart. The young blocks of continental crust, which included volcanic islands that formed over rifts, floated around on the earth's surface like bubbles on top of a mug of hot chocolate, displacing each other and coalescing into larger, more complex masses.

During Paleozoic times, from about 550 to 250 million years ago, several major landmasses formed, incorporating much of the earth's crust. By 270 million years ago, the planet's major landmasses merged, forming the supercontinent Pangaea.

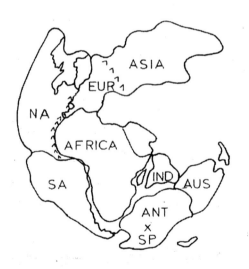

The supercontinent, PANGAEA, at the end of the Paleozoic, with near modern continental outlines for location (Sirkin, 1994).

Supercontinent PANGAEA

Compression of both continental and oceanic crust during this period formed the Appalachian Mountains, which, research suggests, reached elevations on par with the modern Himalayans.

"At the end of the Paleozoic times, Pangaea stood firm with the Appalachian Mountains as its backbone. Southern New England, including the present position of Block Island, was buried under thousands of feet of crustal rock," explained noted geologist, Leslie Sirkin, in his 1994 book, *Block Island Geology: History, Processes and Field Excursions*. This landmass remained intact until Triassic times ended, about 200 million years ago, when it began to split apart. Sirkin continues: "The breaking of the earth's crust into large blocks, or plates, and movements of these plates, made possible by the softening of the rock beneath the continents, coupled with the circular convective flow of heat within the earth, are now believed responsible for both the collision of the continents and their eventual separation. Geologists refer to these processes collectively as Plate Tectonics."

Plate Tectonics

Gradually the Atlantic Ocean formed and filled the abyss left in the wake of separating continents, and North America rotated counterclockwise from an equatorial position to a higher latitude north-south orientation. Around the same time, South America, Antarctica, and Australia all broke away from Africa. Less than a hundred years ago, geologists had yet to explain how coal deposits in western Germany so closely matched coal found in the eastern United States. It was not until the 1960s—and the emergence of plate tectonics as a working geologic hypothesis—that such mysteries began to unravel.

As continental separation continued, the Atlantic spilled into the void, flooding lowlands; eroded sediments settled, layer-by-layer, upon this newly formed seabed. From the Jurassic period to the present, a wedge of coastal plain and continental-shelf sediments—thousands of feet thick—formed. Tertiary Period beds of sediment were not deposited in the Block Island area, as it was above sea level at the time. However, the island does have late Cretaceous sands and clays that contain various elements that formed in ancient wetlands on the oceanic margin of a Cretaceous delta. Similar to those on Martha's Vineyard, Cretaceous sediments at the island's Clay Head area and the southeast corner are nowhere near their original position. These sediments were "bulldozed" into place by mile-high glaciers.

SE Light Bluffs
(Image courtesy of Michael Milford)

Scenic Ocean
(Image courtesy of Zach Harvey)

Glaciers

It began, almost imperceptibly, about a million years ago. On a global scale, weather turned cooler and wetter—perhaps a drop of a few degrees in average year-round temperature, and moisture in cooler areas falling as snow, rather than rain; over time, these snow drifts held longer into springtime. Eventually, snow began to accumulate faster than it melted each year. For decades and centuries, it piled up, until, under its own growing weight, snow compacted into ice. The accumulating ice became so heavy it squeezed "down" and out due under its own weight, following a path of least resistance. For thousands of years the ice grew, moving away from its origin, covering at least all of New England, much of the Midwest and northern Great Plains. Scientists named it the Laurentide Ice Sheet. In time, the ice became so thick even mountaintops vanished.

In comparison, about 35.5 million years ago, long before the Wisconsin glacial period, a meteorite impact gouged out the northern portion of Chesapeake Bay. Formed much earlier (geologically speaking) than Block Island, the northwestern Calvert Cliffs area in what is now Maryland (famous for its fossilized shark's teeth) contains sediment deposits from receding waters millions of years ago.

GEOLOGIC TIME SCALE (0 to 4.6 billion years ago)

(my* = ages in million years) Sirkin, 1994

ERAS	PERIODS	AGE (my*)	EVENTS
Cenozoic	Quaternary	0 to 2	Cyclic glaciation
	Tertiary	2 to 65	Northern Hemisphere glaciation; Erosion of S.New England upland.
Mesozoic	Cretaceous	65-144	Continents move toward modern positions; Buildup of continental shelf.
	Jurassic	144-213	Pangaea begins to split apart 200my; Basins form.
	Triassic	213-248	
Paleozoic	Permian	248-286	Pangaea Supercontinent completed; Appalachian Mts completed.
	Pennsylvanian	286-320	Coal swamps form
	Mississippian	320-360	
	Devonian	360-408	Laurasia and Gondwana begin to merge.
	Silurian	408-438	
	Ordovician	438-505	Laurasian continents begin to merge.
	Cambrian	505-590	Avalonia joins N.A.
Proterozoic		590-2500	Protocontinents develop
Archean		2500-4600	Beginning of Planet Earth, 4600my

Geological Time Scale

As the Laurentide Ice Front crept down over the land, it swept away all moveable material—plants, trees, giant boulders, even forests—but never reached as far southward as Chesapeake Bay. While this was happening, sea levels fell—a result of prolonged precipitation (snow) being compressed into ice. Rivers emptying into what is now Chesapeake Bay ran another sixty miles to their terminus points with the Atlantic. (Canada's oldest ice, called the Barnes Ice Cap, around Baffin Island, is a twenty-thousand-year-old remnant of the Laurentide Ice Sheet.)

Meanwhile, back at Block Island, rocks gathered up by glacial ice were carried hundreds of miles southward, eventually discarded as "glacial erratics," far from the nearest outcrop of similar, matching rock. "Many boulders were carried only a few feet, some a few miles, dropped at random, some perched precipitously on one another," explains Leslie Sirkin. Another prominent New England geologist, Betty Thomson, offers insight into the ways receding glaciers shaped the Rhode Island coastline: "Sometimes boulders were strewn out in a train of broken fragments; such boulder-train fragments have been traced for miles from certain outcrops of characteristic rock. Some of the largest of them are found on the present day shore in Narragansett, RI." I, myself, have seen boulders, estimated by geology experts at seventy-five tons, balanced on the flat bedrock of Narragansett's mainland shoreline.

From the direction of grooves, gouges, and scratches in exposed bedrock, geologists have traced a generally southward movement toward Block Island. "Surfaces that had been polished smooth became streaked with grooves and scratches cut without reference to the grain of the bedrock by smaller rocks frozen into the underside of the moving ice," notes Thomson.

Glacial Moraines

Four times during the past three million years, great sheets of glacial ice came down and covered much of New England. Of these four distinct glacial periods, two were responsible for creating and modifying Block Island, as well as portions of the New Jersey Coast, Long Island, the Vineyard, Nantucket, and Cape Cod. It appears the intervals between glaciers were longer than the glacial periods; the fossil record shows that these protracted "thaws" provided enough time for vegetation to return as far north as southern Canada before the ice returned.

Early on, geologists recognized the superficial strata similarity of the islands from Long Island east to Nantucket. In a century-old *U.S. Geological Survey* paper (1896), Othniel Marsh writes: "That Block Island was once connected with Long Island is suggested by a glance at a map of the New

England coast, that the same great moraine created all is evident from facts well known." Anyone viewing a chart of southern New England waters will recognize Endeavor Shoals as a submerged shoal connecting Montauk Point and Block Island's Southwest Ledge. In an 1898 paper, Lloyd Eaton lays out the particulars of the island's formation: "Examination of Block Island itself proved to me that these glacial deposits were merely a superficial covering, while the main body of the Island was formed of much older beds, the exact age of which offers a most interesting problem." These sediments, he goes on to suggest, appear to be derived from freshwater clays that were deposited in the quiet waters of a (proglacial) basin separated from the Atlantic by a great barrier (hill) that has since been destroyed by erosion and subsidence. These are the rust-colored clays visible today at Clay Head or the south-side bluffs.

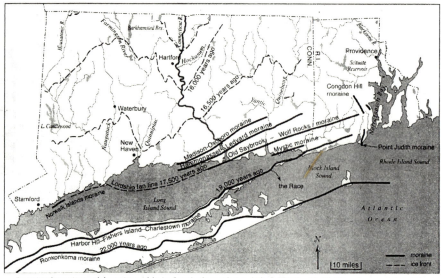

Recessional moraines and the position of the ice front in Connecticut and Rhode Island. —Modified from Stone and others, 2005
Skehan, 2008

CT, RI Recessional Moraines

For several decades, I fished the area called the "Sub Buoy" (now off-limits due to enforcement of the three-mile EEZ striped bass closure); researching the island's geology, I discovered that, following the most recent ice age, the deep water immediately west of Southwest Ledge was actually the submarine channel of the Connecticut River. That theory suggests there must have been a tremendous waterfall where the race lies today. Marsh lays out the evidence: "The character of the bottom over these shoals is hard, with occasional rocky localities. In fact, it is essentially the same as that of the 'bars' underlying Plum Gut and the channels east and west of Great Gull Island . . . [bathymetric clues] between Montauk and Block Island look right for such an origin . . . . Considering the effects of tidal scour during the ebb through the narrow passages [The Race] of the [Long Island] Sound, it is plain that the channel is of this kind."

Approximately fifteen thousand years ago, climate patterns moderated and the last ice sheet retreated northward—the ice "front," like our ocean tides, receding and advancing cyclically as the melt continued. The retreating ice sheet left behind massive deposits of material, or "recessional moraines," along their southern edges—much the way plowing during repeated storms builds massive, layered snowbanks beside a highway. The south shore of Rhode Island has several recessional moraines; the Charlestown Moraine, which courses WSW immediately north of Route One in portions of South Kingstown, Rhode Island, is most easily recognized. In an excellent 2008 book entitled *Roadside Geology of Connecticut and Rhode Island*, geologist James Skehan explains the Charlestown Moraine "is a continuation of the Harbor Hill-Fishers Island moraine, the recessional moraine on the North Shore of Long Island. It was deposited about 19,000 years ago during a cold period that briefly stopped recession of the glacier. Melt-water from the stationary ice flowed into the massive pro-glacial lake that later filled to become Block Island Sound."

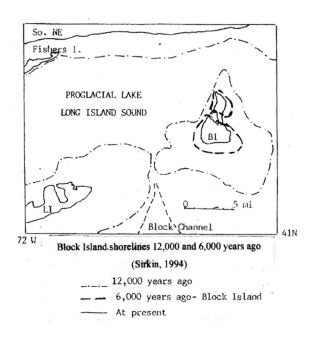

Block Island shorelines 12,000 and 6,000 years ago
(Sirkin, 1994)

_._._ 12,000 years ago
_ _ _ 6,000 years ago - Block Island
———— At present

Block Island Shorelines

The Modern Island

The island's ground is a mix of mineral scrapings (clay, sand, and gravel sediments) deposited in what was once an inland sea filled by glacial runoff and subsequently mounded up by the last glacier's southern "face"—the terminal moraine. Scattered over the surface are stones, rocks, and boulders delivered from as far away as what is now southern Massachusetts. The nearly 365 freshwater ponds on the island (one for every day of the year) identify the locations of arena—and barn-size chunks of glacial ice that have since melted. These craterlike depressions are called "kettles" or kettle ponds. Since the nonporous island clay traps and holds water, numerous ponds resulted.

Research of coastal sediments via seafloor core sampling tells us Block Island was approximately six times its present size twelve thousand years ago. Rapid and continuous erosion has dramatically reduced the island's visible mass, and scientists predict that, by 2300, it will have created two separate islands. For a while, early in its creation, it was two hills separated by sea water; shifting coastal sands eventually linked the two promontories.

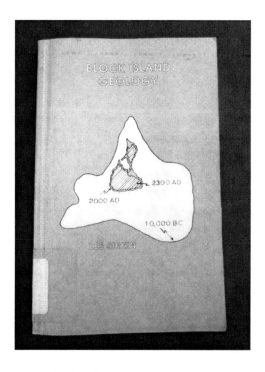

Block Island Geology, Sirkin

The Hudson

Melting water streamed southward from the Wisconsin Era glacier, carrying sediments and gouging out rivers and canyons that stretched to then-distant ocean shores. "During peak glacial advances the sea level was about four hundred feet lower than at present, and the (nearby) Hudson River flowed another 120 miles (southward) across the coastal plain, gouging out the Hudson Canyon of the present day sea floor," explains John Waldman. One can assume other major mid-Atlantic estuarine drainage systems carved similar marine canyons: Delaware Canyon and Hatteras Canyon, to the south, while northward, Block Canyon was about eighty miles distant from the sea.

"The Hudson did not follow the bed it occupies today," continues Waldman. "Gaps in the ridges of the Palisades and Watchung Mountains, carved well before the Ice Age, suggest that the Hudson crossed the Jersey Palisades near Sparkill, a little north of the Harbor, then flowed southwest across the Watchung Mountains near Paterson, NJ, and then to the ocean through the channel of the present Raritan River.

"During the height of the last ice age so much water was piled up upon the land in the form of ice that all the oceans of the earth were several hundred feet shallower." One must assume these geological processes affected river spawning areas of several existing populations of coastal striped bass, including the Hudson River stocks.

The progenitors of our beloved striper were around for many millions of years before Block Island took shape. The biological success of *Morone saxatilis* was undoubtedly tied to the fish's ability to make progressive changes (geographically) to take advantage of redesigned Hudson, Delaware, Chesapeake, and Albemarle Sound habitats, as melting glaciers altered estuarine spawning sites. Today's Chesapeake Bay is fed by fifteen river systems and viewed as the area-of-origin of today's striped bass resource.

I have been looking at the sea floor with my depth-sounders and fish-finders around the island for years. Its geology and modern-day geography, although far different than the mainland, makes a lot of sense but, more importantly, has offered action not only with striped bass but also with a variety of other species, including cod, pollack, and tuna.

*Reflecting on my professional island history, my experiences at the North Rip, unlike those of SW Ledge, were a result of their geological differences. Years ago, the preponderance of lobster gear made Ledge trolling and drifting difficult, possible only during tidal change, whereas steep hard-clay edged mussel beds favored holding different tide-long size and age group bass.

Early career focus favored large fish, which later gave way to conservation numbers marked for science following the Moratorium. Whichever side of the island fished, I've been fortunate to enjoy both, for reasons too numerous to mention.

THE MANISSEANS

*Treat the earth well:
it was not given to you by your parents,
it was loaned to you by your children.
We do not inherit the Earth from our Ancestors,
we borrow it from our Children.*

—Ancient Indian Proverb

There can be little doubt East Coast North American natives were among the first to catch and use striped bass for food, and among the many were the Mashantucket Pequots in Connecticut.

Over a decade ago, while researching my last book, *Over-Winter Striper Secrets*, I learned the primary reason for the location of the Mohegan Sun Casino was the Pequot tribal winter-season camp in Norwich, Connecticut. At the head of the Thames River, food—oysters, clams, scallops, sturgeon,

40,000 B.P.
Modern Humans, *Homo sapiens sapiens*, appear on Earth. (Neanderthal man is now given the designation *Homo sapiens*, while modern man is now classified as *Homo sapiens sapiens*.)

| 40,000 B.P. | 39,000 B.P. | 38,000 B.P. | 37,000 B.P. | 36,000 B.P. | 35,000 B.P. | 34,000 B.P. | 33,000 B.P. | 32,000 B.P. |

HISTORICAL TIME LINE
B.P. stands for "Before Present," and is given in radiocarbon years. By convention, "present" means A.D. 1950, denoting the development of radiocarbon dating at this time.

35,000 B.P.
Homo sapiens sapiens becomes dominant species on earth.

salmon, and striped bass (the latter seasonally and through the winters)—was abundant. Scarcity of upland game in deep winter forced the tribe(s) to depend on several abundant and readily harvested estuarine food species.

The hard, bony remains of sturgeon, salmon, and striped bass littered shell heaps at this tribe's winter camp in Norwich, Connecticut. Radiocarbon 14 dating has indicated deposition five hundred years before Christ.

Upon learning about the near three-thousand-year-old Block Island Year-Long Indian village and the archeological discovery of "middens," which were essentially kitchen garbage dumpsites, I suspected the striped bass would again appear—this time as a summertime food source. As it turned out, Block Island's waters and the striped bass they contained go just a bit further back than one might imagine. Further research unearthed accounts of numerous island expeditions.

Some of this evidence confirms that island natives, along with a number of other Algonquian-speaking mainland tribes, caught striped bass. It was the description of extensive shell heaps by one Professor Marsh, Yale University, in his 1840 paper "The Geology of Block Island," which sparked other early investigations.

Block Island's fame predates the arrivals of the first white men; in fact, many island legends were narrated to its earliest white settlers by original Indian inhabitants. The Manisseans told of long continued wars of conquest, waged for the sake of the island's highly prized fisheries. The Manisseans, who shared genetic roots with the warlike Narragansett tribe, had, when early whites arrived, occupied the island for so long that they themselves had no idea when their ancestors had arrived. Records of Manissean culture were scarce at best; careful exploration of island shell heaps began in 1896.

In an 1898 paper, "The Prehistoric Fauna of Block Island," Eaton states: "On some of the glacial hills near the shore, or around the Great (Salt) Pond, shell-heaps of considerable antiquity may be observed, but so far as I could ascertain none of them have been explored. One may be seen on the south side of the road recently cut through a low hill near the new steamboat landing on Great Pond. The deposits are several feet in thickness, indicating a long occupancy of the place by some of the early inhabitants of the Island. The short examination I was able to give this 'kitchen-midden' disclosed many marine shells, mainly species now living in the adjacent waters, the most abundant of which were of oysters, clams, and scallops. Mingled with these were a few bones of fishes, birds, and small mammals."

| 31,000 B.P. | 30,000 B.P. | 29,000 B.P. | 28,000 B.P. | 27,000 B.P. | 26,000 B.P. | 25,000 B.P. | 24,000 B.P. | 23,000 B.P. | 22,000 B.P. |

Eaton went on to examine three sizeable shell heaps during the winter of 1897. These include the Fort Island shell heap, the Mott shell heap, and the Cemetery shell heap, all of which lie on the shores of what we now call the Great Salt Pond.

From the Mott shell heap, the remains of the following animals were identified: mammals (deer, dog, beaver, otter, various seal species, and small whales); birds (hawks, owls, geese, ducks, grebes, and gulls); various reptiles (snapping, box, and painted turtles); fish in the form of striped bass, cod, tautog, sea bass, sharks, and sturgeon; and shellfish like oysters, scallops, clams, mussels, snails, and barnacles.

2,500-Year-Old Village

Kevin McBride, Rhode Island Sea Grant-sponsored archeologist, who led the Block Island excavation, said, "As far as we know, this is the oldest evidence we have for year-round villages in southern New England—and maybe for the whole Northeast" (Source: "Discovery at Block Island: 2,500-Year-Old Village Predates Agriculture," Carole Jaworski, 1990).

"Five hundred years before the birth of Jesus and 60 years before the Parthenon on the Acropolis at Athens was completed, ancestors of the Manissean Indians—a branch of Algonquian-speaking Indians . . . related to the Narragansetts—settled into permanent, year-round village life on Block Island . . ." (ibid). There is definitive evidence they were catching striped bass, as were a number of other Algonquian Indian tribes.

Human Ancestors

While modern humans (*Homo sapiens sapiens*) first appeared only some forty thousand years ago, it wasn't until thirty thousand years ago they began to penetrate the colder regions of the world. Scientists estimate the earliest arrivals in North America did not cross the Bering Strait land bridge until twenty-seven to twenty-eight thousand years ago.

12,000 B.P.
Human population increases to 3 million. Goats domesticated in Near East.

| 21,000 B.P. | 20,000 B.P. | 19,000 B.P. | 18,000 B.P. | 17,000 B.P. | 16,000 B.P. | 15,000 B.P. | 14,000 B.P. | 13,000 B.P. | 12,000 B.P. |

14,000 B.P.
Dog domesticated from Asian wolf.

Once this migration to North American began, spreading both south and east, a west-to-east movement seemed illogical, thanks to harsh climate and glacial ice sheets covering many inland areas. It wasn't until roughly fifteen thousand years ago—about the time that humans also reached the southern tip of coastal South America—that the retreat of the existing glacial ice sheet allowed access to the Northeast. "When this continental glacier began to melt," writes Carole Jaworski, "its southern edge stood on a line that ran through Long Island, Block Island, Martha's Vineyard, and Nantucket. It wasn't until then that the southern edge of New England was open for the reestablishment of plant and animal communities—and eventually man."

As sea levels rose with the melting of the glaciers, Block Island—then just two hilltops located off the Rhode Island mainland—became two small islands. Dunes, a *tombolo*, properly speaking, eventually connected them and a large estuary formed—an ideal site for human inhabitation (Jaworski, 1990).

It was not an accident that early people chose this site, suggests Connecticut state archeologist, Nicholas Bellantoni. "It was like a Garden-of-Eden, rich with resources," he says.

Gerald Abbott, a Providence physician and member of the Block Island Historical Society, approached the State Archeologist in 1985 for advice on how best to study the island's archeology. Working through the town of New Shoreham, he eventually applied for and received a grant to survey the island's archeological resources. Abbott offered to put up his summer home for the month of June, along with two Jeeps, for use by the archeological team.

Pay Dirt

The survey team found things right away, and they kept finding artifacts near Great Salt Pond. "They knew the Native Americans always located their villages on land that faced south, below the crest of a hill and out of the wind—unlike today, where we locate on the top of the crest for the view. That's one reason the site is still intact. It's not in a place Europeans and Americans would choose for a building site" (ibid).

10,000 B.P. Agriculture begins in Near East as seeds of wild grasses planted with digging sticks.

7500 B.P. Copper smelted by Persians; produces first metal that can be worked, but is too soft to hold an edge.

6000 B.P. World's population reaches 85 million.

3900 B.P. Stonehenge erected sometime in the next three centuries.

1955 B.P. Jesus born.

| 11,000 B.P. | 10,000 B.P. | 9000 B.P. | 8000 B.P. | 7000 B.P. | 6000 B.P. | 5000 B.P. | 4000 B.P. | 3000 B.P. | 2000 B.P. |

11,000 B.P. New Stone Age begins in Egypt and Mesopotamia.

8500 B.P. Wheel invented sometime in next two centuries by Sumerians in Tigris-Euphrates Basin.

7000 B.P. Maize (corn) and beans cultivated in Western Hemisphere.

4900 B.P. Great Pyramid of Cheops at Giza built.

2388 B.P. Parthenon on Acropolis at Athens completed.

A 1980s archeological investigation, led by Kevin McBride, examined shell mounds and campsites at Block Island, and eventually carbon-dated the site as a 2,500-year-old village. "This discovery not only pushes back the date for year-round settlements in southern New England by well over 1,000 years, it also provides evidence that permanent settlements were possible without agriculture, as the use of corn by native Americans didn't occur until the 14th century. The earliest known use of maize (corn) in the northeast did not occur until 1160 on Martha's Vineyard—nearly 1,500 years after people had settled into permanent villages on Block Island. Theirs was a marine resources economy, as food remains were determined to be 90% marine and 10% plant, whereas on the mainland plant utilization was 50% of the diet" (ibid).

Fish were caught using net sinkers—grooved stones that could take plant-fiber-woven nets to the bottom. Once the presence of fish was suspected, investigators believed it was quickly raised to trap its contents. Since deer were limited, seal skins were used for clothing. Porpoise and lobster remains were common as well. Native Indian waterway travel was not uncommon, as reported by minister Roger Williams (1603-1684), cofounder and early settler of the colony of Rhode Island and Providence Plantations. He told of the Narragansett Indians using canoes capable of carrying upward of forty warriors. "The native Americans were very well adapted to ocean movements between Islands, in both Rhode Island and Massachusetts, even in winter" (Ernst, 1932).

With SeaGrant funding, island researcher, Ruth Greenspan, a trained zoo-archaeologist specializing in fish bones, compiled a collection of identifiable fish remains including—yes, you guessed it—skeletal remains of *Morone saxatilis*. Greenspan's discovery forced the question of whether this was a year-round settlement. "The food discovered at the site—the combination of fish, land mammals, sea mammals and seed—indicated year-round use" (Jaworski, 1990).

EXPLORERS AND COLONISTS

The topography of this Island is peculiar; it resembles the sea running high before a Northeast gale, and suggests that the island may have been thrown in some convulsion of nature and has taken its form from waves which it penetrated.

—Sheffield, 1876

    The first people to inhabit Rhode Island probably arrived over ten thousand years ago. These people, the Paleo-Indians, settled in Rhode Island after migrating across the land bridge between Asia and North America. The Paleo-Indians were nomadic hunter-gatherers who lived in a brutal post-Ice Age environment. After a few thousand years, the climate of Rhode Island warmed, allowing expansion of native populations. Is it possible these early inhabitants had near-shore settlements that no longer exist? Could rising sea levels have obliterated any evidence of their existence?
    Over thousands of years before the arrival of European colonists, the Native Americans progressed through many different stages, including the Archaic and Woodland eras. These different eras, bracketed by time, and various technological and/or social achievements, witnessed a fundamental shift from a nomadic, hunter-gatherer lifestyle to a more stable, village-based agricultural existence. The Native Americans who greeted the first waves of European explorers were descendants of these various cultures.

Early Explorers of Rhode Island

Many different European nations have claimed the original discovery of Rhode Island. Some maintain that Irish sailors landed in New England during Medieval times, while others believe the Vikings were the first trans-Atlantic visitors to navigate the waters off what eventually became the Rhode Island Coast. Based on controversial carvings found on the Dighton Rock near the Taunton River, some historians have speculated that the Portuguese explorer Miguel Corte-Real was the first to reach New England.

It was two thousand years after the Block Island Indians (Manisseans) established their first year-round village in southern New England when the Italian navigator Giovanni da Verrazano (1485-1528) became the first *documented* explorer of North American waters and soil. Sailing north from Long Island Sound, in service of the French crown, he "discovered" Block Island in 1524. An entry in his logbook describes the particulars:

> We discovered an island triangular in form, distant ten leagues from the continent . . . full of hills, covered with trees, much populated judging by the continuous fires along all the surrounding shore which we saw made . . . This is the most beautiful people and the most civilized in customs that we have found in this navigation. They excel us in size: they are of bronze color, their face sharply cut, the hair long and black, upon which they bestow the greatest study in adorning it: the eyes black and alert, the bearing kind and gentle . . .

Verrazano is widely acknowledged as the first European since the Norse colonization of the Americas around AD 1000 to explore the Atlantic Coast of North America between the Carolinas and Newfoundland, including New York Harbor and Narragansett Bay. The bridge over the opening of New York harbor, a vessel of the Italian navy, along with the bridge connecting Jamestown and Newport in Rhode Island, are among his numerous eponymous honors. These accolades notwithstanding, it's doubtful that he ever set foot upon Block Island.

In 1523, eager to discover new trade routes, French merchants and financiers from Lyon and Rouen persuaded King Francis I to approach Verrazano and ask him to plan a voyage that would explore the waters between Florida and Terranova (Newfoundland). Like most European nations heading into the Colonial period, French traders were primarily interested in finding safe passage to the Pacific Ocean. Verrazano agreed, and within months, four ships set sail due west for the Great Banks region. A violent storm cost the voyagers two of these vessels; and the remaining two ships, *La Dauphine* and *La Normande*, sustained significant damage that forced them back to port in Brittany, where repairs were completed in the final weeks of 1523. They set sail once again, this time heading south toward calmer—if, thanks to hostile Spanish and Portuguese control, risky—waters before attempting the Atlantic crossing. After a stop in Madeira, complications forced *La Normande* back to homeport; while Verrazano's ship, *La Dauphine*, piloted by Antoine de Conflans, departed for the New World on January 17, 1524. Vessel and crew arrived at Cape Fear on or about March 1 and, after a short stay, reached modern North Carolina and the Pamlico Sound lagoon.

In a letter to Francis I, Verrazano wrote that he was convinced the latter was the beginning of the Pacific Ocean—and ready access, via the Atlantic, to China. This misguided report caused one of many errors in the North America cartography of the time. (The continent would not be fully—read: *accurately*—mapped for hundreds of years.)

Continuing their northward exploration, Verrazano and his crew came into contact with Native Americans living on the coast. It appears he completely failed to notice the entrances to the Chesapeake or Delaware Bays. In New York Bay, he encountered the Lenape Indians and observed what he guessed was a large lake—which was in fact the entrance to the Hudson River. He then sailed along Long Island's southern shores, where he noted an island and named it "Luisa" after Louise of Savoy, the Queen Mother of France, and the mother of Francis I. However, several maps of the era named the island "Claudia," in honor of Claude, the wife of Francis I. Verrazano described Luisa (Claudia) as "about the size of the Island of Rhodes." (In fact, they share similar shapes.) When the founders of Colony of Rhode Island and Providence Plantations surveyed the land, they mistakenly thought that Aquidneck Island was the place referred to by Verrazano.

Needless to say, that is where Rhode Island eventually got its name.

Prevented from landing by poor weather, Verrazano noted in his journal that the island seemed "much populated, judging by the continuous fires all along the surrounding shores" (Jaworski, 1990). Verrazano continued sailing up the coast and entered Narragansett Bay, landing in what is now Newport Harbor. Here, he met and stayed for two weeks with the Wampanoag Indians, who were friendly to his crew. He left the area in May 1524, following the coast up to modern Maine, Southeastern Nova Scotia, and Newfoundland, after which he returned to France in early July.

The Northwest Passage was not found near Rhode Island, and ninety years passed before the next European would explore the area. In 1614, the Virginia settler, John Smith, charted the New England Coast. He sailed past Luisa Island and renamed it after himself—"Smith's Isle."

Adrian Block and the Natives

The next to navigate Rhode Island waters were the Dutch, who eventually settled in present-day New York. The Dutchman, Adrian Block, was sent up the coast in search of a good trading ground, and stumbled upon Luisa/Smith's Isle, and decided to hang his name on it. And Block Island—in a manner of speaking—was born. He became the first European to set foot on the island. However, if he saw any Indians there in 1614, there is no record of it. Although the Dutch and English explored the area in 1614, settlement would not begin for another twenty years.

In 1634, the western Niantic defended their tribe by killing John Stone, a renegade Boston man known for stealing Pilgrim vessels, near the mouth of the Connecticut River. Despite the fact Stone had been actively trying to kidnap native women and children to sell as slaves in Virginia, the colonists became furious (partly due to earlier Indian atrocities against settlers on the mainland by a related tribe). The English demanded that the Pequot Indians (who spoke for the Western Niantic) surrender Stone's killers. This demand was dismissed by the tribe; an action that began the slide toward war. In the summer of 1637, the Western Niantic killed another Bostonite, the trader John Oldham, on a vessel near Block Island. Pequot and Mohegan intrusions in the early seventeenth century left the Niantic Tribe split into two divisions: the Western Niantic, who allied with the Pequot and Mohegan, and the Eastern Niantic, who allied with the Narragansett. "The Island belonged to the Narragansetts and its Indian name was Manisses" (Sheffield, 1876). Perhaps it was the eastern Niantics that merged with the Narragansett people who called Block Island "Manisses," which means "God's little island."

Without consulting the Connecticut colonists, Governor Henry Vane of Massachusetts, in August, sent a punitive expedition of ninety men under John Endicott to Block Island with instructions to kill every Indian warrior and capture the women and children, who would be valuable as slaves. Orders were to "massacre all of the Native men on the island." The expedition killed numerous Eastern Niantic Indians and burned their sixty wigwams in the village and all the tribe's cornfields, and shot every dog. But the Niantic fled into the woods, and the soldiers only managed to kill fourteen of them. Deciding this punishment was insufficient, Endicott and his men sailed north to Fort Saybrook in Connecticut, then attacked the Pequot village at the mouth of the Thames River. There demand was made for one thousand fathoms of wampum to pay for the murder of John Oldham, along with some Pequot children to be held as hostages to ensure peace. This incident was one of several that precipitated the Pequot War.

Following the slaughter of Indians and the destruction of their dwellings at Block Island, the Court of Massachusetts Bay Colony granted ownership of the island to four of its citizens in 1658. "In 1660, these four gentlemen sold their title to the Island to a company of sixteen men who took possession of it the following year" (Eaton, 1898). "It would appear that Indians often did not grasp the notion of ownership as defined by the English. To the Indians, the mere signing of a paper did not transfer exclusive right to a piece of uncultivated land. If the English owners failed to occupy the land and use it, the natives saw no reason why they should not continue their usual activities there. Even after the English had arrived on a piece of property and constructed houses on it, the Indians often clung to their old rights of fishing and hunting. In short, the natives of New England seemed to believe that, generally speaking, the forest belonged to him who was able to make use of it" (Leach, 1958).

In 1662, island tribal natives (Niantics, Narragansett, and Manisseans) numbered somewhere from 1,200 to 1,500. At that time, the Manissean population was believed to be in the range of three hundred to five hundred. But by 1774, nearly 115 years later, only fifty-one Manisseans remained—the rest having either died out or left the island. The last known full-blooded Manissean Isaac Church died unheralded at the age of one hundred in 1886.

At the time of European settlement, the combined population of the Narragansett and Niantics was estimated to be around seven thousand. Encroachment, disease, and warfare due to European settlement caused the population of Rhode Island's native population to drop to approximately two hundred by 1880.

Rhode Island Settlement

English from the Massachusetts Bay and Plymouth colonies made frequent forays into present-day Rhode Island for trading purposes during the 1620s, but it wasn't until 1635 that the first white person settled there. William Blackstone, an Anglican clergyman, built a home near present-day Lonsdale near a river that was later named for him. Blackstone was Rhode Island's first settler, but the first settlement did not develop around him, rather further south, at Providence. Roger Williams and his followers, who were seen as religious extremists to the Puritans of Massachusetts, settled Providence. They left the Massachusetts Bay Colony to find religious freedom in the wilderness of Rhode Island. Securing land grants from the Narragansett, easily facilitated by Williams's friendship with the tribe, these settlers went on to found the towns of Providence, Newport, Portsmouth, and Warwick.

Border disputes were common during this time; conflicts between Indian land grants and royal charters made acquiring land difficult. To secure their land and religious freedom, Rhode Island sent Roger Williams to England in 1643 for a parliamentary patent that united the four original towns into one colony and protected their freedom of worship. Twenty years later, Rhode Island acquired a royal charter from Charles II, who was more than happy to secure Rhode Island's freedom of worship, especially if it angered the Puritans.

English settlers from the mainland first arrived on Block Island in 1661, led by Captain John Underhill—when the island was part of the Massachusetts Bay Colony. Block Island officially became part of the colony of Rhode Island in 1672 and the island government adopted the name "New Shoreham" (named after Shoreham in the County of Sussex in England). A Dutch map of 1685 clearly shows Block Island, indicated as Adrian Block Island ("Adriaen Blocks Eylant").

RECENT ISLAND HISTORY

God helps those who help themselves.

—Unknown

Block Island and the Town of New Shoreham are unique, more distant from either the mainland or from other islands, than any other town along the 1,800-mile eastern coast of the United States.

Although isolated, the island is farther from Rhode Island's State Capital than any other community. In fact, it is the smallest town in the smallest state in the country, isolated from neighbors, one that lacked a safe harbor for two hundred years. As islands go, it's small scale, barely twelve square miles; but were you to check a travel brochure, one would need only to step out their door and be in a land of pleasure, with only minimal travel required.

There is also the human story, of shipwrecks, of lifesavers, of farmers, of seaweed gatherers, of hurricanes, of pirates, of post offices, of sea captains, to name a few, not to mention countless famous visitors.

Block Island is located in the Atlantic approximately twelve miles south of the coast of Rhode Island, sixteen miles east of Montauk Point on Long Island, and is separated from the Rhode Island mainland by Block Island Sound. The United States Census Bureau defines Block Island as Census Tract 415 of Washington County, Rhode Island. As of the 2010 census, the population of 1,010 lived on a land area of 9.7 square miles. The island is part of the outer lands region, a coastal archipelago made by the recessional and terminal moraine that resulted from the Wisconsonian Era Laurentide glacier retreat, about twenty-two thousand years ago.

The Nature Conservancy added Block Island to its list of "The Last Great Places." The list consists of twelve sites in the Western Hemisphere. Approximately 20 percent of the island is set aside for conservation. Notables such as Presidents Bill Clinton, Dwight D. Eisenhower, Franklin Delano Roosevelt, and Ulysses S. Grant visited Block Island.

New Shoreham

The only town on the island is New Shoreham. The island is a popular summer tourist destination and is known for its bicycling, hiking, sailing, fishing, and beaches. Two historic lighthouses, Southeast Light and North Light, still guide mariners around the at-times volatile SE Corner and the North Rip, respectively. Southeast Light has for generations of island and Point Judith fishermen been a source of life-giving hope during the last legs of countless northward steams from offshore grounds in volatile weather. Much of the northwest tip of the island is an undeveloped natural area and resting stop for birds along the Atlantic Flyway.

Every summer, the island hosts Block Island Race Week, a competitive, weeklong sailboat race. On odd years, the event is held by the Storm Trysail Club and on even years by the Block Island Race Week participant Clubs. Yachts compete in various classes, sailing courses in Block Island Sound and circumnavigating the island. While it's a big deal for island tourism, Race Week—right at the height of the June striper bite—is not a favorite among local striper fishermen.

Other popular events include the annual Fourth of July Parade and celebration. During these times, the island's population can triple over the normal summer vacation crowd.

Frederick J. Benson

In this context, it would be unjust to fail mention of one Frederick J. Benson, a native Block Islander for most of his ninety-three years, who presented much island history in his book, *Research, Reflections and Recollections of Block Island*. "Fred is like Block Island's 1867 granite North Light, a monument, a signal of stability," said Connie Larue, fifty-five, echoing the sentiments of many of the island's six hundred residents. "He is a genuine folk hero, a living legend."

A lifelong bachelor, Benson lived there since 1903, when at the age of eight, he was sent there from Boston as a foster child. Since then, he wrote two books, taught high school for fourteen years, and was a commercial fisherman and foreman of a salvage crew working island shipwrecks. He has also worked as a carpenter, cement layer and builder, ran a taxi service, owned and operated the Square Deal Garage from 1917 to 1951, and was the island's undertaker for ten years. He operated the Motor Vehicle Department in addition to his real estate business, was a member of the Volunteer Fire Department, and was vice president of the island's blood bank.

But his list of accomplishments and activities did not end there. He played baseball and coached the island's baseball team and was the island civil defense director for twelve years, police commissioner, first captain of the local rescue squad, president of the Chamber of Commerce five times, and Island Man of the Year.

Fred Benson and Senator William Lewis, 1962
Fred in his prime, posed with the Island's State Senator, William Lewis — their prowess as striped bass fishermen is amply demonstrated in this photo showing the result of one hour of surf casting on Charleston Beach. Fred had to replace the hooks in his plugs with heavier ones when the big fish started biting.

Fred Benson & striped bass

In 1829, the original North Lighthouse was built, but it was replaced in 1837 after it was washed out to sea, making it the second wooden lighthouse claimed by the ocean. In 1867, the third lighthouse that can be seen today was constructed. A few years later in 1873, construction began on Block Island's other lighthouse, Southeast Light. The location of the island's southeast light was initially surveyed by a young Virginia surveyor by the name of George Washington. His job was to determine rates of erosion. He did so for several coastal headlands, including the beacon at Montauk Point, New York, where the lighthouse stands today. Some years back, thanks to more than a century of intense erosion, a major feat of modern engineering successfully moved iconic Southeast Light a good distance north and away from the perilous edge of the steep bluffs.

Since Block Island has no natural harbors, breakwaters were first constructed to form Old Harbor in 1870. Block Island's other harbor, New Harbor, wouldn't be created until 1896, when a channel was dug to connect the Great Salt Pond to the open Sound on west side of the island.

By this time native, timber became rare, thanks to persistent wind and salt spray that reduced primary vegetation to scrub oak.

Deforestation forced locals to become dependent on peat for heat and cooking. It was described by many as a treeless island and remained so until recent times.

Tree-less Island

Trees were absent, but glacial erratics were everywhere, so common they offered the opportunity to create fences, more to demark property lines than anything else. Today these stonewalls collectively reach a distance of three hundred miles.

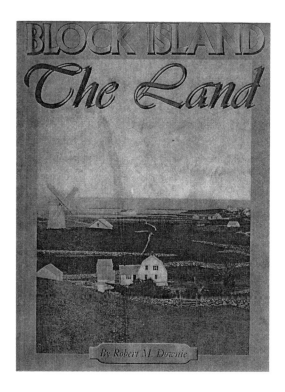

Block Island Stone Walls

The Block Island Boat

One of the most historically renowned American workboats, the Block Island double-ender, came to be on a ten-square-mile island off Rhode Island, northeast of Montauk Point and southwest of Point Judith. While there is no definite proof of the boat's origin and very little is known about when it began plying the waters of New England, a careful study of the lines of this burdensome double-ender and its two-masted unstayed rig suggests a Dutch lineage.

From ROARING BESSIE to SCRIMSHAW

Blk. Is. Double Ender

For a brief time in 1614, the island was named Smiths Isle, after the English adventurer and soldier John Smith; then when the Dutch explorer Adriaen Block landed there and mapped the area in 1614, he named the island for himself. English colonists finally settled in the island in 1661, and in 1672 it came under the jurisdiction of Rhode Island and was renamed New Shoreham. It was officially named Block Island in 1876.

Block Island settler Trustrum Dodge is the assumed founder of the fisheries on the island in 1661. While the details of the boats of Dodge's era are hazy, by the 1840s, the Block Island boat had evolved into a definite type and remained the same until about 1880. With a three-to-one length-to-beam ratio, the boats were built for utility: The smaller ones, at twenty-three feet, were used for daily fishing and transportation; the larger boats, at around forty feet, were the freighters. They hauled all sorts of things, including lumber, window sashes, the mail, and even oxen.

The Island Free Library, Block Island's only public library, was established in 1875. Block Island's school was built in 1933, replacing five one-roomed schools.

During World War II several artillery spotters were located on the island to direct fire from the heavy gun batteries of Fort Greene at Point Judith, which protected the entrance to Narragansett Bay. Lookout positions for the spotters were built to look like houses. The U.S. government offered to evacuate the island, as it could not be effectively defended from enemy invasion. However, the islanders chose to stay. Days before the war ended, the Battle of Point Judith took place seven miles to the northeast of the island.

The island's airport was opened in 1950 and remains open today as a general aviation airport. In 1972, the Block Island Conservancy was founded. The conservancy and other environmental organizations are responsible for protecting over 40 percent of the island from development. In 1974, Old Harbor Historic District was declared a National Register historic district. Discussions of Block Island's old buildings, native islanders, history, and ongoing efforts to conserve the land, together with a collection of eight hundred period photographs of the island spanning the 1870s to the 1980s, are found in four books: *Block Island—The Sea, Block Island—The Land,* and volumes 1 and 2 of *The Block Island History of Photography,* all by historian Robert M. Downie.

Climate

Block Island's weather is greatly influenced by the surrounding ocean and prevailing winds that generally blow offshore. The climate is oceanic, a rarity on an East Coast in the Northern Hemisphere. Because of its temperate climate, cool breezes, and the wide sweeping beaches, the island is often referred to as the "Bermuda of the North." Because the ocean remains cold during the spring and summer months, Block Island stays cooler than the mainland during this period. However, summers can still be hot on Block Island, although July and August average in the mid and upper 70°F, instead of low and mid-eighties that New York and New England experience. Block Island's record high temperature is 95°F (35°C). Block Island stays warmer than the mainland during the fall and winter months when the ocean remains relatively warmer than the mainland. Block Island's record low is —7°F (-22°C).

Beaches

Crescent Beach can be viewed from the Pt. Judith Ferry on the way to the island. It contains three smaller beaches: Fred Benson Town Beach (still popularly known as State Beach due to its former status as one), Scotch Beach, and Mansion Beach, all of which are located on Corn Neck Road. State Beach and Ballard's Beach are the only beaches on the island with on-duty lifeguards. State Beach has a pavilion with food and beach rentals. The so-called Baby Beach begins at the Surf Hotel, near the Beachhead Restaurant on Corn Neck Road. Scotch Beach is located just north of Fred Benson Town Beach and Mansion Beach is located north of Scotch Beach.

North of Mansion Beach are Clay Head and Pots and Kettles. Clay Head is a set of cliffs, which can be seen from the ferry out of Point Judith or New London. This area is rocky and contains iron-rich clay deposits and is a popular area for shell and rock hunting.

Cow Cove, Settler's Rock, and Sandy Point make up the northernmost point of Block Island. Here lies the North Lighthouse and the postcard sunsets. Settler's Rock is located at Cow Cove, where the settlers landed and swam to shore bringing with them the island's first cows, which they pushed off the boats and forced ashore. Attached to the rock is a plaque naming the original settlers of the island. This beach is not ideal for swimming on the ocean side, especially at the point, due to strong rip currents. Opposite the beach is Sachem Pond, a freshwater pond and good for swimming.

On the south side of the island, Black Rock Beach is widely regarded as the best beach for surfing on the island, due to a shoal that creates high surf. However, the beach tends to be very rocky and has a reputation for being a nude beach, despite laws against nudity on Rhode Island's beaches. It is located near the Mohegan Bluffs and Southeast Lighthouse.

Coast Guard Beach is situated between the Great Salt Pond and the ocean on the northwest side of the island. It's a popular beach for fishing and walking, but not particularly good for swimming due to the high numbers of transient boats traveling to and from the island.

Ballard's Beach is on the eastern side of the Block Island Ferry Dock and jetty. Set right in front of Ballard's Restaurant and Inn, popular with boaters and with the young crowd. There are cocktail waitresses on the sand and daily live music outside. There's also a busy volleyball court with daily games and tournaments. There are lifeguards on duty at Ballard's Beach.

Under the Light, Bluffs Beach is accessed by parking at the Mohegan Bluffs entrance, then by walking down the staircase. There are 141 steps to this rocky area, known for its spectacular view. At the foot of these steep, wooden stairs are big rocks leading to the beach.

Some Tourist Attractions

The Harborside Inn is a restaurant and hotel on the south side of Block Island. Southeast Lighthouse is located at the southeast corner of the island on the Mohegan Trail. The lighthouse was constructed in 1875 and remains to this day an active U.S. Coast Guard navigational aid. The lighthouse was moved in 1993, in danger of falling off the bluffs due to erosion. In addition to offering tours of the tower, the lighthouse has a museum that is open during the summer season

The Mohegan Bluffs are located a short distance to the west of Southeast Lighthouse. The bluffs are the site of a pre-colonial battle between the invading Mohegan and the native Niantic in which the Mohegan were driven off the edge of the tall cliffs to their deaths on the beach below. A long staircase of over one hundred stairs leads to the bottom of these clay cliffs and looks out over the Atlantic. On clear days, Montauk, New York, can be seen in the distance from the southern and western sides of the island.

Rodman's Hollow is a 230-acre glacial outwash basin, near the southern shore of the island. The hollow has several walking trails. Even though the hollow is well below sea level, it contains no saltwater, thanks to a clay barrier. Horseback rides through Rodman's Hollow are also offered.

North Lighthouse is located at Sandy Point on the northern tip of Block Island. The North Lighthouse warns boaters of a combination mussel bed/gravel bar extending from this end of the island. The surrounding dunes are part of the Block Island National Wildlife Refuge, home to many species, including the piping plover and American burying beetle. A short walk away from the North Lighthouse lies the tip of the island, with ocean on both sides of a thin, unstable strip of land.

The Block Island Historical Society Museum is located near the downtown area and contains a broad array of Block Island artifacts.

U-853 is a U-boat wreck seven miles (eleven kilometers) east of the island, lying in one hundred thirty feet (forty meters) of water. Recreational divers frequently visit the wreck, though at least three have died therein.

Block Island Bullet Points

* **1524:** Block Island discovered; Verrazano named the region he explored Francesca in honor of the French king.
* **1590:** A war party of forty Mohegan Indians were driven over the bank known as Mohegan Bluffs by Block Island Indians—the Manisseans.
* **1613:** Block and another Dutch fur trader start sailing back to Holland with a cargo of furs. Block's ship, the *Tiger*, catches fire and is destroyed at the mouth of the Hudson River. They built a new ship, the *Onrust* (the Restless).
* **1614:** Trial voyage of the *Onrust*. Block sails through the East River and Hell's Gate into Long Island Sound. Block is the first European to explore the Connecticut River, sailing sixty miles upriver. He then discovers Block Island, later named after him, and returns to Holland.

* **1636:** Island claimed in combat by Massachusetts soldiers, in retaliation for Indians killing trader named Oldham.
* **1637:** The Niantic (tribe) defended themselves at Block Island that summer.
* **1661:** Island settled by sixteen families from the English colony of Massachusetts. The island was forested at that time and had hundreds of fresh water ponds. They established a farming and fishing community.
* **1672:** Island government officially adopts the name "New Shoreham."
* **1687:** Margaret Guthry buried, now the oldest identifiable island gravestone.
* **1690-1704:** Invaded by privateers four times while England was at war with France.
* **1699:** Pirate Captain William Kidd visited Block Island shortly before he was accused of piracy and hanged in Boston. At Block Island Kidd was supplied by Mrs. Mercy (Sands) Raymond, daughter of the mariner James Sands. Story has it that, for her hospitality, Mrs. Raymond was bid to hold out her apron, into which Kidd threw gold and jewels until it was full. After her husband Joshua Raymond died, Mercy moved with her family to northern New London, Connecticut (later Montville), where she bought much land. The Raymond family was thus said to have been "enriched by the apron."
* **1714:** Tree cutting became restricted, later called a "Treeless" Island. Today there are few trees on Block Island.
* **1719:** Dogs owned by the Manisseans were no longer allowed, due to a town act.
* **1737:** Emigrant ship *Princess Augusta* wrecks, leaving Palatine (Germany) survivors and their dead.
* **1775-1783:** During American Revolution, the island was neutral, trading with both sides but stripped of its trees. Block Island returned to previous status following the war.
* **1812:** During the War of 1812 against the British, Block Island was briefly occupied by the British Navy under the command of Sir Thomas Hardy. British vessels included HMS *Dispatch*, HMS *Terror*, HMS *Nimrod*, HMS *Pactolus*, and HMS *Ramillies*. Hardy took the fleet to Block Island in search of food and to establish a strategic position at the mouth of the Long Island Sound. The British were enraged to discover that virtually all Block Island livestock and food stores had been transferred to Stonington, Connecticut in advance of their arrival. On August 9, 1814, Hardy and his fleet departed Block Island

for Stonington Harbor in part to lay claim to the Block Island food stores and livestock. Hardy's predawn raid on August 10 was repulsed with damage to his fleet in a battle that has since become known as the Battle of Stonington.

* **1832:** First island postmaster appointed; office in his bedroom.
* **1867:** The present-day North Lighthouse was built, the fourth Lighthouse at Sandy Point, prior three lost to fire.
* **1870:** Breakwater successfully built on east side, creating Old Harbor.
* **1875-1890s:** Many Victorian hotels and stores built at Old Harbor; now nationally historic.
* **1875:** Island Free Library founded and still operating.
* **1873:** Construction began on the brick Southeast Lighthouse; moved in 1993.
* **1895:** Great Salt Pond channel successfully dug, creating the New Harbor.
* **1907:** Steamer *Larchmont* sinks off Block Island; hundreds dead; islander heroes.
* **1917-1918:** In WWI, from a population of about one thousand islanders, sixty-three go off to war.
* **1929:** Pilot Amelia Earhart visited the island, staying at the Narragansett Inn. As a publicity stunt to further her fame, she dived in a hard hat suit off a U.S. Navy submarine in the Great Salt Pond.
* **1933:** Block Island School built, replacing five scattered, one-room schools.
* **1941-1945:** In WWII, from a population of about seven hundred islanders, ninety-five go off to war.
* **1942 and 1944:** Two U.S. Aircraft Carriers are named *Block Island*; the first sank seven German U-boats.
* **1950:** State airport opens, replacing informal grass fields used since 1920s.
* **1960:** Winter population plunges to 486, the lowest since the 1770s.
* **1972:** Block Island Conservancy founded; one-third of island now saved from development.
* **1974:** Old Harbor village declared a National Register Historic site.
* **1993:** The massive brick Southeast Lighthouse moved 245 feet from eroding bluffs.
* **2000:** Winter population surpasses one thousand for first time since the 1930s.

II

THE STRIPER ECOSYSTEM

STRIPED BASS BIOLOGICAL PROFILE

*By learning you will teach;
by teaching you will learn.*

—English Proverb

Note to the Reader: There are countless fairly good to excellent field guides that can provide a basic snapshot of *Morone saxatilis*, our beloved striper. And then there are the untold thousands of reams of paper devoted to that species—its reproductive biology, its evolution, its social history, and the endless subsections beneath the larger headings. It all begs the question, "Why do I need to read another scientific examination of the striped bass?" I'd argue that if you want to catch striped bass with any consistency, you'd better develop at least a basic understanding of your target's most basic instincts.

I attribute much of my own striper-catching success to a lifelong study of the fish—its evolutionary wiring, its behavioral patterns, its adaptability, and its endless connections to the greater ecosystems it occupies. As you try to improve your catch rate, you'll study the proven elements of a strategy: rip fishing, deep trolling, the timing of moons, tides and migrations, the striper diet (most of which topics are covered elsewhere in this book). But until you can connect these methods (and the big-name spots) with the striper's root motivations, you're ultimately doomed to a one-dimensional approach. It is with that idea in mind that I offer the following section.

Know Your Striper

The striped bass is a typical member of the Moronidae family in shape, having a streamlined, silvery body marked with longitudinal dark stripes running from behind the gills to the base of the tail. The maximum scientifically recorded size and weight was two hundred centimeters (6.6 feet) and 56.7 kilograms (125 pounds), for a female fish taken from a North Carolina net in 1891 (Setzler et al., 1980). The average adult weight is thirty to forty pounds, and stripers have been known to live for up to forty years or more. Individuals larger than fifty pounds are considered an absolute trophy fish and a possibly once-in-a-lifetime catch. The former all-tackle angling record fish, taken in New Jersey in 1982, weighed 78.5 pounds. That mark was broken in 2011 by a Connecticut-caught 81.88-pound behemoth.

Striped bass spawn in freshwater, and although they have successfully adapted to freshwater habitat, they naturally spend their adult lives in saltwater (i.e., it is anadromous). Four important bodies of water with breeding stocks of striped bass are Chesapeake Bay, Roanoke River/Albemarle Sound, Hudson River, and Delaware River. It is believed that many of the East Coast rivers and tributaries that emptied into the Atlantic had at one time breeding stock of striped bass.

Striped Bass Life Cycle

The following chart shows average lengths and weights of striped bass at selected ages. I used several sources (scientific data, my own records, and fellow angler records) of weight to length ratio data and combined them into a table. I then analyzed the data and came up with my best approximation of an accurate weight to length chart. My data suggest today's adult stripers, as compared with the late 1960s, weigh approximately two to three pounds less than weights used by Mansuetti, probably the result of diminished forage. All my striped bass were taken somewhere along the east coast in the northeast area, either in the ocean, Buzzards Bay to Long Island Sound, and associated rivers. Please do not rely upon Mansuetti's chart as an absolute but rather as a general guideline in your effort to estimate weight based on size measurements.

FISH TAGGING PROGRAM
AMERICAN LITTORAL SOCIETY
HIGHLANDS, N.J. 07732

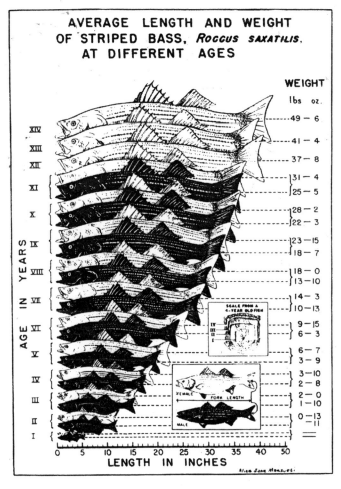

Fig. 3. Graphic summary of average lengths and weights of striped bass, or rock, at different ages.

Striped Bass Length and Weight

Females reach significantly greater sizes than do males; most stripers over thirty pounds are female. Thus, the term "bulls," originally coined to describe extremely large specimens, has been more accurately changed to "cows" in recent times. Males rarely live over ten years, while females can reach ages of nearly twenty years on occasion. The number of eggs produced by a female striped bass is directly related to the size of its body; a twelve-pound female may produce about 850,000 eggs, and a fifty-five-pound female about 4.2 million eggs. Along the Atlantic Coast, the spawning period rangers from mid-February in Florida (St. Johns River) to June and July in the Gulf of St. Lawrence, Canada (Bigelow and Schroeder, 2002).

Females mature no earlier than four years, and some not until six or eight. By contrast, most males reach sexual maturity at two or three years of age. The size of the females at sexual maturity has generally been used as a criterion for establishing minimum legal size limits along the East Coast.

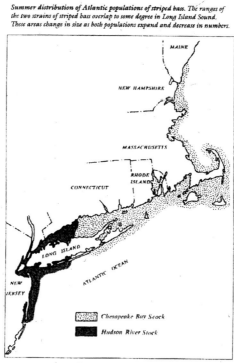

Karas, 2000

Striper Summertime Distribution
(Dated)

The migratory behaviors of coastal striped bass are more complex than those of most other anadramous fish, which spend most of their adult lives in the ocean but migrate up rivers and streams to spawn. Striped bass seasonal movements depend upon the age, sex, degree of maturity, and the river in which they were born. At one time, the Chesapeake Bay and its tributaries were responsible for as much as 90 percent of the spawning ground for the Atlantic striped bass population. While the Chesapeake Bay remains the primary spawning location and nursery area for the East Coast stock (scientists estimate the Chesapeake Region accounts for between 70 percent and 90 percent), spawning activity also occurs in the Roanoke River/Albemarle Sound watershed in North Carolina and the Hudson River in New York. Some spawning activity has been witnessed in the Delaware River and several other smaller river systems along the East Coast. It is widely believed that these river systems, as long as pollution is kept to a minimum, will continue to expand as spawning/producer areas.

In late winter, mature striped bass begin to move from the Atlantic Ocean into tidal freshwater to spawn. Spawning is triggered by an increase in water temperature as well as salinity levels and generally occurs in April, May, and early June in the Chesapeake Bay tributaries, Roanoke River, and Hudson River. Scientists believe that young striped bass do best at a salinity of about 0.6 to eleven parts per thousand, compared with full-strength seawater which has a salinity of about thirty-four parts per thousand. Striped bass have an innate sense of finding the right water before spawning and a strong "homing" tendency toward natal waters.

Shortly after spawning, mature fish return to the coast. Most spend summer and early fall months in middle New England near-shore waters. In late fall and early winter, they migrate south to the North Carolina and Virginia capes.

During summer and fall in coastal waters, the sex ratio is generally 9:1, in favor of females, particularly in the north (Bigelow and Schroeder, 1953). Striped bass catches from Rhode Island, North Carolina Coasts, and Long Island, New York's south shore consisted of 90 percent, 90 percent, and 85 percent females, respectively.

Some Striped Bass Distribution

Striped bass were introduced to the Pacific Coast of North America and into many of the large reservoir impoundments across the United States by state game and fish commissions for the purposes of recreational fishing and as a predator to control populations of gizzard shad. These include Elephant Butte Lake in New Mexico; Lake Ouachita, Lake Norfork, Beaver Lake, and

Lake Hamilton in Arkansas; Lake Powell, Lake Pleasant, and Lake Havasu in Arizona; Castaic Lake, Lake George in Florida, Pyramid Lake, Silverwood Lake, Diamond Valley Lake, East Fork State Park Lake near Cincinnati, Lake Cumberland, and Lake Murray in California; Lake Lanier in Georgia; Reelfoot Lake in Tennessee; and Lake Mead in Nevada; Lake Texoma, Lake Tawakoni, Lake Whitney, Possum Kingdom Lake, and Lake Buchanan in Texas; and in Smith Mountain Lake in Virginia.

They are also found in the Minas Basin and Gaspereau River in Nova Scotia, Canada. Striped bass have also been introduced into waters in Ecuador, Iran, Latvia, Mexico, Russia, South Africa, and Turkey—primarily for sport fishing and aquaculture.

The striped bass is one of the most avidly pursued of all coastal sport fish. Striped bass are native to most of the East Coast, ranging from the lower St. Lawrence River in Canada to the St. John's River in Northern Florida, and from Lake Pontchartrain, Louisiana on the Gulf of Mexico, to the open waters of the Atlantic. The primary range where most recreational and commercial anglers along the East Coast pursue striped bass spans from Maine to North Carolina. However, striped bass are also found in many freshwater inland lakes along the East Coast. The West Coast of the United States also has a healthy striped bass fishery, mainly in the Delta area of northern California. While the East and West Coast striped bass fisheries draw the most attention, striped bass can be found in thirty-one states, facilitated in some landlocked jurisdictions by stocking programs in lakes and reservoirs.

Selected Biological History

Today we have solid evidence supporting the argument that striped bass have a marine origin. In a published 1996 study, Nolf and Stringer, described the strong resemblances of fossil otoliths (inner ear bones) of Percoidei (Perchlike) fishes with present-day Moronidae (family of fish to which striped bass belong) from the Cretaceous Era sandstone deposits (145-65 million years ago). Fossil otoliths identified as being those of Moronidae were recovered from ancient marine sea beds, covering what is presently the southern area of North America (Blue Springs, Union County, Mississippi), long before formation of what we know as the Atlantic Ocean. Contrary to recent popular belief, our striped bass had marine ancestors for millions of years, and did not evolve from a line of freshwater fish, as previous authors had maintained.

Freshwater Spawning

In a paper by Secor (2002) about estuarine dependency and life history evolution, based on phylogenetic evidence, Secor profiles three economically important temperate sea basses, the North American striper (*M. saxatlis*), the Japanese sea bass (*Lateolabrax japonicus*), and the European sea bass (*Morone labrax*), all of which show global distribution. Members of this group not only show strong taxonomic affinities but also near-shore coastal distribution, which support valuable fisheries. Their apparent similarity in appearance is more that superficial, causing considerable debate over their interrelationships. Contrary to the prevailing view for salmonids—namely, that anadromy evolved from freshwater ancestors—Secor asserts that anadromy in our *Morone saxatilis* evolved from a marine-spawning ancestor. *L. japonicus* and *M. labrax* both spawn in near-shore *marine habitats*, and larvae are transported into embayment and estuarine nurseries (Jennings et. al. 1992). Both species are found to occasionally use freshwater habitats for foraging as juveniles and adults.

Facultative Anadromy

In its evolution, *M. saxatlis* developed *facultative anadromy* (leaving saltwater to spawn in freshwater), utilizing numerous, stable North American estuarine environments for both spawning and early development. In all likelihood, this environmental behavior developed to avoid marine predation on young, as well as to make use of abundant estuarine food resources like river herring. *Geological evidence strongly suggests both the European and Asian species lacked similar environments, accounting for the absence of this behavior in those species.*

Temperate estuaries of Europe and Japan are significantly smaller than those of North America. Due to mountain chains and active volcanoes, over geological time, these estuaries represent unstable productive (and reproductive) habitats, whereas the eastern continental divide of North America is characterized by an ancient and highly-eroded mountain chain and corresponding broad coastal plane. This erosional landscape favored creation of the world's largest network of temperate estuaries, that of Chesapeake Bay, which presently supports an abundant striped bass stock.

Further Evidence

Additional research suggesting marine ancestry for the striper also comes from work done by Beitch (1963), who investigated the kidney's role in enabling survival in environments of varying salinity. Their research reported the absence of kidney nephron distal tubular segments, present in most freshwater fish species, but absent from striped bass and white perch—a reflection of the probable marine origin of the latter two.

The ability of fish to live in both fresh and saltwater environments demands specialized kidney function. When a striped bass enters freshwater to spawn, or forages in brackish (or fresh) water, it faces dual problems of depleted salt in the bloodstream, or absorbing too much water. "In order to make the change, the osmotic pressure (a force created by dissolved salts and minerals in the blood stream) must be adjustable," reports author, Nick Karas. "Anadromous fish possess glomerular kidneys, which have the ability to respond to differences in urine volume that result from different (low) salinities. These fish also possess membranes in the mouth cavity that can handle the uptake and secretion of ions in the blood tissue and protect it against undue diffusion. *The glomeruli (small masses of capillaries) within the kidneys take urinary wastes out of the blood, maintain a (constant) isotonic balance, and thus allow striped bass to change environments at will.* In many anadromous fish, this change requires some conditioning time, but in striped bass, it happens rapidly.

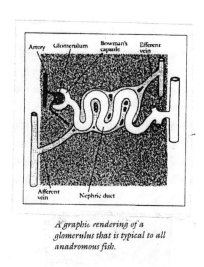

A graphic rendering of a glomerulus that is typical to all anadromous fish.

Striper Kidney Nephron

You may notice Beitch's research used the name *Roccus saxatilis* (striper) and *Roccus americanus* (white perch). Unfortunately, due to prior taxonomic use, the name *Morone* took precedence over *Roccus*, an incorrect, but highly popular, name. Consequently, to the dismay of many in the angling community, the genus name was corrected to *Morone* in the mid-1960s by the International Commission on Zoological Nomenclature (ICZN). The species Latin name *saxatilis* means "dwelling among rocks"—a truly appropriate name for the striper.

Genetic Memory Revised

Upon learning of early transplant stockings of East Coast striped bass into several West Coast areas, I wondered how these Hudson River stock stripers would fair in a totally different geographic and climatic environment, given that they were genetically programmed to forage New England coastal waters. I was not surprised to learn California biologists could find no annual evidence of striped bass following their stocking in Sacramento Bay waters. Not until four years later, when many of these fish became sexually mature, were spawning stripers discovered in its estuarine waters. Olfactory memory was undoubtedly involved, but I suspect sonic "road signs" possibly assisted, allowing them to relocate the Sacramento River for spawning purposes.

Although initially imprinted with coastal New England foraging information that obviously became transformed into West Coast geographical information, transplanting confirms striped bass possess a unique adaptive skill.

Landlocked Stripers

The striped bass became this nation's first official state fish (in South Carolina) with the impoundment of the Cooper River in 1941. Completion of the dam formed the 170,000-acre Santee-Cooper Reservoir; biologists were aware striped bass used the Cooper River for spawning but assumed any impounded fish would die. After World War II, scientists discovered they (the now-landlocked striped bass) were flourishing and reproducing in the huge lake.

Imagine my surprise, when on my way to Florida over a decade ago, I pulled off the highway at a McDonald's in South Carolina and found the dining area packed with statues, murals, giant photos, paintings, and other displays dedicated to striped bass. I soon learned of the importance of this marvelous fish to the economy of the Santee-Cooper impoundment area of the State.

Freshwater Stripers

There are very few successful spawning populations of freshwater striped bass; these include Lake Texoma, the Colorado River and its reservoirs downstream from and including Lake Powell, and the Arkansas River as well as Lake Marion/Santee Cooper (South Carolina) that retained a landlocked breeding population when the dam was built; whereas other freshwater fisheries must be restocked with hatchery-produced fish annually. Stocking of striped bass was discontinued at Lake Mead in 1973 once natural reproduction was verified.

A Plastic Fish

In summary, I've long been impressed with the extraordinary adaptive capabilities of our striper and in fact have often referred to them as "plastic" fish. After all, only a plastic fish could adapt "on the spot" when its routes of seaward escape were dammed, and it became landlocked; only a plastic fish could, within a relative handful of generations, adapt for estuarine spawning, or transition from saltwater to freshwater feeding while chasing herring upriver—punching through brackish water into fresh and not just *surviving* but *thriving*. Only the offspring of a plastic fish could survive these jarring shifts to basic biological wiring.

And it's not just the striper's astonishing adaptability to dramatic shifts within spawning or foraging environments—or the type and abundance of available food sources. It's that striped bass, carried westward across the continent by train, could short-circuit their original East Coast (Hudson River, in fact) genetic memory upon transplant into California river systems—in effect rewiring themselves, inside a single generation, for West Coast living (and spawning). Incidentally, for more on this last fascinating chapter in the "social" history of American striped bass, see the following section on the journey that established a California breeding stock.

Bottom line is that, where our beloved striper is concerned, there's much truth in the old line about change as the only constant. That forty-pound striper you're watching may not have inherited instincts that tell it to ambush three-pound shad in the shadow line of a new bridge, but it's clear enough to see she's not only figured it out but also raised it to a high art form. Understand that our bass will not only adapt to survive but adapt to flourish, even in the face of extreme adversity. Embrace, as the next logical step, the idea that there are precious few hard-and-fast rules dictating striper behavior or—more to the point of the coming chapters—the best times, places, or techniques to catch them.

Transcontinental Bass

In his 1997 book, *The Striped Bass Chronicles*, George Reiger writes: "In 1879 and again in 1882, the striped bass went west with the pioneers when several hundred, mostly fingerlings, were transplanted from a New Jersey river by Dr. Livingston Stone, at the urging of S. R. Throckmorton of the California State Board of Fish Commissioners. They went across the continent via train, wagon, milk cans, and wooden bucket to the upper estuary Sacramento River, feeding San Francisco Bay. Some accounts say one or both California stockings came from the Navesink River; others say from the Shrewsbury River, near Red Bank, NJ. Since the Navesink (flowing west to east) and the Shrewsbury (flowing south to north) ebb together into Raritan Bay behind Sandy Hook, they comprise the same tidal ecosystem. Thus, all Pacific stripers are descended from the same Hudson River-origin gene pool" (George Reiger, 1997).

The transported stripers adapted so well, that by 1889, just ten years after the first stocking of Atlantic fish, striped bass were being sold in San Francisco markets. Transporting fry coast to coast by train today would be no easy task. But in 1879, only ten years after the first coast to coast rail trip was even possible.

All of this came about, thanks to Dr. Livingston Stone, a pioneer in striped bass stocking, who was one of the founders of the American Fisheries Society. Like a modern-day Noah, Dr. Livingston Stone loaded the aquarium train car with an assortment of East Coast fish intending to transport them to California. Dr. Livingston Stone also deserves special recognition for his first-hand account of his disastrous first attempt to transport fish to the Pacific Coast in 1872, in a well-equipped aquarium train car paid for by the California Fish Commission.

Stone and his entourage made it as far as the Elkhorn River in Nebraska, where the train fell from the bridge into the river. Not deterred from his mission to transport fish to the West Coast, and not to be outdone, Dr. Stone immediately set out for the Hudson to procure young fish for another attempt.

An impossible trip for most men, but Dr. Livingston Stone of the U.S. Fish Commission (forerunner of the U.S. Fish and Wildlife Service), was not like most men; he was up to the challenge. He had the vision and attitude that he could do it. His charge was to get the striped bass to California alive. The fish were carried in wooded barrels and milk cans, and cooled by ice, Dr. Stone's crew changed the water every two hours when possible and agitation was done by hand twenty-four hours a day. After days of continuous care, almost all of the fish arrived in good shape. In the 1881 trip to California, Dr. Stone had devised a cylinder with tiny holes in the bottom when filled with water and held over the cans released a fine spray of air-enriched water.

Despite Indians, rickety bridges, poor rail beds, dry plains, and the Rocky Mountains and having to improvising ways to keep the fragile fingerlings stripers alive he accomplished his mission. Today the striped bass is one of California's top-ranking sport fish. With about three hundred thousand anglers fishing for stripers annually catching over two hundred thousand fish, adding over $24 million to the economy all directly related to striped bass fishing.

In the late 1800s, Dr. Livingston Stone of the United States Fish Commission (a forerunner of U.S. Fish and Wildlife), at the urging of the California State Board of Fish Commissions, began transporting the bass from New Jersey to the San Francisco Bay. In milk cans and wooden barrels, first-hand agitated and refreshed, later afforded a crude oxygenation system, the first stripers made their way to the West Coast. The striper is now one of California's top ranking sport fish. Found in relative abundance in the early 1900s, the fish numbered approximately three million adults in the early 1960s; by the early 1990s, the count dropped to about 775,000, with 30 percent of those hatchery-reared. Still fished as far as the Columbia River in Washington State, the Sacramento Delta fishery, where the fish migrate biannually, remains troubled by Delta water diversions, pollution, illegal take, exotic aquatic organisms, and bay-fill projects. Last-ditch efforts are being made to restore the western fisheries.

SOME STRIPER PROBLEMS

Science never solves a problem without creating at least ten more questions.

—Anonymous

The study of fish diseases is of major importance for several reasons. Many fish populations have declined drastically over the last several decades. Scientists are attempting to discern the cause of these declines to prevent more fish from dying. Environmental pollution appears to be playing a large role in the development and/or exacerbation of disease. By understanding fish, with respect to health and disease, fish populations can be used as sentinels to monitor water quality, to evaluate human impact on the environment, and to serve as harbingers of changes in human health.

Lymphocystis

Lymphocystis is probably the best-known viral disease of marine and freshwater fishes, including the striper. It is characterized by the presence of small irregular, solitary, or confluent nodules of an off-white color on the skin and fins of affected fish. It is not caused by a parasite.

Principal transmission of lymphocystis is by waterborne virus; the virus enters the fish through the gills or skin abrasions. The disease is chronic, rarely fatal, and has an early-spring seasonality in many species. The symptoms of the affected fish include missing scales, reddened areas, and milky coverings that give the fish the appearance of having been rolled in flour. This skin virus is spread from fish to fish when one fish rubs against another, particularly among overwintering fish that occupy the warm-water discharge areas of power plants along several northeast river systems. It is usually not fatal to the fish unless other organisms like bacteria invade the lesions. The virus itself is not harmful to humans and anglers who would otherwise consume the fish have nothing to fear from the virus itself. However, most—witnessing an infected striper's less-than-appetizing appearance—choose to pass on that specimen's culinary attributes. There is no harm in touching or handling a fish that has lymphocystis.

Lymphocystis (lymphocystis disease, lymphocystis virus infection) is a chronic, self-limiting, viral disease affecting up to 125 species of teleosts (bony fish) worldwide. Freshwater, estuarine, and marine fish in warm-water, cool-water, and cold-water environments are susceptible to this disease. In general, lymphocystis is a disease of more evolutionarily advanced species of teleosts, such as herrings, perches, basses, flounders, snappers, and damselfishes. Because of viral replication and subsequent inhibition of mitosis in the host's connective tissue cells, affected individuals develop macroscopic, nodular lesions that somewhat resemble warts. The greatly hypertrophied cells, called lymphocysts, typically occur on the skin or fins. Rarely, these lesions may develop in internal organs.

In 1874, J. Lowe documented the first case of lymphocystis in European flounder. Since then, scientists have performed considerable research on this disease, its host range, and repercussions of infection.

Lymphocystis infected striped bass

Although lymphocystis disease has a low mortality rate, it may leave an individual disfigured. This disfigurement can have several consequences. If the gills are affected, the fish can have difficulty breathing. If the lesion is located around the mouth, the fish may have difficulty in feeding or may be unable to feed. Also, infected fish in confined environments or in the wild may be more likely to be targets of aggression or cannibalization. In addition, lymphocystis may be complicated by secondary bacterial or mycotic infections.

Mycobacteriosis

Mycobacteriosis, an infectious disease affecting striped bass in Chesapeake Bay, was first diagnosed in 1997 based on the presence of granulomatous inflammation and acid-fast bacteria in skin and spleen. The disease is caused by a group of naturally occurring bacteria, which are widespread in aquatic environments, called *mycobacteria* (five species). But a few species of mycobacteria, particularly *Mycobacterium shottsii*, can cause disease in both animals and humans. It has never been reported in a wild population on the East Coast until 1997, when scientists began seeing it in the bay's striped bass.

For thousands of years, perhaps 80 percent of all the Atlantic Coast stripers were actually spawned in the tributaries of the Chesapeake. It is not mere coincidence this spawning and nursery area for striped bass also happens to be the same for menhaden. It probably goes without saying that striped bass—particularly within the Chesapeake—have a complex ecological relationship with this all-important food source. Frankly, though, it has taken *way too long* for the ASMFC to comprehend the importance of *whole ecosystems* in fishery management—particularly the interdependence of species.

In his groundbreaking 2007 book, *The Most Important Fish in the Sea: Menhaden and America*, H. Bruce Franklin's mentions Jim Price, a fifth-generation waterman, former charter skipper (now retired), who still continues to fish mornings before breakfast. In 1997, Price caught a fish that carried the signs of myco and is quoted as saying: "I've never seen anything like that in my life. It was so sickening it really took something out of me." After depositing several similar fish to the Cooperative Oxford Laboratory, he began his own study. Sometime later, Price commented, "I've been looking in the stomachs of rockfish for forty years, but I couldn't believe what I saw—nothing, nothing, absolutely nothing. Not only was there no food, but there was no fat. Everything was shrunk up and small."

Many scientists now believe that the rockfish are sick because they're malnourished—they're not getting enough menhaden, a high-fat, high-calorie food source.

The Virginia Institute of Marine Science (VIMS) estimated in 2005 that 76 percent of the bay's rockfish are infected with *myco*, and there may be ten or more forms of *myco* infections.

How does mycobacteriosis affect striped bass in the bay? In infected striped bass, mycobacteriosis causes inflammation, tissue destruction, and formation of scar tissue in one or more organs. The first signs of infection usually show up in internal organs such as the spleen and kidney. Small, grayish-white nodules called granulomas form in an attempt to stop the infection. As more granulomas form, the striped bass's normal organ tissues are lost to scar tissue. Some infected striped bass also have shallow, reddened, or dark-colored skin ulcers. (Please note that not all skin lesions on striped bass are caused by mycobacteriosis.)

Mycobacteriosis has been called a "wasting disease" because it causes striped bass to slowly lose body mass and significant amounts of weight. "We don't know a great deal more about why this disease is in the striped bass population than we did several years ago," said Phil Jones, a fisheries manager with the Maryland Department of Natural Resources. "It's not clear why other fish species in the Chesapeake Bay are not being affected."

Since 1997, ongoing surveys have found that as many as 60 percent of striped bass in the Maryland portion of the bay are infected. In the Virginia portion of the bay, mycobacteria (mostly *M. shottsii*) were found in the spleens of 76 percent of striped bass collected between 1999 and 2001.

The bottom line is that seven years after mycobacteriosis was first identified in the bay's striped bass, scientists remain almost as baffled as ever about why it's here—and the degree to which it poses a threat to striped bass, a fish normally considered to be one of the bay's success stories since populations rebounded from record low levels in the 1980s.

Last fall, bacteria cultures taken during a multiagency striper survey indicated that 81 percent of the fish in the Potomac were infected, 67 percent in the York, 61 percent in Rappahannock, and 54 percent in the Nanticoke. Meanwhile, new figures from the Virginia Institute of Marine Science's ChesMAPP survey—which uses a standardized method to collect fish from the mouth of the bay to the Susquehanna Flats five times a year—shows that the infection rate seems to get higher as fish get older.

Meanwhile, new figures from the Virginia Institute of Marine Science's ChesMAPP survey—which uses a standardized method to collect fish from the mouth of the bay to the Susquehanna Flats five times a year—shows that the infection rate seems to get higher as fish get older.

But striper researcher, Anthony Overton—who conducted some of the early mycobacteria studies in the Chesapeake—said it is important to not only look not at the disease, but why the striped bass are infected to begin with. Through the 1990s, he noted, a variety of bacteria were found in striped bass—often infecting large parts of the population—until mycobacteria infections became the dominant problem.

"We concentrate a lot on the bug itself, but I kind of think there should be a shift toward looking at the ecosystem as a whole," he says. "Why is this happening? There was always some bacteria popping up."

A popular theory is that a huge number of striped bass in the bay are stressed and therefore susceptible to disease, because they don't have enough to eat. Their most important prey item, menhaden, is in short supply.

And because today's striped bass can't be caught until they reach eighteen inches—the legal size used to be twelve inches—there are more big fish in the bay than ever before, requiring even more food. Several recently published studies suggest a growing imbalance between menhaden and striped bass populations.

Striper with Mycobacteriosis

CAPTION: This striper has the deadly disease mycobacteriosis. It's thought to be nearly always fatal to striped bass, and that more than 75 percent of rockfish in the Chesapeake Bay are infected.

(**Author's Note:** Stripers Forever, the conservation group solely dedicated to the conservation of the most popular saltwater game fish, has started the *Mycobacteriosis* Research Initiative in hopes to find a cure for this deadly disease. The questions and answers that follow—broken down into three categories—are designed to help readers make sense of the real-world implications of what appears to be a near-epidemic of the disease among Chesapeake Bay—origin striped bass.)

FAQs: Myco and Striped Bass

Q: *What is fish mycobacterium?*
A: Mycobacteriosis is an infectious disease caused by bacteria in the genus *Mycobacterium*. These species of "marine mycobacteria," such as *Mycobacterium marinum* and *M. chelonae*, are ubiquitous in the environment. Newly identified species such as *Mycobacterium chesapeaki* and *M. schottsii* have only been described from the Chesapeake Bay. At least ten species of mycobacteria have been isolated from striped bass lesions.

Q: *How does mycobacteriosis affect fish?*
A: Mycobacteriosis is a bacterial infection that results in inflammation, tissue destruction, and formation of scar tissue in one or more organs. Signs of infection are first noted in internal organs such as the spleen and kidney. Nodules (called granulomas) composed of inflammatory cells and fibrous connective tissue form in response to the bacteria in an attempt to stop the infection. An increase in the number and size of granulomas leads to the formation of extensive scar tissue and eventual loss of normal tissue architecture. This disease progresses slowly in fish and has been characterized as a "wasting disease" due to loss of body mass and emaciation. It is not known how many fish die or if any fish recover from this disease in the Chesapeake Bay.

Q: *Are myco symptoms always externally visible?*
A: No. Mycobacteriosis in fish is generally first found in internal organs. In mild cases of this disease, signs of infection may only

be evident microscopically. As the disease progresses, additional internal organs may show signs of disease. In severe cases, virtually all organs and tissue are affected including the skin and muscle. Mycobacteria have been isolated from young-of-year striped bass, but no visible signs of disease have been found. Infected one—and two-year-old fish typically exhibit mild to moderate signs of the bacteria. However, three—to five-year-old fish have the highest incidence of mycobacteriosis and occasionally exhibit severe infections, including emaciation and scar tissue formation on the skin. It is important to note that striped bass are susceptible to other viral, bacterial, and parasitic infections; therefore, not all striped bass with lesions on the skin have mycobacteriosis.

Q: *How many fish are affected?*
A: The Maryland Department of Natural Resources (DNR) and Maryland Department of Agriculture's Animal Health Laboratory at College Park first diagnosed mycobacteriosis in the Chesapeake Bay in 1997. This prompted a bay-wide striped bass health assessment survey that continues today. Currently, DNR surveys indicate that as many as 60 percent of striped bass in the Chesapeake Bay have this disease. This infection rate has more than doubled since 1998 when this survey began. Fish are probably exposed to these bacteria early in life with infection rates increasing with age: 11 percent in one-year-olds and 60 percent in three—to five-year-olds. Differences in reported prevalence of mycobacteriosis may be due to variation in diagnostic techniques employed.

Q: *Are certain species more prone to mycobacteriosis?*
A: Mycobacteriosis has been documented in more than one hundred sixty species of fresh and saltwater fish worldwide. However, there is no evidence that mycobacteriosis is common in any Chesapeake Bay species other than striped bass. In 2001, surveys were conducted with white and yellow perch, and so far no fish were found with the disease. Additional species will be added to this survey in the future.

Q: *What is the DNR doing about mycobacteriosis?*
A: DNR, along with state and federal partners, initiated a health survey of striped bass in 1998. This general health survey involved collections of striped bass from the lower, middle, and upper Chesapeake Bay including numerous tributaries and was designed to identify problems in the population. Complete examinations were performed on

these fish and samples were processed for microbiology (pathogen identification), histopathology (visible signs of disease at the cellular level), nutritional status, and parasite load. Results indicated that the disease of concern was mycobacteriosis, and that the infection rates were rising. In addition to mycobacteriosis, resident fish also exhibited ulcers or areas of hemorrhage on the skin, termed "ulcerative dermatitis syndrome" or UDS.

Starting in 2003, DNR and its partners began a more detailed study of mycobacteriosis in striped bass, involving younger age classes of resident fish as well as migratory fish. Fish from all areas of the bay are being examined. Experiments are under way to determine how this disease is transmitted to fish. In addition, fisheries managers are taking a close look at the population structure to determine what population level affects may be evident. DNR and its partners (NOAA, USGS, VIMS, and UMD) are currently planning a conference to discuss current state of knowledge and future research concerning mycobacteriosis.

Chesapeake striped bass migrate from Maine to North Carolina, and their catch is controlled by very tight quotas in coastal Atlantic States. Population numbers remain high, and to date, scientific analyses have not shown an increase in the number of stripers dying of natural causes; any kind of disease would be considered a natural cause. Fisheries managers in all the coastal states are continually monitoring catches and collecting data that would detect an increase in mortality associated with mycobacteriosis.

More FAQs: Myco and Humans

Q: *Can humans get mycobacteria?*
A: Yes. Mycobacteriosis is zoonotic, which means it can be transmitted to humans. Mycobacteriosis is also called "fish handler's disease" because of cases involving people associated with fish hatcheries, aquaculture facilities, the aquarium industry, as well as sport and commercial fishing industries.

Q: *What is fish handler's disease?*
A: Fish handler's disease is the human form of mycobacteriosis. It is contracted through direct contact with infected fish or water.

Q: *How are humans affected?*
A: Infections in human are generally limited to the extremities such as fingertips and feet, but may involve the joints, bones and lymph nodes. Individuals with cuts or scrapes are at higher risk for infection. The most frequent symptom is the formation of a persistent bump or nodule under the skin. Additional symptoms may include the formation of ulcers, swelling of lymph nodes, and joint pain. This disease can be treated with antibiotics. A health care provider should be contacted if any of the above symptoms develop following direct skin contact with fresh or salt water or after handling or processing fish. If you have any questions or general concerns, please contact a health care provider.

Q: *How can anglers and fish handlers protect themselves?*
A: Individuals that handle striped bass should wear heavy gloves (made of leather of heavy cotton) and boots to avoid puncture wounds from fish spines and wash hands thoroughly after handling or processing striped bass. Open cuts or scrapes on hands and arms should be thoroughly cleansed and bandaged. Again, this disease can be treated with antibiotics, and any persons with questions or concerns should contact a physician.

Fish Prep and Consumption

Q: *Can I get mycobacteria from eating a "tainted" rockfish?*
A: A recent check of the published medical studies on this kind of infection in human beings shows that eating properly prepared and cooked rockfish has not been associated with human mycobacterial illness. (**Author's note:** DHMH recommends that people not consume any raw rockfish or any fish that appears diseased.)

Q: *Should I be concerned about preparing rockfish?*
A: No. Use common sense when preparing your fish fillet. Fish with open, reddened lesions on the body or with signs of hemorrhage or darkened patches in the fillets should be discarded. Fish that appear to be healthy and are properly cooked are safe to eat. DHMH recommends that people not consume any raw rockfish or any fish that appears diseased. While handling an infected rockfish, especially if the skin is cut or scraped, can lead to skin infections, simple hygiene precautions can prevent this.

Q: *Should I be concerned when handling raw fish?*
A: When handling any type of fish, use a few practical and simple precautions:

- *Protect broken or vulnerable skin.* If cuts, scrapes, or other open or inflamed areas of the skin are present, cover hands and wrists with an impermeable barrier (like a rubber or vinyl glove) to prevent any bacteria from getting into the soft tissue under the skin where *Mycobacterium marinum* organisms are known to cause infections.
- *Dispose of any leftover fish parts after preparing raw fish.* Wash off all cutting boards, surfaces, knives, and other utensils used to process raw fish with warm soapy water and rinse thoroughly.
- *Stop any infections early.* If red, itchy, or ulcerated bumps appear on the skin—especially on the hands and forearms—after processing or handling fish, contact a health care provider. Those with underlying medical problems, including a weakened immune system, should also contact a health care provider.

Fish Lice

A final subject area worthy of at least brief consideration under the larger heading of striped bass diseases is fish lice. Obviously, while an infestation of fish (sea) lice on a striped bass is *not*, properly speaking, a "disease," the study of these parasitic copepods may well shed light on a number of variables affecting the present and future health of bass—at either an individual-fish level or stock-wide. The parasitic organism can provide a unique lens into the biology of the host organism.

To help readers get a handle on these ubiquitous bass bugs, I've provided a handful of common questions I've fielded for charter clients over the years, along with answers I've supplied. Some of the latter have changed significantly over the years, mirroring an array of changes in striped bass spawning behavior, habitat, migratory patterns, and so on.

Q: *Where do striped bass pick up fish lice?*
A: Dense, open-ocean wintertime schooling—as with pre-spawn aggregations in outer Chesapeake Bay from December through March—facilitates the transmission of lice from one fish to another; eventually, nearly all schooled fish are infested. Carriers of lice

include cod, salmon, and several kinds of herring. In fact, eighty different North Atlantic fish species are known to carry the same lice migratory striped bass typically display at the time of their arrival at Block Island.

Fish Louce; *Caligus elon gatus*; Female #1 with egg strings

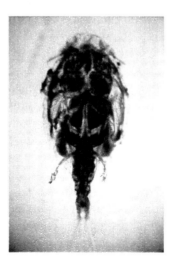

Fish louce; *Caligus elongatus*; Male

Q: *Under which conditions will stripers shed fish lice? Does it relate to water temp, salinity, or something else?*
A: Salinity is the key. Most fish lice will vacate a host fish when, during a migratory period, it reaches coastal waters and dramatically reduced salinity. In the case of striped bass, the run into natal rivers to spawn will clean fish of all lice—regardless of the degree of prior infestation.

Q: *What about the conventional "wisdom" that says the presence of sea lice indicates a striped bass is a "fresh" migratory arrival?*
A: Sexually mature female stripers that have overwintered in Mid-Atlantic offshore waters typically enter freshwater to spawn, thus shedding their fish lice. (Research has confirmed that parasitic copepods will leave a host fish immediately once that fish has entered freshwater.) However, several factors—including out-of-synch hormonal timing or a lack of suitable (in quantity or quality) prespawn forage—may prevent some overwinter females from spawning, consequently resulting in heavy infestation. That is, without the freshwater "purge" spawning provides, fish that winter-over in ocean waters may wind up seriously infested with parasitic copepods.

Q: *Do parasitic fish lice pose health problems to their striped bass hosts?*
A: Research has shown that several species of striper lice tend to attach to the host fish on or around the gills, where they have immediate access to blood supply. Heavy gill infestations can debilitate a host quickly, causing death via increased exposure to predation or greater-than-average susceptibility to other diseases. Other fish lice species feed mainly on the host's layer of protective mucus; heavy surface infestation can erode skin areas, leaving a striped bass prone to life-threatening bacterial, viral, or fungal infections.

Q: *How might we draw parallels between presence of certain sea lice and striper spawning or winter staging locations—or even spawning success?*
A: During spring/summer 2010 and 2011, island observations on recently caught, lice-infested female stripers (destined to be filleted) bore minimal or absolutely no post-spawning signs, suggesting that—for whatever reason or reasons—these reproductively mature, Chesapeake, Delaware, or Hudson River-origin origin females had failed to "sow the next crop." Though copepod infestation would have no direct bearing on a female striper's spawning capability, it does suggest

that some part of the reproductive puzzle is missing from the striped bass stocks spawning puzzle. Some in the scientific community have posited that only little energy was available for egg production—the consequence of minimal or nonexistent late-season forage in the form of river herring or menhaden.

STATE OF THE STRIPER

*Tomorrow belongs to the people
who prepare for it today*

—African Proverb

NOTE: The following question-and-answer section was extracted from a tweaked dialogue between your author, whose questions appear in bold and italic typeface following the initials **AA**, and noted striped bass biological authority Dr. John Waldman of Queens College (New York), a former expert with the Hudson River Foundation (HRF). The hope here is that Waldman's observations (responses denoted by initials **JW**) may help to shed some light on the current "State of the Striper," so to speak. To be clear, this dialogue was actually modified from one of Waldman's lectures during a "Maine Striper Symposium." Also included in a brief sidebar at this end of this abbreviated chapter are brief entries on the 2010 and 2011 Chesapeake Bay striped bass Young-of-the-Year (YOY) indexes for 2010-2011.

AA: *Is the large decrease in numbers of schoolie (2-10 pound) striped bass also being seen elsewhere along the Atlantic Coast or is Maine unique?*

JW: It's more pronounced in Maine, but it is being seen everywhere along the "Striper Coast." There are myriad accounts of noticeably to dramatically lower numbers of striped bass along their whole coastal range, but chiefly of younger, smaller age classes. For example, the phenomenal winter fishery for schoolies in the Thames River, Connecticut, recently collapsed. In spring 2011, residents of Martha's

Vineyard asked, "Where are the stripers this year?" Even near the mouth of the Hudson River, a striped bass population center, spring and fall fishing for smaller stripers has been dismal in the last several years.

AA: *Which striped bass stocks contribute to coastal Maine fisheries?*
JW: The great majority of anadromous (i.e., spawned in fresh water, go to sea) striped bass that occur in coastal and estuarine waters of Maine originate from the Hudson River and Chesapeake Bay, with a likely much smaller contribution from the recently recovered Delaware River population. Various studies suggest that a great Chesapeake year class swamps a great Hudson year class, but that a great Hudson year class can exceed a poor Chesapeake year class. (Contribution from North Carolina's Roanoke River is either nonexistent or trivial.) Together, these three populations support the *Atlantic Migratory Striped Bass Stock*.

All three populations behave similarly, with adults spawning in their natal rivers and then exiting them and migrating north, before wintering in the ocean between New Jersey and Cape Hatteras. Many younger, immature striped bass also migrate northward. There may be some minor contribution from reproduction in the Kennebec River, but it is unlikely to have more than a local effect.

AA: *Why do striped bass numbers in Maine fluctuate so widely?*
JW: The history of striped bass fisheries and tagging studies show that the Atlantic Migratory Striped Bass Stock is density-dependent in its coastal movements. Density dependence means that the more striped bass there are competing for resources in marine waters, the farther they spread out to reduce intraspecific competition. For two examples, tagging studies in the 1960s suggested that striped bass from the Hudson did not move past central Long Island. But tagging studies in the 1990s (a time of record year classes and high catches in Maine) showed that Hudson stripers were traveling as far as the Bay of Fundy. Also, in 1997, I visited Grand Manan Island, at the mouth of the Bay of Fundy. Stripers were being caught and were actually visible in the clear waters, but they had only crossed the four-hundred-foot deep channel and shown up there for the first time in recorded history the year before; indeed, local fisherman didn't even know what they were.

AA: *Can good Atlantic Coast striped bass fishing still occur these days?*

JW: Yes, for two reasons. One is that even under density dependence, some habitats are optimal for striped bass (e.g., Cape Cod, which still offers respectable striper fishing), and others are suboptimal, only inhabited when densities are extremely high (e.g., Grand Manan Island). The other is that stripers aggregate to food resources. Surfcasting along most of the Striper Coast was poor in autumn 2010, but central Long Island had the best schoolie fishing in decades because of the ongoing presence of a great abundance of sand eels, while party boats had remarkable catches of midsized stripers just offshore.

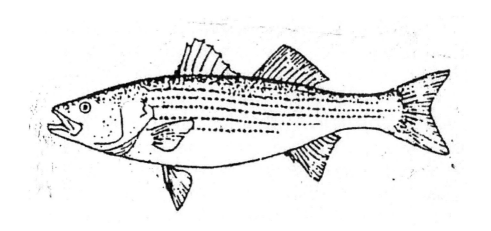

Striped Bass-Small

AA: *What is the current state of the Atlantic migratory striped bass stock?*

JW: Unbalanced. We have the still sizeable remnants of the dominant year classes of the 1990s and early 2000s, which are now midsized (fifteen to thirty pounds). But fishing is off in most coastal locations because these sizes don't behave the same as smaller stripers. Good coastal striped bass fishing is sustained in most locations by schoolies, with an occasional larger fish in the mix.

The problem is that we have had lower year class production, with no dominant year classes (taking for the sake of convenience dominant to mean a geometric mean catch of ten juveniles per net haul) in Maryland waters of the Chesapeake since 2003. However, between 1993 and 2003, there were four cohorts that exceeded a juvenile index value of 10, reaching almost 18.0

in 1996. In fact, larger Maryland index year classes in recent years were only about as high as almost all of the smallest year classes between 1993 and 2003. (The Virginia juvenile striped bass index for lower Chesapeake Bay shows a similar pattern.) In the Hudson, the 2007 Hudson cohort was strong, but from 2004 to 2010, juvenile indices have generally been lower than the mid-1990s to 2003. Without these multiple dominant year classes, we have perpetuation of the populations but not the sheers numbers of schoolies that sustain coastal fisheries and that push out to northern waters.

AA: *Is this like the population crash of the 1980s all over again?*
JW: No. In the 1980s, we had very few large striped bass left in the Chesapeake population, and thus, not enough eggs were produced even when ecological conditions were favorable. Today, we have many midsize spawners—which implies no shortage of eggs being spawned—but they have not been generating dominant year classes. This doesn't mean that we should squander these larger stripers; they are being reduced annually by fisheries and natural mortality, and they are "money in the bank" until we see dominant year classes again. "Keeper" as applied to striped bass is an unfortunate term; there is no need to keep legal striped bass.

AA: *What controls striped bass year class size?*
JW: Assuming sufficient eggs are produced during the reproductive season, year class size is set during the larval and juvenile stages. Primary is the match of the larvae that have just finished depleting their yolk sac to the availability of dense patches of plankton in space and time. If the match is good, there is high early survival.

Important new research (CBASS) in Chesapeake Bay also revealed a link between long-term climate effects and the success of its anadromous fishes. There is a weather cycle called the Atlantic Multidecadal Oscillation (AMO) that varies on the scale of thirty-five years or so; its warm phase produces more precipitation into estuaries than the other state and this results in larger, lower salinity nursery areas that favor recruitment of anadromous fishes. The AMO flipped to the phase less favorable to striped bass five years ago, which is coincident with low production there through 2010.

The year 2011 is providing some good news (and support for the CBASS theory). Despite being in the less favorable, drier AMO phase, 2011 was a very wet year, beginning with a large melting snow pack and continuing with above average rainfall. The Maryland juvenile striped bass index is just below 10.0, its highest value since 2003, and the Virginia Index also is strong.

AA: *What other factors are influencing the abundances of individual stocks?*

JW: Beyond fishing, there are ecological factors that have been implicated or at least suggested to be affecting striped bass abundance. In Chesapeake Bay, these include low abundance of menhaden prey (menhaden are at record lows in the Atlantic) and a disease, mycobacteriosis, that may or may not be linked to lowered condition of striped bass because of the scarcity of menhaden. In the Hudson, colonization by Eurasian zebra mussels beginning in 1991 has been shown to be depressing abundance and growth of juvenile striped bass by strongly reducing the phytoplankton available to striped bass larvae.

AA: *What is the long-term future of striped bass fishing in Maine?*

JW: Uncertain. Schoolie striper fishing will remain poor until there is at least one dominant year class produced again (but 2011 may qualify), and it may require multiple dominant year classes for there to be sufficient density dependence to generate first class fishing again in Maine. Fishermen in Maine need to accept that they are at the northern margin of the summer range of the Atlantic Migratory Striped Bass Stock, which is highly dynamic in the long term given the vagaries of management and ecology that control striped bass numbers. It would be a mistake for residents of Maine to believe that the excellent fishing of the 1990s and early 2000s reflects the normal status quo for striped bass abundance. Mainers should remain especially vocal in striped bass conservation because their fishing is more sensitive to the size of the Atlantic Migratory Striped Bass Stock than are locations nearer to the producer populations.

Chesapeake Spawning Success, 2008-2011

The Maryland Department of Natural Resources Fisheries Service performs a Juvenile Striped Bass survey each year, in Chesapeake Bay, where they document annual spawning success for young-of-year (YOY) striped bass. Results for 2010 showed a mean catch per haul of 5.58—below the long-term average of 11.7. A low relative index indicates a probable scarcity of stripers in future years when these juveniles reach maturity. In contrast, results for 2009 were up somewhat with a mean catch per haul of 7.87 versus 3.2 for 2008—a significant jump, but still below the long-term average.

Thankfully, and much to the surprise of many vocal critics of recent striped bass management, 2011 results for the Virginia's Institute of Marine Science (VIMS) 2011 YOY survey indicate more than twenty-seven fish per seine haul, significantly higher than the historic average of 7.5 in the Virginia portion of Chesapeake Bay. Correspondingly, Maryland's 2011 survey yielded a 34.6—well above the long-term average of 11.9, more than five times 2010's results of 5.9, and in fact the fourth highest measure of striped bass spawning success in the Chesapeake Bay in the survey's fifty-eight-year history. Delaware's 2011 survey met the average mark, as did New York's Hudson River YOY survey.

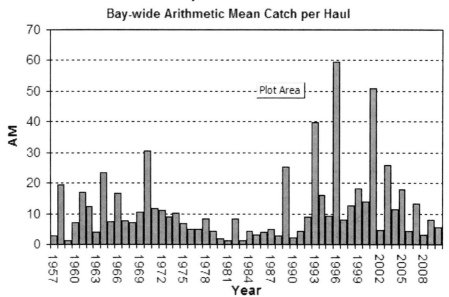

YOY Striper Abundance

THE AMERICAN EEL

*Thousands passed the lighthouse that night,
on the first lap of a far sea journey—
all the silver eels, in fact,
that the marsh contained.*

*And as they passed through the surf and out to sea,
so also they passed from human sight
and almost from human knowledge . . .*

—Rachel Carson,
Under the Sea-Wind, 1941

My interest in eels began when I started using them for both day—and nighttime striper fishing. During the first winter after moving to Rhode Island from Long Island, New York, I'd visit small coastal ponds to watch them being "gigged" through ice thick enough to support parked vehicles. Gigging involved a multipronged trident-like spear fastened to an eighteen—to twenty-two-foot wooden pole long enough to probe a tidal pond's soft bottom. It wasn't until years later that I learned local farmers had once harvested numbers of overwinter stripers through coastal-pond ice—a bit of local history I profiled in my last book, *Over-Winter Striper Secrets*.

Despite actively charter fishing decades ago for oversized stripers, it was only recently that I bothered to delve into their biology and history, although I felt I knew it fairly well. It so happened a close friend and fishing partner, W. H. Krueger, who is a noted ichthyologist and eel expert at the University of Rhode Island (now retired), knew more about them than most, and agreed to assist my request for help.

Early in my saltwater bass fishing, I became friends with a local "Swamp Yankee" by the name of Clifford Tucker. He was better known as "Dubie," a nickname ascribed by his parents to "do-be-good." In his later years, he trapped eels in Narrow River for a living. The Pettaquamscutt River Estuary, or Narrow River—as it's called locally, is a small ten-mile long estuary watershed in southern Rhode Island, fed at its headwaters by the freshwater of Gilbert Stuart Stream and empties at its tidal inlet at the Narragansett Town Beach. It has several freshwater brooks along with a major feeder stream, demonstrates a moderate saltwater wedge, along with numerous marshes, flats, and estuarine lakes, all of which empty into lower Narragansett Bay and Rhode Island Sound. Historically, it has also hosted a sizeable contingent of Hudson River-origin overwinter striped bass (Anderson, 2009). For further Narrow River information, go to: www.narrowriver.org

Map of the Narrow River Watershed

Life History

The American eel (*Anguilla rostrata*) is classified as a freshwater fish, with a range encompassing much of the East Coast. It's one of the few fishes that spawns at sea and spends its adult life in lakes, rivers, and estuaries. To my knowledge, our eels are one of only two fish that travel far offshore to the Atlantic's deep-ocean abyss (Sargasso Sea) for the purpose of spawning—a behavior known as catadromy.

Even today, how and why an eel becomes male or female remains a mystery. Just over a decade ago, my fishing partner and friend, Professor W. H. Krueger and his doctoral student, Ken Oliveira, published a paper on the eel. "For at least two decades, males predominated in the Annaquatucket River, RI, with no significant variation in mean total length in either sex. Because the species in panmictic (random breeding), this consistency suggests environmental sex determination (ESD). Most yellow eels (feeding phase) under 12 inches (300 mm) total length in the Annaguatucket are sexually undifferentiated. And in contrast to all other published sex ratios, males generally outnumber females [three-to-one].... Estimates of yellow eel population densities are four to ten times greater than published values for other habitats."

Krueger and Oliveira (1999) propose that yellow eel crowding may suspend sex differentiation *and* suppress femaleness. Evidence links high population density to high proportions of males among Atlantic Anguilla; reciprocally, low density yields a preponderance of females. This ESD (Environmental Sex Determination) may be adaptive, resulting in vast numbers of small males in coastal habitats (closer—relatively speaking—to the high-seas spawning area), while the much larger fecund females occupy most of the available estuarine (i.e., upriver) habitat.

Getting back to the American eel, its snakelike body with a small pointed head contains tiny pointed teeth, is typically brown along the back with a tan-yellow color along the belly and lacks pelvic fins. It is very similar to the European eel, but the two species differ in a number of ways such as spawning period, chromosomes, and number of vertebrae.

Once spawned in the Sargasso Sea, it takes nine or ten weeks for the eggs to hatch. Months after hatching, young eels move toward North America and randomly enter various freshwater systems to mature. The eel lives in fresh water and only leaves this habitat to reenter the Atlantic Ocean for spawning. The female can create up to four million buoyant eggs a year but, like males, dies after spawning.

The eel is found along the Atlantic Coast, including Chesapeake Bay and Hudson River. It prefers to hunt at night; and during the day, it hides in mud, sand, or gravel very close to shore, in roughly five—to six-foot depths.

American eels have become economically valuable to the East Coast and rivers where they travel. Eels caught by fishermen and sold, are eaten, or kept as pets. They help maintain the Atlantic Coast ecosystem by eating dead fish, invertebrates, carrion, insects, and if hungry enough in captivity, to cannibalize each other.

Although many anglers are put off by the snakelike appearance of these catadromous fish, eels are in fact fit for human consumption and are frequently caught by anglers fishing for something else. The IGFA World Record weight for the American eel is 9.25 pounds, caught in November 1995.

AMERICAN EEL / *Anguilla rostrata* (LeSueur 1817) /
Common Eel, Silver Eel, Freshwater Eel, Elver (juvenile) / Bigelow and Schroeder 1953:151–154

Figure 60. American eel *Anguilla rostrata*. Connecticut River, Mass. Drawn by H. L. Todd.

American Eel

Eel Stages

The life stages of the American eel start with the egg, then the leptocephalus larva, then glass eel, then yellow eel, and finally, silver eel. Hatched eel eggs produce tiny, flat, transparent larvae with long, narrow heads (called leptocephali); following an extended larval period during which spawned eels drift/migrate toward land and their eventual freshwater homes, these "hatchlings" metamorphose into glass eels. Glass eels develop pigmentation as they move into brackish or freshwater estuarine environments. Usually by two years of age, small, pigmented eels make the transition into yellow eels. Yellow eels inhabit fresh, brackish, and saltwater habitats where they feed mostly on invertebrates and smaller fishes. Sexual maturity occurs sometime between ten and twenty-five years of age. When yellow eels reach sexual maturity, they begin a "downstream" toward the Sargasso Sea spawning grounds. During this migration, yellow eels metamorphose into their adult, silver eel phase, undergoing several physical changes. Adult silver eels are believed to spawn in the Sargasso Sea during winter and early spring then die.

The freshwater eel, of the genus *Anguilla*, evolved more than 50 million years ago, giving rise to fifteen different species (Prosek, 2010). Freshwater eels may have originated in the tropics, because two-thirds of the recognized *Anguilla* species inhabit the tropics, while only five species are from temperate regions (Tsukamoto and Aoyama, 1998). In fact, phylogenetic evidence strongly suggests that the place of origin for freshwater eels was the western Pacific in the vicinity of Indonesia.

Both the American eel (*Anguilla rostrata*) and the European eel (*Anguilla anguilla*) spawn in the same area. However, it was once postulated that there is a shift of spawning times that creates reproductive isolation; that theory identified February as the peak spawning season for the American eel and April for the European. Subsequent work by researchers Castonguay and McCleave (1987) revealed that both species spawn simultaneously in an overlapping area (spatiotempral sympatry). Underlying reasons for reproductive isolation remain unclear.

Following spawning, eel larvae then emerge from eggs suspended in the Sargasso Sea, a subtropical gyre in the North Atlantic somewhere East of Bermuda. Named after the prolific oceanic weed, the Sargasso Sea encompasses two million square miles of the Atlantic. The only reason scientists know this is that dense bodies of larval eels have been found drifting near the ocean surface thousands of miles from any shore.

Krueger, he informed me the most important Atlantic *Anguilla* paper ever published, sad to say, was also the most overlooked. That's because it was published not in a journal, but in a book, *American Fisheries Society Symposium 1* (1987). The paper, "Reproductive sympatry of American and European eels and implications for migrations and taxonomy," was authored by James D. McCleave, Robert C. Kleckner, and Martin Castonnguay. It was based on more than two thousand leptos five to ten millimeters long, captured over a huge area. The Euros were taken from 23-30 N latitude to 48-74 W longitude; the Yanks from 19.5-29.0 N to 52-79 W, a huge overlap. Both species were frequently taken in the same nets. Furthermore, a 1987 paper by Castonguay and McCleave cited here showed that, based on small leptos caught with opening-closing nets, the two species spawn at the same depths as well: the upper few hundred meters. The above then is the probable spawning area. Reproductive isolation must be by behavioral means or by distinctly different odors (pheromones) in the ovarian fluids. There is some published biochemical evidence for hybridization.

The first paper also suggested that abrupt changes in temperature and salinity experienced by the silver eels as they cross the North Atlantic Subtropical Convergence tells them to stop migrating and reproduce (McCleave et al., 1987). ALL of the specimens were taken in or below this front, which apparently concentrates the eels in a relatively limited area.

Where salmon are best known to "imprint" on a natal river, or young striped bass return to genetically imprinted overwinter estuaries, scientists have yet to identify the mechanism whereby adult American eels locate the Sargasso Sea ten to thirty years later—or how eel offspring may or may not locate the estuary that reared the parents, which die post spawn.

A MYSTERIOUS FISH

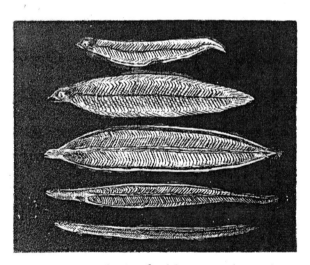

Metamorphosis of eel larva to glass eel

Prosek, 2010

Leptocephali larvae transition to glass eel

We can only guess how long it takes for eel larva to reach the New England Coast, as no one has yet been able to track a juvenile eel's progress from the deep ocean to shore. It has been suggested that baby eels, as small as matchsticks and clear as glass, find their way into southern New England streams around mid-March, then ascend various estuaries (rivers, salt ponds, creeks), moving from salt well into freshwater. These migrants are believed to be in their second year—hatched from eggs in the Sargasso between February and April the year prior.

By the time they reach freshwater, they have slimmed from their leaf-shaped larval stage, but still transparent, except for two black dots for eyes. Referred to as glass eels, they move into estuaries at night, passing docks, homes, bridges, even transiting fish ladders meant for other fish. After several days to a week in freshwater, they become pigmented and resemble thick, black shoelaces.

These eels, now called "elvers," feed and grow, taking up residence in an estuary, river, or lake, a specific part of which they may occupy for up to one hundred years, depending on the species. "When they are of age to migrate and spawn, they undergo physiological changes that prepare them for their sea journeys. Their eyes get bigger and take on a bluish cast, their skin becomes thicker, and their pectoral fins elongate. Steel-colored, with black backs like many ocean fishes, these migrating eels, fat and strong, are referred to by biologists and fishermen alike as silver eels" (Prosek, 2000).

Some biologists theorize eels know their spawning location due to "imprinting" when they're born—possibly due to some geomagnetic sense. It has been proven eels and other fishes, like tuna, have a magnetic sense, which may enable them to locate their oceanic spawning site.

Overfishing

Through the 1990s, Japan severely overfished its native eel (*Anguilla japonica*) populations to the extent that available supply plummeted, driving price into the clouds. Consequently, the abundant and mostly unregulated North American eels became a prime target—and a hugely lucrative one—for export to Asia.

For a few years in the mid-1990s, the world commercial and aquaculture eel harvest soared to 205,000 metric tons, with an economic value of a staggering $3.1 billion. "A single eel farm in Canton, China, was capable of raising, cleaning, grilling, freezing and packaging 8,000 tons of eels annually, most of which were shipped to Japan" (Prosek, 2010).

On our shores, the cost of shipping live American eels to Japan posed a logistical problem. It didn't take domestic dealers long to figure it out: Instead of shipping adult eels, they shifted focus to the capture of glass eels, which they could ship by the millions to farms in China and Taiwan. The farms could then raise these juveniles to a preferred size. In what amounted to an unregulated, fully above-board eel gold rush, stateside commercial fishermen were soon receiving $250 a pound for glass eels.

However, state biologists and conservation officials soon woke up to the mass exploitation of the resource, and the export business was shut down. In the late 1990s and again in the mid-2000s, the American eel was considered by the federal government for a formal Endangered Species Act (ESA) Listing, but backers couldn't assemble enough credible eel data to support the designation. Since the American eel inhabits many different bodies of water (and thus management jurisdictions) throughout its life and passes through so many distinct life stages, it has proven extremely challenging to manage the stock.

The American eel, found in freshwater, estuarine, and marine habitats from Greenland to South America, has disappeared from portions of its historical freshwater range over the last century, mainly as a result of dam building through the 1960s. Habitat loss and degradation, excessive harvest, and hydroelectric turbine mortality have contributed to localized population declines as well. In 2010, Greenpeace International added the American eel to its seafood "Red List," which identifies commercially important species likely to be sourced from unsustainable markets/fisheries.

If you've been wondering how those eels you like to feed to Block Island stripers ever went from "two-for-a-nickel"—the going rate in the 1960s—to more than two bucks apiece you now pay at the tackle shops, you now have your answer.

What's Next for Eels?

In an October 2011 issue of *The Fisherman* magazine, longtime conservation writer Al Ristori reported that American eels are once again being considered for ESA listing under either threatened or endangered status, a move, he suggests, "that would likely eliminate their use as striper bait." The U.S. Fish and Wildlife Service issued a ninety-day finding on September 28, 2011, setting in motion a new formal investigation of available science.

"There already have been suggestions in ASMFC meetings," Ristori continues, "that the use of eels as bait may be the first to go if more severe regulations are considered to be necessary. That would be a *big* problem for some striper addicts, as most of the largest [bass] caught in recent years—including the recently-accepted IGFA World Record have been hooked on live eels."

Canada, facing a 99 percent decline in migratory eel counts through the upper St. Lawrence River, is also prepared to act. Ontario has already closed its commercial and recreational fisheries, and Canadian government regulations have set a goal of reducing eel mortality by 50 percent from all sources.

Home Waters

Early in my saltwater bass fishing career, I became friends with a local "Swamp Yankee" by the name of Clifford Tucker, better known as "Dubie," a nickname drawn from his parents' constant admonition, "Do be good!" In his later years, he earned a living trapping eels in the Narrow River. Formally the Pettaquamscutt River estuary, the "Narrow River" is a small, ten-mile-long estuarine watershed in southern Rhode Island. Fed at its North Kingstown headwaters by freshwater from the mill stream below Gilbert Stuart's birthplace, the Narrow River discharges into Rhode Island Sound through a winding tidal inlet at the north end of Narragansett Town Beach.

Two for a Nickel

Standing on the hard packed gravel launching ramp at "Swede" Enquist's Middle Bridge Bait and Tackle Shop some forty years ago, Dubie Tucker had just dumped fifty squirming and twisting bass eels into my seven-gallon bucket. Alongside, hauled partway up the ramp was Dubie's battered wooden skiff, littered with Narrow River eelgrass, several eel pots and a nearly full eel car. Closer inspection revealed several live horseshoe crabs—bait for the next set of traps—beside the bailing scoop.

The eighteen-horsepower Evinrude outboard tilted up at the transom had seen better days but still did the job. That job was setting and tending several hundred eel traps, most of whose yield would be sold as bait to people like me, who chased large striped bass. The bulk of my eels would soon reside in an eel car Dubie had made for me a year prior. It was a simple, rectangular cage—a rough-sawn pine frame wrapped in quarter-inch galvanized wire mesh, with access via a trap door at one end. Hung by a cord off a dock, it would keep several dozen eels lively long enough to supply my nighttime ventures along Narragansett's rocky ledge shoreline. More about that later.

The remainder of Dubie's bass eels went to local bait and tackle shops, where they were stored in aerated tanks behind closed doors for those clients wanting live bait for striper fishing. More specifically, the eels were for those fishermen looking to catch larger stripers—the "bull" bass, which were actually—properly speaking—"cow" bass, females that far outweighed their male counterparts.

For those who targeted school-sized striped bass, the refrigerator behind the tackle counters held large cardboard flats of damp rockweed and recently dug clamworms shipped weekly from the mudflats of MA and ME. A flat held twelve dozen sandworms and sold for six dollars. These days, a flat sells for nearly $45.

At any rate, most eel tanks had either a 110V or 12V electric air pump that oxygenated the water and kept the baits lively. It wasn't uncommon to see both shore and boat anglers leaving shops on a Friday evening with a dozen or more eels in their bait buckets. Like some other big-bass-minded fishermen, I had specific requirements for the eels I offered to unwary striped bass. Not only did these eels have to be between twelve and fourteen inches, they also had to have a specific coloration—grey-green back and snow-white belly. Mind you: eels that came from other rivers might occasionally have that "correct" pigmentation, but it wasn't anything you could count on. Eels caught in the Connecticut River by another commercial supplier had tan bellies and weren't favored by locals. Little did we know, the age and sex of an eel determined its size and appearance. Funny thing about bass fisherman—once they get an idea in their heads about the success or failure of a particular color eel (or anything else, for that matter), they form an opinion that's hard to change.

Dubie Tucker

I'd often visit Dubie while he worked out in the garage behind his Pond Street residence. The garage housed—among many other things—the tools he used to build his eel traps, which numbered in the dozens. The *Narragansett Times* profiled Tucker in July 1996: "He was a man of many skills, from raising turkeys to weaving cloth. Wakefield, RI, was a mill town in the early 1900s, and he learned to weave in local mills before he left school. For a time, he owned a bait shop in Galilee and spent years on Point Judith Pond, both eeling and shellfishing." After some years, he moved his eel trapping efforts into the Pettaquamscutt (Narrow) River, where I first met him.

Once his pots were in the water, he'd tend them every two to three days, empty their catch, and rebait them. It was then I learned eels could live out of water so long as they were kept wet, allowing them to exchange gases through their skin.

For those with specific preferences, Dubie offered eels in various sizes and colors—some silver-bellied, some yellow-bellied, some exceeding twenty inches in length, others less than ten inches. Admittedly, at that point, I had little insight as to why such a variety existed. Dubie allowed me to choose the size and color I wanted, and things were fine for a couple of years.

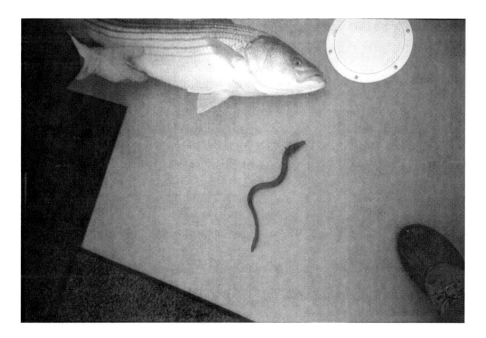

Still Watching That Eel

R. J. Schaeffer Fishing Contest

Back in the sixties, the Scituate Salt Water Anglers was but one of many Rhode Island saltwater fishing clubs but differed in that the majority of its members targeted larger striped bass, doing much of their fishing from boats along the Newport shore, Narragansett Bay's western shore, and South County's south shore westward to Charlestown. At this point in my career, I'd yet to discover the striper mecca of Block Island. Frankly, I'd had no reason to look elsewhere.

During the time the R. J. Schaefer Salt Water Fishing Contest, run by the Brooklyn, New York-based brewery, then in its seventeenth or eighteenth season, was offering the state's saltwater clubs a well-organized platform to pit their striper fishing success against what "the other guys" were catching. Boat and Shore Divisions, with points generated on the basis of fish size, made it all the more interesting. A fish had to be over fifteen pounds to qualify and if caught from shore was worth twice as many points as one taken from a boat. Affidavits had to bear weights off certified scales and witness signatures required approval by club directors prior to submission.

I was proud to be a member of this elite striper club, as we were State Champs three years running. Many in the club, including me, wore "Nifty Fifty" and "Super Sixty" R. J. Schaefer Contest patches denoting the catch of fifty—and sixty-pound-plus striped bass.

Late that summer, I was at Swede's (Swede Enquist, owner of Middlebridge luncheonette) early one morning weighing up a striper I suspected to be over fifty pounds. The cross-member of the frame that supported the scale was decorated with a large silhouette of a leaping striper, painted white. I studied it each time I delivered a good fish to the scales. In fact, at my request, my father had cut that plywood bass out and painted it for me, so all would recognize a place locally caught stripers could be weighed.

The scale beneath did right by me that morning: When I hung the largest fish from my toils the prior evening on the hook, it read 53 ½ pounds. (Among the rest of my respectable catch were several fish in the low—to mid-forty-pound range.)

Back then, I had a large, low-profile open plywood box that was bolted to roof racks on my beat-up Chevy. Anyone who handled as many stripers as we did soon learned not to use the car's trunk, as the odor it soon generated would attract not only after-dark prowling cats but also raccoons, skunks, and other critters.

Just then, Dubie Tucker pulled up in his pickup, jumped out, and wandered over, his gnarled hands working a piece of line. "That's a good one," he mumbled. "Fifty-something?" I nodded. Looking down, he pushed some gravel into a pile with his foot then explained he had some bad news about his eels. "I gotta go up on the price," he said sheepishly. "Price of gas is up, trap wire's up, and someone's been raiding the traps I got out. Hate like hell to do it to you—feel like I'm takin' advantage of you . . ." I awaited the bad news.

"Can't do two for a nickel like I have been," he announced. "I gotta get a nickel apiece from now on . . ."

Other Fish to Fry

There was a brief period in the sixties when I couldn't get eels from Dubie, so I fell back on buying them from the new owners of Babcock's Marina on Point Judith Pond. Its original owner and namesake, Elmer Babcock, was a dyed-in-the-wool Swamper of the first order.

Babcock was a local fixture. He'd feed the same line to anyone who'd listen: "Fella could make a good living working the local salt ponds for fish, crabs, clams, and selling bait from his shop and small boat marina."

The new owner at Babcock's, a gal with two young daughters as helpers, ran the marina and shop, selling new boats and outboard motors, bait (like worms, squid, mummies, clams, quahogs, live eels, etc.), as well as ice cream. Not wanting to handle any eels, she'd send the youngest one out to the docks to dump some eels into my bait bucket.

After buying a dozen eels or more, I'd be sure to finish up with the purchase of a double-dip vanilla ice cream cone and hang around for a bit. Funny how things work out: That gal later sold Babcock's and landed a job at another marina. Some years later, I wound up dating and eventually marrying that girl, inheriting two daughters in the bargain.

As anyone knows who routinely uses live eels, they're tough to handle, thanks to their incessant squirming and copious mucous covering. A quick hand and a dry rag (or Scotch-Brite pad) are the main way to successfully wrangle one onto a hook. From there, the angler risks discovering that his bait has tied itself in a ball and in the process decorated the leader with a half-dozen slime-dipped overhand knots—rendering the whole setup more or less useless, pending repairs.

For years, we prevented that aggravation by storing eels in a small, ice-filled bucket, which slowed them down, making them easier to handle. Even after an extended tour on the hook, the baits are remarkably hardy: if there's even any curl to the tail, the eel's still alive. And if the eel's still alive, a striped bass will have no trouble finding and engulfing it—even in the turbid nighttime blackness at current-swept depths of forty, fifty, to one hundred plus feet. The reason? Although the eel isn't visible to the bass until the very last second, the striper's ultra-sensitive lateral line can detect prey movement yards away. That's why, in many cases, fresh, spunky eels catch better than near-lifeless ones.

III

TACKLING ISLAND STRIPERS

WIRED FOR ACTION

Failure to prepare is preparation for failure.

—Unknown

Anyone with some years in the business of trying to consistently land Block Island bass knows that there's a world of difference between catching fish when the bite's wide open, and catching them when the conditions are tough, the fish are scattered, or, for whatever reason—whether it's dogfish or an abundance of other available feed—the fish aren't willing to take eels. The difference between the guys who catch most days and the guys who get skunked most days is a willingness to do what it takes to *make the fish eat*—to hunt them and ultimately make them an offer they can't refuse.

There's no cute way around it: if you're looking to improve your season-long catch rate, you're going to have to learn the finer points of controlled-depth fishing. And pleasant as it is to get 'em on downriggers, you really can't get around the need to drag wire. With that certainty in mind, the following two pieces lay out (1) the connections you'll need to rig your own wires and (2) a build-it-yourself device that will let you precisely measure your lengths of stainless line.

The Wire Connection

Knowing how much wire line to troll is key to success. Gone are the days I feared having an angler suffer a parted wire upon hookup—whether at the wire leader connection, the marker, the wire itself, or the backing connection. If a wire was lost, I was embarrassed. Sure, some clients were unaware they'd created a kink, but that's part of the game. At day's end, I have the mate run the wires out for inspection, visually inspect them myself, or, if necessary, retire a suspect outfit for a "section" replacement.

Over the years, I've come to learn how some other skippers deal with wire line connections, and I'm both amused and horrified. Reason being I've been around long enough to know what works and what doesn't. If you've been troubled with wire line connections, consider the following.

Wire to Leader

Most mono leaders tend to be short, there's only little stretch to absorb the pressure of a hook-up or the antics of a sizeable fish boat-side. A leader connection has to be able to "grease" through a tiptop—one reason using a small swivel for that junction is a poor choice. True, a no. 10 swivel is rated at thirty-five-pound-test and can pass through a large tiptop but frequently hangs up and is weakened by rod tip forces (even the miniscule 130-pound-rated Spro swivels are murder on rod tips). And those who use a clinch knot to connect their leader to a wire loop know wire can cut it.

Prowler wire-to-monofilament-leader connections use a "nail knot," so called because a tool, such as—you guessed it—a nail, is used to assist in creating it. I learned of this connection years ago from a Montauk skipper and in all honesty can claim I've never had a properly tied one part on me, no matter how much pressure was applied.

This knot will take a little practice, along with some patience, but once you get the knack for it, you'll find it's the best wire-to-mono connection you'll ever create. Reason being the mono is snelled to a bend in the wire in such a fashion it cannot be pulled off. Try this—about three inches of the monel or stainless wire is bent upon itself and the mono is snelled onto it. The nail is initially placed alongside the tie to keep the wire from bending, and assist with the mono finding its way under the wraps then carefully removed prior to pulling both mono ends up tight. Make sure the mono has passed through the loop in the wire line end.

Pulled up tight using saliva to moisten it, the five or six complete turns of mono comprising the knot is snipped close, and the wire is finished off with a tight whip.

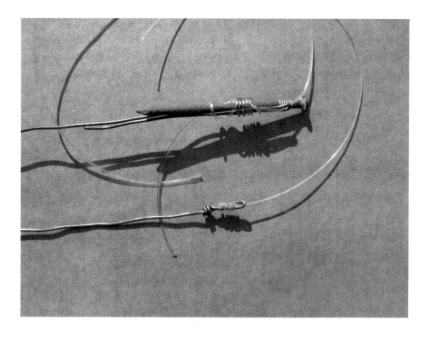

Nail Knot

Wire to Markers

You mark your lines so you know how much wire you're fishing, right? If not, you're probably unable to consistently repeat success. Markers can be colored, but forget that sticky tape that easily jams a rod guide. Instead, try using either hollow core two-hundred-pound-test test Dacron or colored eighty-pound-test mono as a marker, tying it in via a nail knot. Using Dacron is slightly quicker and easier, and a busy tackle shop can make a few yards available to you.

I use hollow-core two-hundred-pound-test Dacron for markers on my three-hundred-foot wire line outfits, one at one hundred feet, a second at 150 feet, a third at two hundred feet, and a fourth at 250 feet, with the end of the wire marking three hundred feet.

The connection is simple. Using a twelve-inch section of Dacron, I insert the end of my fifty-pound-test wire about an inch into its hollow core, carefully poking the wire end out a couple of inches into the Dacron. Then, bending the wire sharply back on itself with pliers, the wire is pulled snug prior to whipping four to six turns around the Dacron. Make sure the cut wire end is tucked back into the soft Dacron with needle-nose pliers, lest you bloody up your thumb when deploying it later. With a match, seal the "fuzzy" end of the Dacron, which melts and fuses it, preventing any possible loss.

Another option is using monofilament as a marker; clear, fluorescent-green, and red mono have worked well for me in the past. Since I use soft (fast) tip rods for wire line jigging, there is no stiff tip to compromise (harden) that portion of the wire. Those who use stiff rod tips simply don't get it.

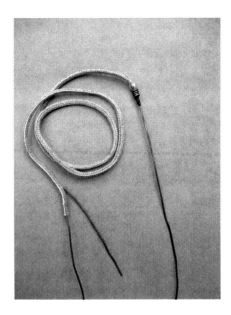

Hollow-core Dacron Spice Connection

Go Haywire

A haywire twist can be used to temporally connect one end of a wire to another while fishing, should a bad kink, snarl, or potential break occur while a wire is deployed, only a temporary fix if properly done, but one that should last for the day.

Using pliers—this takes a little practice—tightly twist both wires around each other for a minimum of three to four inches overlap then finish each end with a tight whip. After catching a fish, you'll know you did a good job if the whips don't move.

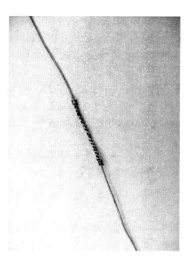

Haywire Twist Connection

Spares

For years, I've spooled spare wires in reverse onto small spools, so once connection is made to the backing, the new wire and its markers can be wound onto the reel. If you're not up to doing something like this at home or in the garage, check out www.polyjig.com or call Ed Shea at (401) 885-4441. Premade custom-length shots of wire with markers are available to buyer's specifications.

Wire to Backing

Today my wire line outfits use 130-pound-test Dacron backing, spliced into a three-foot shot of two-hundred-pound-test at the wire end. Reason being, depending on depths being fished, we may deploy up to three hundred feet of wire, and we jig the 'chutes on the heavier Dacron. Again, should I choose to refresh the connection, it takes less time than if I were using monofilament backing.

At the Reel

I've fished jigs and frames on wire for years in rips as deep as sixty feet, using Penn 113HLW reels. I favor this model for several reasons: not only is it lightweight, the spool also holds plenty of line, even with three hundred feet of wire deployed. Consequently, the spool diameter remains large, providing tremendous mechanical advantage upon retrieve. One turn of the reel handle returns as much or more line as reels twice their weight, an important factor when jigging long wires. Also, Penn reel parts are readily available, should one need repair. So the next time your buddy loses a fish to a busted wire connection, show him one of yours and smile.

Wire-Winders

Not long ago, numerous RISAA members debated/hypothesized, via e-mail, various ways to measure and mark the length of a wire line deployed for trolling, several of which were hilarious. Many suggested line counters were the answer. Others confessed theirs had fallen off the reel, then overboard, or didn't work well for lefties, or rusted and fouled due to salt corrosion, or lasted less than a season, and so on. One genius posted they work well when fishing a color-marked lead core line (?), while still others suggested using downriggers instead. Not that I haven't successfully fished wire line outfits from down-riggers in deep water for years, but I've got to assume jigging that downrigger had to be *exhausting*.

I've come up with a much simpler solution to the problem—a homemade line-winder for measuring wire lines either at home, shop, or garage instead of in a field or between dock pilings. This simple device does a multitude of jobs and best of all creates repeated catch success. Another style allows lines to be quickly reversed.

Wooden Line Winder for measuring wire and mono

When Precision Counts

Ever wanted to place marked-length wire on your reels, or inspect them for threatening kinks? Ever wanted to save a few bucks by reversing one end of a mono or wire line that's only slightly used or damaged? Ever mark a mono or spectra-fiber line for presenting a diamond at depths tuna are marking? Ever wish you had a spare spool of marked wire for the one that just parted off—the spare reversed on a spool so all you had to do was connect it to the backing and wind it up?

Ever redo your wire line marks after a hard day's use to prevent parting? Ever place one or more Dacron splices into a shot of wire to mark lengths fished? All these are possible with just a few minutes of your time, using the wooden wire/mono winder.

Spool Options

I use two types of spools, one hand-powered, the other cordless-drill-powered. The wooden hand powered winder uses a half-inch plywood for the sides, soft pine for the drum spokes, and a carriage bolt for a spindle. This winder allows me to slowly remove and inspect lines from my reels, whereas a cordless drill does it quicker, but it's difficult to accurately measure length with one. More about that shortly.

Wooden Winder

Cut two circular pieces of half-inch plywood with a ten-inch diameter, drilling a 3/8-inch, centered hole in each. Using eight pieces of ¾-inch by 1 ¼-inch by six-inch pine, equally inter-space, nail and glue each one inch from the outside edge. Be sure to glue, as the compression forces of mono will destroy a weak joint. Next, drill a 5/16-inch hole two inches from the edge of one plywood "side-plate," then locate a 5/16-inch by three-inch bolt and nuts to create a handle using a 1 ¾-inch piece of 3/8-inch diameter PVC pipe for a handle sleeve.

3/8-inch by ten-inch carriage bolt, with washers and nuts, allows easy and convenient mounting. If desired, either a steel spring or drag washers between the steel washers can provide tension. Use a hacksaw to make several inch-long cuts into the plywood's radial edge for holding a line end. Despite constant use, mine has served me well for years. Consider mounting it on the side of a workbench, with a rod holder facing it. Not having to remove a reel from a rod hastens service and simplifies life!

Whatever size winder you make, you'll need to accurately measure a shot of wire to calibrate it (number of turns equals distance). Forget using mono, which stretches. Once calibrated, you can make up a chart, post it, and refer to it in the future. For example, with my winder, twelve turns puts twenty-five feet of line on the drum, twenty-four cranks, fifty feet, forty-eight cranks puts one hundred feet on, and so on.

Plastic Spool Winder

Check with your local tackle shop to secure one or more empty one-pound capacity (or larger) bulk mono spools. Typically with a 5/8-inch center hole, they can be converted for use with a cordless variable speed drill to simplify and speed up line reversing, inspection, or removal.

Simply secure a 5/8-inch wooden dowel, measure the width of the plastic spool, then cut the dowel about 1 ½ inches wider. If a drill press is handy, bore a dead-center, two-inch-deep hole in the dowel at one end to receive a ¼-inch-diameter bolt. Leave about 1 ½ inches of the bolt exposed and hacksaw the head off, filing down any burrs. Next, press the dowel, which should fit snuggly, into the spool hole prior to applying some five-minute epoxy to both the exposed dowel ends and sides of the spool. If done correctly, there will be little or no wobble of the spool at high speed.

Reversing a line from a fishing reel will require two spools—one to receive the damaged end, another to reverse the line prior to making the necessary backing connection. To ease spooling line onto the reel, the 3/8-inch bolt spindle is placed into a 7/16-inch, workbench-drilled hole.

Battery Powered Winder

Spare Wire

If you do enough wire line striper fishing, there will come a time you wish you had a spare wire to replace the one you just dropped. Fret no more. Simply check with friends or your local tackle shop for empty ¼-pound plastic monofilament spools.

Use the newly created wooden line winder to create a duplicate or two of your original wires, marked at distances you prefer. Using a 3/8-inch by 4-inch bolt, washers, and nuts, secure the empty quarter-pound spool on the bolt. Hacksaw a slit in the spool side for starting the reverse end of the line, chuck it up into the drill, and you're ready to wind on your spare shot of wire before using waterproof tape to hold the wire in place.

Since you probably use mono backing on your wire reels, finish the spare wire backing-end with a short mono tail now on top of the spool. Make sure to start winding the spare spool with the leader end, then the marked wire, ending with the short section of mono (tail end) on the top. This spare, reversed line can then be blood knotted to your backing before winding it on, maybe spooled onto your empty reel in less time than it takes your buddy to land another fish! Better yet, have him hold the screwdriver and spool as you feverishly wind it on. One other important point: be sure to stow the spare wire aboard before you depart.

Spare Spools of reversed wire with Mono Leaders

Headers and More

Last season at day's end, we watched a wealthy vessel owner strip all the eighty-pound-test mono off several reels at dockside, gather it up, and dispose of it. New line was then spooled on, finishing a job that had begun an hour prior. If I had to guess, his line had less than a dozen hours use on it, but this guy was loaded, so apparently cost didn't matter. Chances are the line deep on the spool was perfectly serviceable; in fact, he could have created a "header" or "top-shot" of mono with it, saving himself both time and money.

Carefully tying a blood knot offers 90 percent of line strength and would have afforded him the opportunity to reverse, say, a 150-yard shot of line, providing a fresh mono "header" for the next few outings.

Next time your trolling mono becomes "tired," strip and cut that section off onto your winder. After you've reversed it with a plastic line spool winder, carefully connect it with a blood knot. Reversing lines for headers saved me hundreds of yards of mono a season, not to mention time and money. Guess what, I haven't lost a fish to a knotted connection since bubblegum was invented, and I bet you like to save a buck too!

I recently pulled the fly line backing off my Penn 4G-AR fly reels used for tuna fishing. Using my wooden winder and a black magic marker, I marked off fifty-yard increments of the yellow Micron backing (single mark   fifty yards, double mark—one hundred yards, triple mark—150 yards). Now, no more guessing how much backing is in the water.

Wire Sources:

American Fishing Wire
440 Highlands Blvd.
Coatesville, PA 19320-5808
1-800-824-WIRE (9473) www.americanfishingwire.com

Malin Company, Inc.
5400 Smith Road
Cleveland, Ohio 44142
(216) 267-9080
Toll Free: 1-800-967-9697 www.malinco.com

Millard Specialty Strip and Wire Co.
449 Warwick Industrial Drive
Warwick, RI 02886
(401) 737-9930 www.millardwire.com

Brookfield Wire
PO Box 248, Route 9
Brookfield, MA 01506
(508) 867-2579 www.brookfieldwire.com

Wire-Line Specs:

Pound Test	Diameter	Feet per Pound
15	0.014	1,913
20	0.016	1,465
30	0.020	935
40	0.022	770
50	0.024	645
60	0.028	475
80	0.032	360

WIRE LINE DEMYSTIFIED

*Experience is a terrific teacher,
But she sends in terrific bills.*

—Minna Antrim, 1902

Note: *The following section, penned by Zach Harvey, outlines the nuts-and-bolts of wire lining. It is included here in hopes it might help you troubleshoot the steeper stages of your own wire-trolling learning curve.*

There is absolutely *nothing* cutting-edge about wire line trolling. Every couple years, someone will come up with a new way to mark wire or a new lure to troll with the stuff, and that's about as much innovation as you'll encounter. Trolling wire is certainly not the most appealing or sporty way to catch stripers or blues, but year in, year out across a huge swath of East Coast waters, there are very few methods that are as consistently effective—a big reason you should know how to use it if you're serious about catching bass.

Unfortunately, outside the explosive shallow-water scenarios of spring and fall, the best of the bite will be out in the deeper water, and your success will hinge on your ability to hunt big bass where they live. Wire line is not the only method of trolling deep, but where stripers are concerned, it is the most versatile. You can hate the stuff all you want, but if you want a crack at big fish when and where they're most accessible—late June, July, August, the Race, Block Island, Montauk, the Vineyard—you'd better consider investing in a pair of wire line outfits.

Specialty Alternatives

Lead-core line can get your trolled lures or baits to depth in shoal water, from maybe ten to thirty feet if you're willing to send out a lot of line—or if you've got your throttle control hand trained to the point where slow-trolling is as natural as driving your car. Unfortunately, the formula for lead-core is three to five feet of depth for each one-hundred-foot color, where the same length of wire will get you ten feet of penetration. Lead-core is nice stuff in that it's fairly easy to tie, simple to manage, and gives you excellent feel when you connect with a fish. Like wire, it gives you a direct connection to your rig. If all your trolling haunts are tight to beach or very shallow, you might be able to avoid the steel. Problem there is that—sooner or later—the cows will stack up on deeper real estate and the beach will enter the doldrums.

Downriggers—the other viable controlled-depth system—give the advantage of letting you troll deep with mono, adding to the sport of trolling. Downriggers also let you get offerings to depth without a ton of line trailing astern. Some charter guys will break out the riggers when they're trolling depths of over fifty feet—because it's not too practical to send out more than four hundred feet of steel. They'll also use riggers in areas congested with lobster gear—again, because they can weave through the maze with much shorter lines. Problem with downriggers is that they're complicated to deploy unless you have a full-time mate on every outing. They also prohibit offerings—parachute jigs, for example—that require rod action by you to impart action to the lure. Every charter boat I know in Point Judith has downriggers; few skippers use them more than a couple times a season—a fact that speaks volumes about the hassles of downrigger fishing.

Still other guys are exploring trolling with braid, usually through the use of drail or keel sinkers. Again, this can work in shallow water, but the technique has a couple of major drawbacks. First, keel sinkers fished ahead of lures like tubes show fish additional junk before the actual lure moves past—less is more when you're targeting bigger bass. Second, unless you've logged a multitude of hours on trial-and-error detail, and you've found a successful way to mark your braid, depth precision can prove mighty elusive.

It Is Your Destiny

So it's pretty hard to cheat your way around the old standby. Wire, for all its inconveniences, fishes a variety of lures, rigs, and baits well—presents them convincingly. It's really the only way to go with jigs for reasons obvious.

When you're trolling wires, you can predict with fair accuracy running depths of your lures or baits, and get lines back in quickly when the bite materializes. It's that last point that separates the best fishermen in your marina from the worst: when it finally comes together, you don't want to waste any time fussing with unpredictable or unnecessarily complicated gear. Wire's tough to work with at points, but it's predictable and conceptually simple.

Wire Fundamentals

If you're new to wire-lining, a few basic concepts will minimize headaches. First, wire's kryptonite is the kink. One kink—one errant coil that's come tight on itself—will part a wire under only minimal strain. So when you're retrieving loose line, pay very close attention to the line as it passes through the rod tip. If you see a coil come up, take a second to uncoil it. A coil's no problem until it comes tight.

Another key is to be sure you "educate" your crew's thumbs, ensuring that—fish on or no fish on—line gets packed onto the spool tight and even. Unfortunately, level-wind reels are tough for wire, so you'll need to stay on your deck mates about manual level-winding. Ninety percent of all wire backlashes—which tend to be memorable—are the result of careless cranking.

Another prime suspect in the backlash lineup is a bulky knot or a cumbersome mark that won't pass through guides smoothly. Be sure the knots you use are narrow in profile, short in length, and be sure all tag ends are clipped very close. Generally, when you're setting out, you want to feed the leader and first forty or fifty feet out carefully, pulling the line off with your front hand and feeding it out slowly. It's usually easier to set heavier lures like umbrellas, jigs, or plugs, since their weight will get the line moving. With lighter items like small Drone spoons, J-Plugs, or tubes, you'll need to feed the line out much more carefully.

Obviously, communication between the helm and cockpit are vital in any controlled-depth fishing and wire-lining particularly. The reel man needs to be attuned to the captain, who will have an eye glued to the electronics. Hanging a wire on the bottom—or even just touching down long enough to foul a lure with weed—will waste precious fishing time. With heavier rigs like umbrellas, it's wise to come tight to the rig every fifty or so feet, so the rig won't plummet toward bottom. Especially when the rig is approaching the zone, break the spool regularly and let the rig out slowly. Finally, make depth adjustments as quickly as possible. Hanging up and, in the worst-case scenario, parting off a wire could well cost you that setup for the remainder of a trip and will most certainly tack a tedious hour onto your workbench time at trip's end.

One final note: setting lines out is major source of line-related cluster-you-know-what. It's during that time that the cockpit man must know exactly what's happening in bridge man's head. Often, the mate can't see what's ahead, so the captain must communicate clearly his intentions to make a turn. If you have the luxury of two competent guys or gals manning the rods, you can set them out simultaneously while the boat's moving straight ahead. During a turn, or when you're setting lines out one at a time, you always want to set the closest line (the rig with the least line off the spool) into the outside of the turn—and never on the inside of a turn. The latter will cross lines up and end badly. Obviously, it's important that the crew understand the overall trolling pattern, so they can anticipate good and bad times to put lines out.

TO FISH A RIP

A bad day of fishing is still better than a good day of work.

—Author Unknown

Despite a staggering number of feature stories, editorials, columns, fishing reports, blogs, videos, and seminars that have addressed—directly or incidentally, over a period of decades—the particulars of rip fishing, it continues to amaze me how many New England anglers have navigated their entire lives without internalizing a single ounce of the accumulated spoken, written, and recorded wisdom on the subject.

I've watched so many vessel operators who appear oblivious to the well-known fact that fish like striped bass and bluefish congregate near the visible "face" of rips. Ignorance among amateurs is one thing; what *really* bothers me is the multitude of so-called experts, including more than one "professional" charter skipper, whose total cluelessness not only sabotages their own attempts to catch fish but also effectively eliminates the possibility that the rest of us might succeed. In the world of Block Island striper-catching, it's amazing how many boats can successfully work a given spot if everyone works together and extends fellow fishermen a bit of common courtesy. It's equally amazing how quickly one or two boat—and rod-wielding morons can wipe out the productivity of an area that's holding untold hundreds of stripers on a wild feed.

As a reference point, before the Coast Guard began to enforce the three-mile, state water limit—that is, the closure of federal waters, also called the Exclusive Economic Zone, or EEZ, to all striped bass fishing after 9/11—I spent many hundreds of hours plying those rips that make up in the tide-swept, structure-rich stretch of water between the island and Montauk. I learned fast—had to. Faced with a dim-bulb or two who threatened to spook a rip's fish or otherwise gum up the works, Montauk's old guard would strike quickly, sending the offenders home—usually with less line and fewer lures.

For those new to the rip racket, the number 1 no-no is putting your vessel directly over the rip "face," the seam where a rip's stationary, standing waves meet the slick calm, where fish often bunch up to feed. Naturally, not all rips are the same. Prime examples are "googans" (my colloquial name for "idiots") who keep their vessels directly over the rip face, totally ignorant of the fact they have spooked any fish holding station there. Now, water depth is critical; but if shallow, like the North Rip's inner bar, or several of the Ledge's high spots, those individuals will catch few, if any fish, totally destroying any chance of success by others fishing the immediate area.

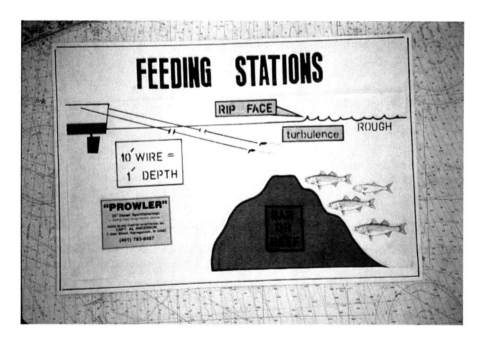

Under The Rip face

In case you're wondering, I began learning how to fish rips by simply watching (granted watching *very carefully*) what some of the best trollers on this coast did. Yes, those were charterboat skippers fishing the roiled waters around Montauk, New York. Early on, I simply joined in and did what they did. It wasn't too long before I too learned how and why to mark my lines, learning that boat speed affected lure depths, and so on. More about that later.

Thanks to those long-ago, now-submerged glacial moraines discussed in earlier chapters, numerous rips were created between Montauk Point and Block Island. These rips were formed by glacial forces that created recessional moraines—moraines that lay nearly parallel to one another, thanks to repeated glacial advance and retreat. Remember, a ridge of *terra firma* once connected the eastern end of Long Island to Block Island; over millions of years, seawater filled in then bored out that ridge of recessional moraine, creating in the process numerous rips that would one day attract cod, pollack, bluefin tuna, bluefish, weakfish and striped bass, as well as other species.

Jack Marshall & Mate Seamus

Once I'd begun fishing the tide-swept island grounds with some regularity, it didn't take me long to realize rips were areas many hungry game fish species congregated. Long ago, Jerry Sylvester, who at the time ran a tackle shop in Narragansett, told me our striper fishing would be much better if only Rhode Island's coastline had rips like those at Montauk or Buzzards Bay.

Outside of a few scattered rips in the bay and along the south shore, most of which make up exclusively during moon tide periods, the only major Rhode Island tidal rip is at the north end of Block Island. The following section is a reconsidered and completely overhauled piece I wrote a number of years back. Its purpose is to help a rip-fishing neophyte grasp the basic concepts he'll need to understand the all-important interplay between spot, current, known rip-dwelling fish behavior, forage, boat-handling, and angling methods.

Get Ripped

As we approached Block Island's North Rip that morning, I could see the NW-running flood tide was already in progress, with white water showing due to a light northerly breeze. Staying up-tide of what I call the Middle Rip; and some distance ahead of the turbulence, we deployed two-ounce chartreuse Andrus parachute jigs to the 150-foot mark on my special wires. My mate directed anglers to begin a fairly brisk jigging rhythm. From experience, I knew the lures were running tight to the bottom at twenty-two to twenty-five feet—right over the mussel bed that is responsible for this rip. The current was quartering over the bar as we slowly trolled "upstream" more or less "jogging in place," holding the standing-wave turbulence at a distance of twelve to fifteen yards astern as we swung across the rip face. The jigs, pulsating above the seabed, must have imitated perfectly—in profile and action—a small squadron of Loligo squid holding their ground in the tide. Suddenly, one rod, then a second, arched over, signaling head-shaking stripers had locked-on.

Meanwhile, other boats, jigging along aimlessly down-tide of the rip, continued their cardio training, fishless. Still others meandered around the area, oblivious to the immediate location of area game fish.

Rip Rudiments

Arriving back at the dock daily with an impressive catch is not luck, but a consequence of knowing where, when, and how to catch fish. Arguably, one of the most consistent sources for stripers, bluefish, fluke, codfish, and a host of other local favorites are tidal rips. Learn how to fish a rip, and you'll consistently outfish others. For cultivating the skills involved—the rigging, the technique, the boat handling—will teach you a great deal

Today's reader will find this hard to believe, but ages ago, I started my lessons on April's early morning running tides at the island's southwest corner bell buoy, as formations of birds (gulls and terns) worked over that rip for several hours. Under all the birds were codfish and pollack that were "bustin'" on the surface, simply demolishing schools of sand eels. This was before the umbrella rig came into being; instead, small two—to three-ounce diamond jigs were the ticket.

There's a lot to learn, whether you wire line or downrigger-troll a rip, diamond jig, or drift baits for gamesters. If your memory is like mine is now, you'll need to start by taking a few notes.

First off, identify a rip by name, but if you're unaware of one used, give it a name and note the time of high or low tide at a nearby location. Also, record the time and stage of the tide you are fishing it, the direction of flow (on both the ebb or flood), the water depth beneath the rip face, and its location (GPS Phantom Loran numbers). Note also the numbers for the ends of the rip or any breaks in it. You may come to discover fluke frequently hang out at both ends of a rip, or stripers take up station at breaks in a rip. Note also wind direction and character of the rip. Frequently, the rougher or more turbulent the rip, the better the striper fishing will be—up to a point. Strong wind conditions can mask the tell-tale signs, concealing a rip's position; saved waypoints have saved my hide more times than I care to admit. One other point, if you have all the above info, there's nothing to prevent you from fishing it under low-visibility, foggy conditions, while your buddies wander the four corners of the ocean hoping to get lucky.

Fish Behavior

Some rips have more to offer at peak current velocities, but most fish better the first and last third of either the flood or ebb tide. Keep in mind that fish have to work harder to hold station in a rip when the tide's roaring at peak velocity; should pickings be slim, they'll move off-station. A striper's survival depends on calories spent versus calories consumed.

For stripers, the bigger the water, the bigger the fish. The logic is simple: Large stripers are stronger swimmers than their smaller brethren. Smaller fish tend to arrive early or late in a tidal rip, simply because they cannot match the performance of larger fish, which will vacate an area when opportunities to ambush struggling prey diminish. In other words, bass won't stay unless available feed offsets the calories spent to hold that ground.

Boulder-strewn bottoms and the current breaks they create offer more options for structure-seeking stripers than simple, soft-bottom edges do—a big reason is that there are more prime big fish berths scattered along SW Ledge's broken seabed than at the North Rip. The compromise, in terms of overall fishability, is that southwest houses tons of problematic lobster gear that can wreak havoc when strong moon tides suck trawl-end buoys subsurface. The North Rip is typically free of lobster gear.

Ambush-feeding fluke will congregate behind structure right through peak tidal flow; when current eases, they'll readily chase bait. In my experience, codfish will pull a disappearing act when tidal currents peak then reappear and chew again during slower flow. Again, it's Mother Nature's ground rules: energy gain must exceed energy expenditure.

Trolling a Rip

When trolling a rip, record numbers where action occurs. Stay up-tide of the rip face, walking lures along the structure. Don't waste your time, energy, or fuel trolling down-tide of it—only googans do that. Remember: fish most often congregate under the rip face, and by trolling along in front of the rip face—your lures swinging slowly across the front of that zone—you greatly increase your chances of jolting strikes. If helm duty prevents you from fishing, have a buddy hook one for you before you slide off the rip.

Boat speed is critical. Particularly important is understanding the difference between speed through water and speed over (relative to) ground. Consider: If you're under way directly into a four-knot current, you will have to make four knots of forward progress just to hold your position relative to the bottom. In this scenario, you can be traveling through the water at four knots (gauges connected to your engine will confirm this) while traveling at zero or 0.2 knot per your GPS. I typically employ troll valves on my engines to reduce shaft rpm, thereby slowing the boat to let wire line offerings to probe deeper. In and out of gear will work also, as will making a turn to allow the "inside" lure to slow and settle. If you make a turn up-tide in a deep rip and get strikes, don't hesitate to practice that technique—then make a note of it.

Draw what you've learned and carry it with you the next time you go. Chances are good and you'll add some info to what you already have; multiply that process out over months and years, and you have the makings of a sharpie.

At The RIP; FISH ON..!

Casting a Rip

Many times, fish hold station on the down-tide, rough-water side of a rip over a bar or ledge, so don't make the mistake of setting up on top of them and casting up-tide—where they *are not*. For one thing, if the water's shallow, you'll probably spook them with the boat. Besides, retrieving a lure down-current multiplies lure speed, killing your odds.

One thing that can be tricky early in your rip-fishing learning is that the visible "seam" where calm water meets rough moves relative to the actual structure that causes it through with the acceleration and deceleration of tidal current. Simply stated, the harder the tide runs, the further down-tide the rip face. Conversely, as the tide eases, the rip face will retreat closer to the structure that creates it.

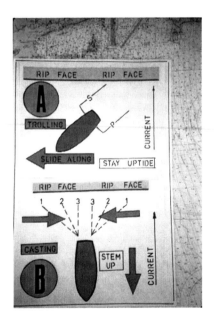

RIP Trolling & Casting

Best bet when plugging—or fly-casting—a rip is to stem the current well up-tide of the face and cast either right or left, retrieving the plug or fly along the edge or in front of the rip face. The more rip face you cover, the better. Fish lying under it are constantly "looking up" toward the surface; offerings behind them in the rough water go unnoticed, lost in the "noise." Perhaps you now know the reason for the eyes of a striper being located where they are!

Drifting a Rip

Approaching your rip in drift mode—perhaps for some nighttime eeling—jot down the numbers for the start of your first drift, noting wind direction and velocity, as it will affect your movement. Be aware that strikes usually come around the time you reach the rip face. Once through the rip, if you get no strikes, run back up-tide to your starting point and repeat the drift. If you're still fishless (or rather, you've had no positive signs), choose a new starting point nearby to create a new drift track. Note the GPS numbers of any action area. Yeah, yeah, I know: you'll be too busy hanging on to your rod to do it. Do it anyway! In the future, you'll be glad you did, as most "spots" repeatedly hold fish on repeat tides, especially under similar conditions. One side note: If you're marking fish on a drift, but not catching them after a few passes, you may need to start your drift a bit further up-tide—especially if the drift's very fast. In that latter scenario, you need to be sure your bait has hit bottom well ahead of the life you're marking. That is, if you set up right on top of—or just a hair up-tide of—the marks, your bait, still in its descent, may still be thirty feet from bottom when you cross over the fish and finally touchdown when you're twenty feet down-tide and out of their zone.

If you can stem the tide, matching current velocity so that the boat remains in one spot, note how far up-tide of the rip face you are when the diamond jigs you're squidding astern receive strikes, along with speed and direction of the current. You may come to see that tidal current direction and velocity change over the course of a tidal period, making structure more or less productive—and quite likely changing your drift track relative to your various starting points. Be sure to make notes about all that, too.

Note your depths, weight of sinkers or diamond jigs used, path of drift, tidal stage, and, of course, any and all results of your efforts—good, bad, or otherwise. Learning, like experience, is cumulative and ongoing.

Develop Options

Years ago, in late April or early May, when open waters east or south of Block Island were simply too rough to fish for cod or pollack, I'd fish tidal rips in its lee. There were days when trolling or diamond-jigging a rip or two would secure all the fish the party wanted. That's right, troll up half-a-hundred cod or pollack by noontime. Those rips still exist, but instead of early-season groundfish, it's stripers or bluefish or fluke.

Fishing the island on a given high-summer weekend, I'm not always convinced the majority of anglers ever got the well-publicized message that structure like lumps, bumps, ledges, and boulders attract game fish, particularly under the influence of moderate to strong tidal currents. Seems the turbulence that results from these structures disorients all sorts of potential meals, meals like squid, shrimp, sand eels, and silversides. Perhaps that's why striped bass become more aggressive as rip conditions intensify.

Whether you target striped bass, fluke, bluefish, cod, weakfish, school tuna, or bonito, knowing how to fish a rip can increase your batting average dramatically—particularly when weather conditions limit your options. More than once, several rips in the lee of the island or mainland allowed us to get the day in when others stayed at the dock. In rough conditions, consider fishing that tide—and only that tide—where the current and wind direction align. Rough-but-still-fishable conditions often yield good results. Keep in mind knowledge about a few rips can give you a big edge, so make plans to get started now.

SPRING STANDARD: SAND EELS AND UMBRELLAS

Wishin' I'd gone fishin' . . .

—Unknown

It was a late May morning last season at Clay Head, Block Island, and Rhode Island Sound waters were flooding hard northwest. High above, terns, gulls, and shearwaters were wheeling and fluttering, others jinxing and diving; while seals and porpoise occasionally broke the calm surface. In the midwater depths below, total havoc unfolded as massive clouds of iridescent sand eels struggled to evade the zooming maws of recently arrived striped bass from the Delaware Bay region. If any situation called for offering tubes on an umbrella rig, this was it!

Fast forward to our second pass: one of my anglers—who'd just accepted the "set" rod from my mate—had his hands full, his rugged wire line outfit bent from foregrip on up. Once the heavy-mono leader showed at the surface, my mate motioned for assistance. Shortly, one bass was led into the landing net; while a second stout bass, locked onto the trailer and still in the water astern, awaited its destiny. Soon, the two stocky teen-sized bass had been unhooked, measured on the tagging board, and placed on a soft deck mat with wet rags over their eyes to ease stress while they awaited tags. Inside of a minute later, the satisfied angler watched as my mate liberated one, and then two, stocky low-teen 'linesiders' - each now carrying a bright new yellow ALS "lock-on" tag behind its first dorsal.

The abundance of sand eels, or sand launce (*Ammodytes dubius*), clouding the waters around Block Island, had focused the attention of many striper addicts on the use of umbrella lures sporting latex or vinyl tubes. By June's end, nearly four hundred keeper-sized striped bass had swam away bearing my ALS tags and well over one hundred bass had been retained; by the end of July, that number swelled to over seven hundred bass tagged and released. Judging from the many spring e-mails inquiring about the best way to imitate a sand eel, I thought a story about a lure I've used for years might be of interest.

Sand Eel City

Although experts offer several reasons for their cyclical abundance, they're still unsure sure why sand eel populations fluctuate. Spring, summer or fall, Northeast stripers have several prime food sources to target; sand eels are among the best. Should you encounter spring-time stripers foraging on this bait and be armed with small tube-armed umbrella frames, you could enjoy some of your best early-season action ever.

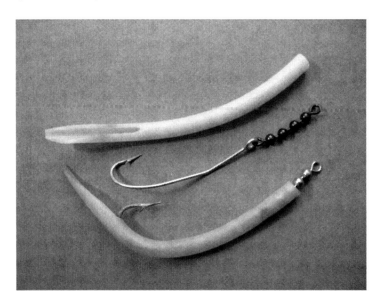

Sand eel latex tube, swivel and hook

Tubes that imitate the size, shape, and action of sand eels are easy to make and not a closely guarded secret. Those who fish with me know I use bead chain swivels to impart superior action to the tubes on my frames—not only in the hook tubes but in teasers as well, which together create outstanding results.

Most umbrella frames sport four arms, each with a teaser placed about a third of the way out from the center weight. I prefer a four-arm frame manufactured locally by Osprey Tackle. Traditionally, a single barrel swivel connects each teaser, usually 1/8-inch diameter tubing, and is held in place by no. 5 Sevenstrand crimps on either side. For superior action, replace the single barrel swivel with a no. 101, seventy-five-pound-test, plain bead chain swivel. Side-by-side, in-water comparisons at slow-trolling speed, the bead chain teaser, if properly shaped, far "outswims" those rigged on single barrel swivels, triggering dramatically more strikes.

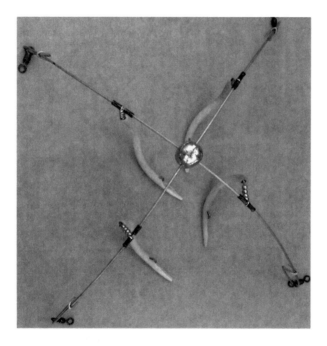

Frame with Teasers attached

As for the tubes with hooks, Limerick-style works best, but you should replace the usual single-barrel swivel with a no. 131, 175-pound-test swivel. This bead chain swivel does two things: first, it imparts more action; and second, it accommodates a slightly longer that better appeals to heavyweight fish. Be sure to cut your ¼-inch ID tubing short enough so that it leaves three beads of the chain showing for superior action. It's a good idea to connect each tube by means of a twelve—to eighteen-inch, sixty—to one-hundred-pound-test leader to a single 1/0 barrel swivel at the end of each umbrella arm.

One final point: Thick-walled latex tubing retards the action stripers love. Since mature sand eels range from four to six inches in length, I use ¼-inch ID, 1/16-inch wall amber latex tubing for hook tubes, typically cut six inches long with a two-inch tail notch. Preferred tubing for teasers is 1/8-inch ID by 1/16-inch wall, 4 ½ inches long with a one-inch tail notch, inside of which the bend is maintained by a section of hardware store soft steel wire.

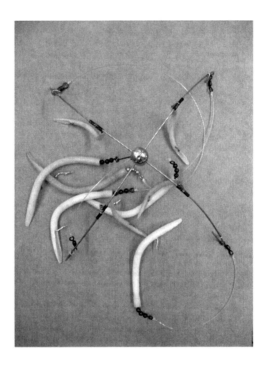

Tubes (4) & Teasers (5) attached

Beefy Tackle

Mustad Limerick hooks, style no. 1022, are fashioned from relatively soft wire and can open under the strain of a sizeable striper. Try a slightly larger hook such as an 8/0 or 9/0, taking care not to crank down on reel drags.

We fish umbrella rigs from beefy outfits, seven-foot silicon oxide guided graphite Tsunami (TSCC 701XXH) sticks, 4/0 Penn Special Senator HLW reels loaded with sixty-pound-test stainless wire (0.028 diameter), Vicious fifty-pound Spectra backing, and Vicious low-vis, clear eighty-pound-test mono leader. How come? We frequently troll areas loaded with lobster gear, and if I hang up on an up-and-down line, I like to get rigs back. We also probe depths approaching fifty to fifty-five feet that routinely hold heavyweight fish, and multiple catches, especially in a rip, will definitely test every connection. Consider marking wire lines, but fishing them shorter by adding a two—to six-ounce trolling sinker. No doubt an umbrella rig set up in this fashion is a bit more costly, but the rewards more than make up for the extra pennies spent.

Trailers

Do yourself a favor and fish only four hooks from an umbrella rig frame. We once fished five, but there's really no need for you to suffer the aggravation that results. Instead, fish a slightly larger teaser down the center.

An article published years ago in *Scientific American* on fish behavior described placing a trailing lure behind others when creating the "bait school effect," which triggered strikes that would not otherwise occur. Remember what I said, and that you read it here. Fish three hook tubes, say with twelve-inch mono leaders, and the fourth with an eighteen—to twenty-two-inch leader. Let me know how bad you out-fish the next guy and how many of those fish were on the trailer. Of course, it may not make much difference when fish are thick, but when fewer or large-for-their-size, it'll make all the difference in the world!

Tune 'Em Up

Would it surprise you to learn a striper's lateral line is sensitive to the sonic vibrations made by an undulating sand eel? Even in inky-black depths, stripers can "sense" a school of baitfish approaching long before they see it. But that's another story.

To best advertise the presence of your umbrella-sand-eel tube lure imitation, each should spin freely. With five teasers and four hook tubes, believe me, they're making a sonic "racket."

The better a tube's action, the better your chances for a strike. Be sure, once you lay the rig in the water, to check that each tube is spinning freely at the same speed—that none of the leaders are tangled—before the wire carries the deal downstairs. Be equally careful that the rigs swimming at depth off your stern remain free of seaweed, eel grass, or other junk that trolled wires tend to harvest from the water column. If you watch the wires track through a pocket of vegetation, know that whatever weeds you "rake" through will ride the wires like elevators all the way into the sub-basement, eventually hopping off on the umbrella frame. And beware the high cost of laziness in a weedy rip: there's *nothing* rewarding about retrieving an umbrella-rig-turned-combine gunked up with an entire farmer's market worth of North Rip salad.

During the course of fishing, my anglers observe either the mate or I adjusting the position of the latex tube over the hook and bead chain swivel, or adjusting the bend of the teasers after each fish. Occasionally, fish strike the teasers, which mangle them out of the right shape. Maintaining the "compound curve" of both tubes and teasers takes a little practice, but the time and effort spent is well worth it. Hard to describe, but that gentle curve of the tubing due to the bend in the Limerick hook shank should be followed by a gentle right-angle curve at the hook bend, just behind the point.

Since you're looking to create a "catchy tune," be sure you've got harmony in your chorus of teasers and tubes. All it takes is a quick check, and if not, tune 'em up. One other thing, be sure to hang onto those outfits firmly.

Umbrella Materials:

Capt. Joe Wysocki
Osprey Tackle
Niantic, CT 06357
(203) 739-4129
(osprey.38@snet.net)

Merrick Tackle www.merricktackle.com
1-800-628-8904 sales@merricktackle.com

Vicious Fishing Line
www.Vicious-Fishing.com

LITTLE SHOOTERS

Science is simply common sense at its best.

—Thomas Huxley

As we slid across the standing face of North Rip, my anglers free spooled line from the light graphite wire setups we affectionately call the "Little Shooters." I suspected the building rip harbored stripers from schoolie size into the high twenties and knew the larger specimens could challenge the skills of this charter crew. With one hundred feet of thirty-pound-test wire running aft off the three shooters (each armed with a small chartreuse bucktail jig and red Uncle Josh pork rind), we worked to establish appropriate jigging tempos, and I reminded anglers to allow a sizeable striper to take some line in the event of a hook-up.

On the "numbers," we had three bites and stuck two. Shortly, the smaller taker was tagged and released as the other angler worked a larger fish toward the transom. As my mate readied the net, hoots and hollers erupted in the cockpit, and a moment later, a forty-inch bass flopped onto the deck.

"I never thought this outfit could handle a fish that size," the angler later commented—not the first time I'd heard that. At trip's end, the angler offered to pay me for the outfit and take it home. Unfortunately, we needed it for a twilight trip later that day.

Over a decade ago, I profiled these light tackle wire line outfits for audiences at various striper shows. Unfortunately, then as now, few anglers equate wire line and light tackle. Believe me, these outfits have changed a lot of minds—the reason I'm once again writing about them.

Don't for one minute think I dreamed these diminutive wire sticks up. Credit for my having them goes to Marshall Greene at Sea Link, Ltd., who gave me a rod as a gift. A short time later, Capt. Kerry Douton, of J & B Tackle fame, showed me another, informing me he'd designed them for trolling bonito in the eastern reaches of Long Island Sound.

We soon pressed the rod into jigging service, again demonstrating the power of these outfits. It wasn't long before J&B Tackle provided three additional ones.

Capt. Kerry Douton, owner and master rod builder at J&B Tackle in Niantic, Connecticut (www.JBTackle.com) kindly provided me with component specs for this rod. The blank is a seven-foot graphite Calstar GF 700XL blank, color gray. The guides are Fuji BNLG—one no. 20, one no. 16, two no. 12, two no. 10, with a BPLT no. 5.5 tiptop. Reel seat is a Fuji FPSD no. 18 or no. 20, and the gimbal is a FUJI GC22. Grips can be either Hypalon or cork. For component lengths, guide spacing, and wrapping details, refer to the accompanying diagram.

For those of you who'd like one or more of these sticks built by J&B, plan on a cost of about $225 and allow two to three weeks for delivery. Given component cost alone (around $175), the Little Shooter is quite a bargain.

Little Shooter's are fun

My shooters carry Penn 320 GTi reels with level-wind mechanisms removed. These I load with two hundred feet of thirty-pound-test (0.020 diameter) stainless steel wire line atop roughly three hundred feet of fifty-pound Vicious braid (www.vicious-fishing.com). This model reel was chosen for its lightweight (19.5 ounces), speedy high gear ratio (4.5:1), and superior drag system. As noted, I forego the level-wind mechanism, as wire line markers can hang up on bars. With a little practice, anglers' thumbs can be trained.

Leaders are typically fifteen-foot, sixty-pound-test mono, connected to wire via a nail knot so the splice greases through the guides. At the first one hundred feet, and at every increment of fifty feet thereafter, the wire is marked with a colored Dacron splice to let clients or crew know how much line has been deployed.

Easy for Jr. Anglers to score also

I use the Little Shooters frequently in depths less than thirty feet and usually arm them with parachute jigs of two ounces or less. My favorite jig for the light wires is a chartreuse, 1 ½-ounce chartreuse Andrus 'chute. At night, I'll sometimes use these rods to drag Luhr-Jensen J-Plugs (size 5)—their double-treble hook configurations replaced with a single 4/0 treble up front. Naturally, other small plugs work well, too—particularly when the bass key in on smaller forage.

In my business, I have to catch fish for all my clients, including juniors, by the most enjoyable fashion possible. As most bassmen already know, trolling wire has long been a go-to method that produces fish when no other method can. However, traditional wire line jigging for striped bass means cumbersome gear. Jigging a combo like that for any length of time will have your muscles telling your brain your arms will soon fall off. Sure, we fish heavier gear when fish or conditions call for it. But whenever it's possible to use them, the Little Shooters offer a greater challenge and more excitement—they're just more fun. Isn't that what fishing's all about? Maybe they'll prove just right for you too.

DANCE A JIG

*We need education in the obvious
more than investigation of the obscure.*

—Oliver Wendell Holmes, Jr.

Diamond jigs—simple, clean, basic, fast, and tooth-proof—are one of the deadliest weapons for catching those Northeast sport fish sporting stripes. Using diamonds means no hooks to rebait, no chewed-up surface plugs to discard, and no mauled bucktails or soft plastics to replace. Unlike a swimming plug with multiple dangling treble hooks, a diamond jig's body offers a sturdy and safe handle for lifting and unhooking feisty fish. If you don't have them in your arsenal, you are missing out on a lot of action each season. When the conditions are right, diamond jigging ranks among the most effective ways to catch striped bass. For example, when sand eels and squid cloud the North Rip in late May or early June, there are times when a four—to eight-ounce diamond will outproduce even live eels.

While some fish hold behind reefs, the majority will pile up in the "sweet spot" up-tide of the rip, just yards ahead of the structure where it juts up from a flat bottom. Because it takes time for the upwelling water to reach the surface as it moves down-tide, the "sweet spot" is positioned well up-tide of the rip line's standing waves, not directly beneath them—one reason a depth-finder is vital to diamond-jigging success.

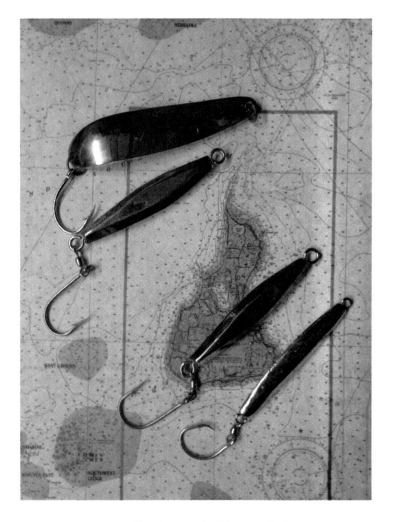

Krocodile Spoon & Diamond Jigs

Once you've found a rip, the best tactic is to jog up-tide while watching your depth-finder. When the bottom flattens out, pull the throttle back and drift toward the rip line. (Drifting, rather than anchoring, enables you to thoroughly cover a reef while also keeping pace with the tide-swept lure.) Quickly free-spool your jig until it bumps bottom then immediately engage the reel and start your retrieve; a curious fish will lose interest if the jig sits for more than a couple of seconds. Resting the jig too long also allows the hook to drag and snag bottom.

Different Strokes

I prefer to fish chrome lures a bit differently than many do. Diamond jigs and weighted spoons like Luhr-Jensen's Krocodile in the three—to five-ounce range are more effective than heavier models because they "flutter," better imitating an injured baitfish. A four—to five-foot upward sweep of the rod at moderate speed is all you need, followed by slack line as the jig falls (it's important to maintain subtle "contact" with a falling jig—but not enough to hamper the jig's action). No reeling is involved. Most strikes come on the drop. Those anglers who don't provide enough slack for their lures to flutter back down receive few, if any strikes. A common mistake is overzealous jigging. Strike zones are typically small, so jigs should be worked close to the bottom where stripers are holding station. Keep in mind it best serves your success to constantly check where the bottom is and then bounce it. If there are bluefish mixed in with bass, they'll often tell you when you're jigging too fast, or—if you're squidding the jig—coming up too far from bottom. Bass tend to favor a lazier stroke and a jig within a few feet of the bottom, while blues will chase them up.

Bass & Blues Like Diamonds

Whatever size jigs you favor, hook selection's important. Many diamonds come from the factory with a treble hook; consider replacing it with an 8/0 single. Single hooks make catch-and-release easier, hang up less on rough bottom, and are safer when unhooking a toothy critter in a pitching boat. A single hook also has less water resistance, letting a jig drop faster (and bowing out less in hard current); a single is also less likely to foul on the line as it sinks. On the other hand, some three—and four-ounce jigs come rigged with thin-gauge 7/0 singles. Unless you are catching only small schoolie bass, replace the stock 7/0 with a heavy-gauge 8/0, lest it straighten on a big fish—since one of the benefits of jigging, especially with a smaller model, is that it will catch a twenty-four-pounder's eye as readily as a twenty-four-incher's. If the action is really hot, file or crimp the barb for easy releasing. Or try a new trend—using circle hooks.

As a rule, the smaller the diamond jig, the better it produces—despite many anglers' tendency to go the other way. They choose a giant lure that sinks like a stone (or—oddly enough—a piece of heavy metal). Forget the huge diamonds: Slinging a sixteen-ounce jig at the island is a great way to practice "active conservation"—working awfully hard with the rod and catching *nothing at all*. I prefer four—to eight-ounce diamonds—the exact size dictated by water depth and current speed—and prefer braid to mono, especially when the tide's hauling in deep water. Other sharpies I know claim best results running braid with a fifteen—to thirty-foot topshot of mono or fluorocarbon leader material. That system combines the braid's diameter advantages and sensitivity while the mono enhances jig action, facilitates knot tying, and minimizes headaches associated with braid tangles. Or you might try affixing a medium snap-swivel to the terminal end of the braid. Although some anglers, fearing trouble with bluefish, use wire leaders, I prefer a short section of sixty-pound fluorocarbon (if blues are thick, you could go as heavy as eighty or even one hundred), as I feel finicky fish see the wire and avoid the lure (consider that fish seldom swallow the entire jig, anyway). Consider attaching jig to fluorocarbon leader via a loop knot, rather than a clinch, to enhance lure wobble.

Capt. Ricky Mola, owner of Fisherman's World in Norwalk, Connecticut, is credited as the first expert in our area to experiment with circle hooks on diamond and butterfly-style jigs. Mola noticed that during feeding frenzies, some bluefish and striped bass were getting deep-hooked in the throat or gills—a drawback of using J-hooks, and a common problem when numbers of bass or blues are feeding aggressively. Captain Mola thought using circle hooks might reduce the injury rate but suspected they might also dramatically reduce the catch rate. Further investigation revealed that, at least with a slow squidding action, a circle hook can be quite effective, provided the angler fights the instinct to set the hook with a snap of the rod, and instead continues to reel steadily through the hook-set and into the fight.

North Rip versus the Ledge

I've successfully jigged diamonds on both the Ledge and at the North Rip for bass, but my favorite spot is the Double Hump just east-southeast of the 1BI buoy. Obviously, bird activity can be a dead giveaway to developing action—and a good D-jigging scenario—anywhere around the island, but it occurs with greatest frequency in the North Rip. Time to be there—North End or Southwest—is first light, a time when any point on the Ledge can quickly turn into a hotspot. Sand eels are the typical forage in the spring, while herring (bluebacks first, and in the very late innings, sea herring) dominate in the fall.

One other point: When fishing the Ledge, note carefully the locations of lobster trawl buoys, since associated "up-and-down" lines will be lurking immediately up-tide to foul lure, lines, and/or—worst of all—a substantial fish attached to the former two.

Diamond jigs aren't for every Block Island striper scenario, but when the right combination of time, tide, feed, and fish arises—birds and bait and bass creating a churning chaos some still June dawn—you might just discover that Marilyn Monroe isn't the only one with a thing for diamonds.

IV
"CONDITIONING" ISLAND BASS

ISLAND TIDES AND CURRENTS

The Moon's the North Wind's cooky,
He bites it, day by day,
Until there's but a rim of scraps
That crumble all away.

The South Wind is a baker.
He kneads clouds in his den,
And bakes a crisp new moon
That the greedy North Wind eats again!

—Vachel Lindsay

    Block Island's geographic position places it between Montauk, Long Island, and the Rhode Island mainland, close to the "mouth" of Long Island Sound. Because Long Island Sound is a U-shaped basin, facing into the direction of the incoming tide, it can compress and focus the incoming water to form higher tides and hence stronger currents. For example, moon tide ranges in the western Sound at Bridgeport, Connecticut, typically exceed eight feet or greater, whereas at Block Island, tidal heights typically range from 3.5 to 4.0 feet

2012 Eldridge Tide & Pilot Book

Few realize the island's location places it under the influence of tidal flows entering and leaving Long Island Sound at the Race, and reason why those in the know consult their copy of the yellow-covered *Eldridge Tide and Pilot Book*. It's for this reason they are slightly ahead or behind tidal times at the island, and not Newport, Rhode Island.

For purposes of familiarizing the reader with several aspects of fishing full and new moon tides in the island area, I've modified a story submitted to *The Fisherman* magazine. Zach Harvey, its NE editor, asked me, along with Tim Coleman, to draft a question and answer article for its striped bass readers in 2011, which in part goes like this.

Al Anderson on the Striper Moons

by Tim Coleman

TC: *Why is striped bass fishing better on moon tides?*
AA: Tidal ranges are generally greater; hence, currents are stronger, attracting various game fish to undertows and rips that typically increase foraging opportunities.

TC: *Which moon phases—full or new moon—offers better fishing?*
AA: Contrary to popular belief, full moon tides are not the correct answer. For example, during the spring of 2011, the full moon tides will be stronger than new moon; but this coming fall on October 26, the new moon tides will be stronger. For several months during the year, full and new moon tides' strengths alternate. Also, conditions such as wind direction, wind velocity, brightness and phosphorescence, as well as time of year contribute to the moon tide success or at times lack of it.

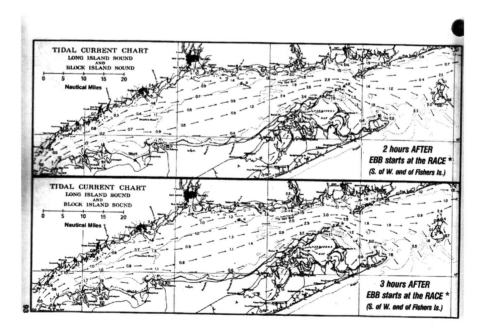

RACE vs BLOCK ISLAND

TC: *If you had to pick one moon during the season, which moon during which month would it be?*

AA: The month has to be June due to reduced foraging resulting from migration—fish arriving hungry, so to speak—but August ranks second. Female striped bass from many areas come to this region to replace energy used in reproduction.

TC: *Do spring bass usually come in on the flood tide on a moon and leave on the ebb during a fall moon?*

AA: Our first stripers at Block Island show up on an ebb tide running to the east-southeast, which is normally two to three degrees warmer than the flood tide. The same is true at Montauk or Monomoy. By the way, in this part of New England, many ebb currents run east opposite the fall migration direction that is west-southwest.

TC: *Any truth to the fact that fishing improves three days before and after a moon?*

AA: Yes, there is typically a three-day period on either side of a full moon when currents are stronger, and that triggers active feeding. Catching bait like squid and sand eels in heavy current is what the maw and tails of bass were designed for. Many anglers like either fishing up or the downside of a moon but either can produce exceptional action.

ELDRIDGE TIDE AND PILOT BOOK

PHASES OF THE MOON 2012 E.S.T.

● New Moon, ◐ 1st Quarter, ○ Full Moon, ◑ Last Quarter, A in Apogee
P in Perigee, N, S Moon farthest North or South of Equator, E on Equator

January	February	March	April	May	June
◐ 1 1am	N 3 3am	N 1 noon	E 4 4pm	E 2 2am	P 3 8am
A 2 3pm	○ 7 5pm	◐ 8 5am	○ 6 2pm	P 5 11pm	○ 4 6am
N 6 5pm	E 9 8pm	E 8 6am	P 7 noon	○ 5 11pm	S 4 noon
○ 9 3am	P 11 2pm	P 10 5am	S 10 4pm	S 8 2am	E 11 1am
E 13 noon	◑ 14 noon	S 14 9am	◑ 13 6am	◑ 12 5pm	◑ 11 6am
◑ 16 4am	S 16 4am	◑ 14 8pm	E 17 noon	E 14 6pm	A 15 8pm
P 17 4pm	● 21 6pm	E 21 7am	● 21 2am	A 19 11am	N 18 1pm
S 19 9pm	E 22 midn	● 22 10am	A 22 9am	N 22 7pm	● 19 7pm
● 23 3am	A 27 9am	A 26 1am	N 25 1am	N 22 7am	E 25 4pm
E 26 3pm	◐ 29 8pm	N 28 7pm	◐ 29 5am	◐ 28 3pm	◐ 26 11pm
A 30 1pm		◐ 30 2pm		E 29 10am	
◐ 30 11pm					

July	August	September	October	November	December
P 1 1pm	○ 1 10pm	E 1 5am	A 4 8pm	A 1 11am	◑ 6 11am
S 1 11pm	E 4 8pm	A 7 1am	N 5 9pm	N 2 5am	E 6 6pm
○ 3 2pm	A 9 2pm	◑ 8 8am	◑ 8 3am	◑ 6 8pm	P 12 6pm
E 8 10am	A 10 6am	N 8 2pm	E 12 midn	E 9 10am	S 12 11pm
◑ 10 9pm	N 12 5am	E 15 2pm	● 15 7am	● 13 5pm	● 13 4am
A 13 noon	● 17 11am	● 15 9pm	P 16 8pm	P 14 6am	E 19 7am
N 15 9pm	E 19 5am	P 18 10pm	S 19 2am	S 15 11am	○ 19 midn
● 18 11pm	P 23 3pm	S 21 7pm	◐ 21 11pm	● 20 10am	A 25 4pm
E 22 10am	◐ 24 9am	◐ 22 3pm	E 25 6pm	E 21 6pm	N 26 noon
◐ 26 4am	S 25 2pm	E 28 noon	○ 29 3pm	○ 28 10am	○ 28 5am
A 29 4am	○ 31 9am	○ 30 2pm		A 28 3pm	
S 29 8am				N 29 10am	

Midnight is the *beginning* of the day.

see p. 235 for daily moon phases throughout the year

White & White, 2012

2012 PHASES OF THE MOON

TC: *Some people use a three-way rig after dark with eels, others a fishfinder. Which one is best and why?*

AA: I favor a fishfinder, paired with the smallest sinker you can hold bottom with, since bass won't feel the weight of the sinker and spit the eel out.

TC: *What basic factors influence moon tides?*

AA: Tidal height is influenced by the moon phases, with highest during full and new moons. Second is the moon's distance from the earth, strongest when moon is closest, called perigee tides, and last by the moon declination north or south that can create different tidal heights on the same day.

TC: *What is the difference between perigee and apogee?*

AA: When either full or new moons occur at perigee, tides and currents will be spectacular. However, when the moon is on the equator, a.m. and p.m. tides and currents will be nearly equal.

TC: *Some people in smaller boats that like to cast into shorelines after dark say, "A bright moon over shoal water catches few fish." Is this so?*

AA: Not to my way of thinking; maybe in very flat water—but conditions like wind and wave action control the normally aggressive, nocturnal feeding nature of bass. Catching and eating food is the primary goal of this animal.

TC: *Along a beach, do you think you'll find fish busting on top after dark during a bright or dark moon?*

AA: In shallow water under calm, starlight conditions during the new or dark moon, we frequently find feeding bass busting into bait. You can't seen them, only hear them, casting toward the sounds.

TC: *How does one obtain information and moon tides and currents?*

AA: The best bet is to go to the Internet and Google publications such as *Tidelog* (www.tidelog.com) or the *Farmer's Almanac* (www.farmersalmanac.com) or the U.S. Naval Observatory (www.usno.navy.mil) or purchase a copy of the 2011 *Eldridge Tide and Pilot Book* (www.eldridgetide.com) from any local marine shop for $14.

TC: *What is the best plug/lure for spots after dark during a bright moon or during the dark?*

AA: Much depends on the size of fish targeted. We've spent hours casting into the southwest corner of the island with lazy swimmers that heavyweight fish often hit. As long as there is minimal phosphorescence, neither moon phase seems to matter if wind and wave action are similar.

TC: *How can one know the approximate tidal time at a favorite spot without looking at a chart?*

AA: A handy tip is during the seven days during a week, the tides will be reversed from what they were at that spot a week prior. If one Sunday had a low tide at noon, the following Sunday will have a high tide around noon.

TC: *Why is fishing more productive at night on moon tides?*

AA: The moon p.m. tides after dark are stronger than daylight. This is helped of course by the nocturnal nature of the fish, and if you have wind and against the tide that creates white water, the fish love it.

TC: *Why are some moon tide areas productive, say, on the ebb but not the flood?*

AA: Steep-sided bars and ledges are good holding stations, creating areas of reduced flow where stripers can hold out of the current whereas the opposite side of the structure may not be similar. Also, the current flow over the structure may not be in the opposite direction. For those reasons, some spots are good only on the one tide.

TC: *What about fishing in our tidal rivers and salt ponds?*

AA: In early summer as temps rise above sixty-seven degrees, fish move out into the cooler, deeper water of bays and sounds; so fishing may not be good in those spots around the moon.

TC: *If you fished, say, off Point Judith Light during the full moon after dark, what depth would you fish and what side of the light, using what?*

AA: I'd test-drift several ledges that are twenty-five to thirty feet deep on the east-northeast side of the light on the ebb tide with prevailing summer winds from the southwest using eels. If the wind was from the west or northwest, I'd drift the area west of the light starting at the

East Wall in twelve to fifteen feet of water. If that wasn't any good, I'd drift an eel at the apex of the Center Wall on the ebb tide in thirty to thirty-five feet of water as there are several rock piles there that hold sizeable fish.

TC: *Around a breach way or inlet, why does the current continue to flood into the breach way when the tide outside is falling?*
AA: It's called the Lag Effect. Even though the tide is falling along the beach, the sea level is still higher outside a breach way and will continue to run into a pond or inlet for some time. Decades ago, I spent hours waiting during the flood tide so I could get a favored spot on the first of the ebb at Charlestown Breachway. Casting position was key to success.

TC: *Can a moon tide adversely affect striper fishing?*
AA: Yes, depending on conditions: some of my favorite areas have currents that become so strong they suck under pot buoys, making them invisible. Not only, then, do fish take up other feeding stations, but we also risk loss of tackle or worse on the buoys. And if say you are trolling a tube and worm during the day but tides are so strong that your offering is falling down-tide, it's time to give up and relocate. Stripers will return once velocities diminish. Knowledgeable striper addicts favor early and late efforts on strong tides. It involves energetics: if fish have to expand more energy than they gain, they leave a rip during peak flows.

TC: *Which Block Island spots have produced best for you during the moon?*
AA: The North Rip and Southwest Ledge areas, early and late in the tides, for reasons stated above.

* * *

This second piece, portions of which ran in the same magazine not long ago, delves a bit further into the particulars of tides, moons, conditions, and timing as these variables play into the quality of the striper fishing on most island grounds.

Block Island's Striper Moon Tides

by Capt. Al Anderson

The eastern sky was showing first light on this Block Island night trip as our WNW drift-line approached North Rip's "double hump." It was early in a new moon flood tide, and suddenly our live eels became nervous, signaling pending strikes. Moments later, my three anglers had heavyweight stripers "thumping" rods and running off line. But that bite soon ended, as our drift-speed in the tide had now nearly doubled, confirmed by declining numbers of fish marking on my fish-finder. Experience told me our quarry would vacate this spot all together once current velocities peaked.

As daylight broke a "rookie" skipper appeared alongside with his party, curious as to why we were headed home, contrary to what his Newport, RI tide chart indicated. Stunned to learn about our late-night success, including the releasing of a few tagged keeper-sized bass, and that he was still three to four hours away from the popular ebb tide, he departed in disgust.

Timing Block's moon tides plays a major role in my charter fishing success. Read on if you want to get in on some of what I've picked up over 40-plus years in the racket.

Timing the Tide

Early in my career, I discovered knowing the Island's tides was critical to success. The most common angling mistake is thinking high tide in Newport is similar to that at Block Island. True, high water at Old Harbor is only 15 minutes behind Newport, but because of the Island's shape and location, tidal currents continue to run for up to 3 hours at several spots. Because Long Island Sound is an immense tidal basin, and Block Island lies just to the east of it, Island waters are under the influence of the Sound's flooding and ebbing tidal currents.

All too often those unfamiliar with the Island's currents arrive long after a tidal stage began, missing the best action created by the early part of a tide. Also, current velocity and flow direction influences striper behavior more than many anglers realize. Others compound their error by fishing one spot on both tides, unaware the nature of the bottom and its relation to current flow may attract sizeable fish on only one tide.

Moon Tides

Anglers who pay attention to detail know that in the course of a week (seven days), the tides are similar to the reverse of the previous week. If on a Sunday it's low tide around noon, the following Sunday will show high tide around noon.

How much ocean tides rise and fall depends on three conditions. First, when the sun and moon are in a line with the earth, their gravitational forces combine to produce a greater tidal range than usual. This occurs at both full and new moons, but don't blame your buddy for thinking they're equal. For several months of the year, new moon tides are higher; and then the same becomes true for full moon tides, the significance of which you are about to read. Second the moon's orbit around the earth is elliptical, ranging from about 252,000 miles at Apogee down to 221,000 miles at Perigee. Hence the position of the moon in its elliptical orbit is very important to tidal heights and hence current velocity. Third, the plane of the moon's orbit about the earth is inclined to the plane of the earth's equator. The moon therefore travels north and south of the equator, and only twice a month is it directly above the equator, resulting in the day's two high tides being nearly equal. When the moon has northern declination and is over the U.S., this high tide will be the greater of our two daily high tides. As a result, tidal currents will be the stronger of the two, frequently attracting larger fish for a longer period of time.

In summary, the height of the tides is influenced most by the moon's phase, with full and new moon tides creating the highest tides and strongest tidal currents. Second, by the moon's distance from earth in its elliptical orbit, tides being highest when it is closest (Perigee vs Apogee), and last by its declination, north or south of the equator, creating tides of different heights on the same day.

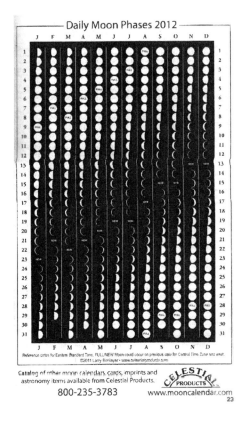

2012 DAILY MOON PHASES

Rip Behavior

Tidal current rips concentrate bait and is reason why various game fish concentrate there. Years ago in May we fished for striped bass and slammer pollock at Clay Head on the WNW flooding tide. But not so on the ebb, as no rip formed there. Ask any old-time Island lobsterman and he'll tell you Clay Head is best for "bugs" on the flood.

Knowledgeable striper addicts target several rips when currents first start, then again when current velocities ease. The inner and outer rip at the Island's North End, on a moon tide, run too hard at mid-tide times for most stripers to hold there. The same is true on Southwest Ledge; lobster trawl buoys there become sub-surface, threatening loss of gear if not detected, which at night is nearly impossible to do.

Pot Buoy in the tide

Experience has taught me winds can delay the start of a tidal current by up to a half hour, or cause them to commence earlier with greater velocity, all dependent on wind duration and direction.

Before your next visit to the Island, secure a copy of *The Eldridge Tide and Pilot Book*. I bookmark the page 86 showing the current table for The Race with a section of masking tape, so I don't have to "hunt" through it . . . If plans indicate a Moon tide, fish intended areas either early or late in their tidal flow. If sequentially arranged, chances are you'll catch better while saving the cost of fuel in the process, so good luck with your fishing.

ISLAND STRIPER WEATHER Q&A

*If you don't like the weather,
just wait a few minutes.*

—Unknown

This brief dialogue relates to the famously volatile, yet somewhat predictable if you've watched them over enough years, weather patterns by which we live and die as anglers. Everywhere under the weather heading are cruel ironies: the same fronts that often spark the wildest striped bass blitzes also wipe out any chance of our getting "across" to see—or cast into—them.

In an attempt to tap into an institutional memory longer than my own, I asked your author, Capt. Al Anderson, to comment on the finer points of island weather as it relates to the hunt for striped bass.

Of course, it will be up to you, the reader, to cultivate your own understanding of island weather. That process may involve some soakings, some bruises, and of course, as you try to develop your own working theories on the relationship between weather and striper, a great many "roads to nowhere." Mother Nature has a finely tuned sense of humor, after all, and it's a fool who tries to shoehorn her antics into rigid atmospheric laws.

Your own striper fishing success will relate—as noted many other places in this book—to your work ethic as a recorder of data. That is, over the course of months and years and decades, your detailed logbooks (of which consistent weather and "conditions" observations will be a big part) should begin to show you some undeniable patterns. Two absolutes apply: There's no substitute for experience, and if you're entrusting all your hard-won lessons to your memory, your learning curve will prove steep indeed. Live it, love it, and for God's sake *write it down.*

For reasons of clarity, "questions"—whether or not they end in question marks—are preceded by my initials: **ZH**. The answers provided by your author are introduced by his initials: **AA**.

—*Zach Harvey*

ZH: *What do you say to the old "west is best, east is least bit?"*

AA: Long ago, thanks my experience and that of others, I discovered gentle easterly winds crush offshore fishing success. For some as yet unexplainable reason, that's true with island striper fishing as well. However, during the early stages of a developing nor'easter aggressive striper feeding behavior blossoms. However—depending on the size and intensity of the gale—building, disorganized seas quickly stir up the bottom and stripers seem to stop feeding to ride it out, and most sensible skippers follow suit, heading for the barn.

ZH: *What's one general forecast that will get you on the phone re: your next day's planned charter to bag the planned mission and reschedule?*

AA: The second or third twenty-four-hour day of strong east-northeast forecast wind, even if it's sunny and relatively warm. Sea conditions reach an uncomfortable level and turbid weed-laden waters carried by tidal currents usually predominate, delivering the miserable one-two punch: *unfishable* and *fishless*.

ZH: *Where, around Block Island, do you see reasonable odds to bail out a trip when the wind's screeching out of the west?*

AA: Perhaps early in the ebbing tide at the North Rip, otherwise in the lee from the Clay Head area down to southeast light.

ZH: *Same basic question as above, only this time the wind's wailing out of the east.*

AA: Again, if early in the flood, the North Rip, otherwise from Logwood Cove south to the island's southwest corner.

ZH: *Lay out the conditions of a borderline to over-the-line day off the southwest corner out to the three-mile line.*

AA: Try to think of every individual component of the overall conditions as its own "force." Wind direction and strength, sea conditions (e.g., a leftover north—to northwest-running heave), the part of the tide (flood tides run generally northwest over the ledge, while ebb tides run south-southeast), and moon phase (which greatly affects tidal current strength). Fishability of the area is about much more than forecasted wind speed; it's about the sum effect of all the forces. Consider this quick case study: On the full moon, with a leftover sea still running from the passage of an offshore storm two days prior, and an ebbing tide, the wind is blowing southwest, ten to fifteen. The wind sounds doable, and conditions as you run down the west side of the island may look fine. When you reach the Ledge, the place is a horror show . . . Why? You had wind against the tide, the leftover sea directly against the tide, and the wind approaching that whole mess is now from another direction. And the full moon means that tide will be running much harder than usual. The place is, in effect, a washing machine. Bear in mind also that conditions can improve or deteriorate scary-fast on the changes of tide. In general, best sea conditions will be when wind, tide, and other forces are all working in roughly the same direction; worst, and frequently dangerous, conditions develop when Mother Nature's various forces are clashing. No matter what, if you plan to fish the place with any regularity, be realistic about the size (and seaworthiness) of your boat, the experience of your crew, and your own capability at the helm.

ZH: *What's the relationship between the big seas rolling north onto the south side and the tendency for such days—rich as they often are in whitewater—to give the surf diehards and a handful of sharper skiffmen (or not-so-sharp skiffmen with a serious death wish) a legitimate shot at forty-pound bass all the way shoreward to just outside the wash?*

AA: At no other time—other than at night—would the seamanship of a vessel operator be at such risk for disaster. Experience is the key to safety, but don't assume all spots are equally dangerous. Doesn't hurt to take a cautious look, and if it appears fishable outside "combing" areas, at least give it a try. Just remember to keep the bow pointed seaward—always with a very sharp eye for those malicious, early-breaking, or giant sets—regardless of whether a fish is hooked.

ZH: *Lay out two "perfect" weather/tide/timing/tactics scenarios for heavier bass at the North Rip.*

AA: Both scenarios would be under the cover of darkness, preferably on light southwest wind, at the inner bar on the flood, and over the Double Hump on the ebb, on either full—or new-moon tides.

ZH: *Under what conditions would you expect to see numbers of bigger bass stacked up on the well-marked spires of higher ground outside southeast light?*

AA: Ideally, when daytime birds indicate bait presence under cloudy or foggy conditions, and light northeast winds exist with a building sea developing.

ZH: *Try to lay out a theoretically perfect day for eeling your career's heaviest bass during daylight hours. Where? When? Which methods? What are you looking for?*

A. We had an actual great late July (perfect) day on the ledge a few years back under cloudy, foggy (low-light) conditions with light northeast winds, almost no other boats, and four experienced anglers fishing fish-finder rigs, three rods at a time, in an area just west of The Boulders, using small (ten—to twelve-inch) live eels. Fishing short drifts, they had bass ranging from the high twenty-pound class to nearly forty pounds, keeping five fish (two of them bleeders). The crew was *very* busy tagging twenty-nine clean, solid fish until the tide quit.

ZH: *Suppose subtle shifts in wind, weather, or gut feeling get you thinking you should pack it up and head home before all hell breaks loose . . .*

AA: Oh, yeah, I've been there: "Look skipper, we're paying customers and this is the best fishin' we've had in a long time, and we've been fishing for 30 years. Whadaya mean *leave?*" Twenty minutes later, a vicious squall was underway, with lightning, rain, and wind so hard it has blown the sea flat and now had it building the other way. I hear this: "dam . . . good thing we left when we did—does it always get this bad?"

THE FORAGE FACTOR

Wishin' I'd gone fishin'....

—Unknown

Striped bass show up in the unlikeliest places—the spots that get you mystified as to exactly what they saw, what in an otherwise run-of-the-mill mud flat with no discernable charge of tide suited their feeding needs and other instincts. Later, you learn from a quahogger that the place has tons of mantis shrimp—or you find signals of a worm hatch there—and it all makes sense. There are a million specialty spots, spots bass will spend a tide or two, or a week. Then they move on. As often as I think, in the course of a season, that there must be big fish right under my nose, I start running odds and eventually resign myself to the unshakable truth that not all striper haunts are created equal. Sure there are bass—some big fish, even, in parts of Narragansett Bay, along the Newport oceanfront stones. There are more bass—bigger fish and total fish—at Block Island.

The great striper outposts—the Montauks, Fishers Islands, The Races, the Block Islands, the Cuttyhunks, the Squibnockets, the Chathams and P-Towns, the Canals—all have their seasons (not all of them every season), and they all have their issues of time and tide, forage arrivals and departures, known conditions, and certain moons that bring it all together. These places have what many of the other occasionally—or intermittently—productive places up and down the coast do not: They have rips; they have boulder-fields, ledges, gullies, mussel beds, deep water close to shore, open-ocean wave action. They have diverse types of striper-favored structure. And yet, without one key element, they'll stand in a given striper season's background—a great spot with an off year.

BI's Forage Draw

The last few seasons have witnessed some frightening shifts in striped bass abundance, leading many to question the real-world health of that resource. Even as the Vineyard and the Outer Cape found themselves "between bass," Block Island has turned out an almost alarmingly steady supply of big stripers, including—since 2008—two seventy-plus-pound fish and a number of sixties. In fact, even through the Moratorium Years of the 1980s, Block Island had—relatively speaking, of course—quite a few stripers. You could almost get the idea the place is special—that it's blessed.

It's actually *both*. Among its many striper-attractant qualities like abundant, diverse structure, and unique tidal influences, the island is blessed, especially in recent seasons, with a tremendous, multilayered abundance of forage—huge shoals of sand eels, squid, butterfish, and silversides cloud the North Rip and the SW Ledge each spring. The last two summers, when other stable baits had begun to thin out, the same grounds witnessed huge influxes of the offshore baits Atlantic Saury and halfbeaks, whose arrival set off wild surface feeds. In the fall, all manner of waves of feed that summered in Narragansett Bay or along the mainland beaches filters through island waters, followed by the late bait—more big sand eels and sea herring and mackerel and whiting. And all of this is just the "run" bait.

Through the course of a season, you'll find some degree of sand eels and squid in the rips on both ends of the island. Butterfish make scattered appearances. But on some level, it's not even these big-name bass baits that give Southwest Ledge its power over big bass. It's what's there between the runs of this or that when the island shines. For the place plays host to all kinds of what might be called "ambient" or "subsistence" bait—the other, less glamorous menu items that can support a significant striper population through high summer, when the fish are—by their basic biology—banished to the bottom by escalating water temps.

There—amid the kelp, the ridges, wrecks, rock piles, and boulder fields carved or dropped by retreating glaciers eons ago—stripers get by with no trouble. Cunners (choggies), juvenile scup and sea bass, smaller bluefish, tautog, flounder, fluke, ling, sea robins, mole crabs, red crabs, Jonah crabs, sand crabs, sea worms, lobsters of all sizes—all call the diverse patches of sea bed along every flank of the island, home. When all else fails, when there's no high-calorie, slow-moving grub at their disposal, there's no chance whatsoever that the island's migratory striped bass population is going to starve. Through decades of incidental stomach-content analysis, I've gotten a pretty broad view of what constitutes the striper diet.

Then again, it could probably be argued that most of the bass that follow ingrained migratory instinct to the island grounds each season arrive—and likely depart—with the major bait "runs." Among the many foraging options within an island striper's reach, several species are key: sand eels, squid, and blueback herring, of which perhaps sand eels are the easiest bait to imitate—the most appropriate look-alike the umbrella rig, or "frame," as some call it.

Not that I haven't attempted creation of multihook lures composed of small squids, or small PET spoons, but each has a similar problem; they "pull hard" when deployed, making it difficult to keep the rigs down in the water column. Besides, when the blues decide to invade your pet rip for a tide, you might as well toss your shell-squid rigs and PET Spoon rigs into a woodchipper. So I've confined my school-imitation rigging efforts to fine-tuning a damn-near-perfect sand eel duped, spending literally years monkeying around with umbrella rigs. For one thing, armed with simple tube teasers and minimal metallic drag-creating eye candy, a frame tows better; they're simple enough to fix or tweak with minimal effort; and, finally, they catch fish, plain and simple. For a more specific look at sand-eel-style umbrella rigs, check out a chapter dedicated to their use in a subsequent chapter.

Sand Eel Snapshot

Let's take a moment to review some information about this key island forage species. First, there are two subspecies of sand lance: the larger of the species, known as the offshore sand lance, *Ammodytes dubius*, is a slender, elongate, small—to medium-sized fish, with a body of nearly uniform width (from gill opening to anus), and a long, straight lateral line bisecting its flank. Head is long with a sharply pointed snout, lower jaw extends beyond the upper jaw; and the dorsal fin is low and long, lateral line long and straight. Color is bluish to blue-green across the top, transitioning down the side to a silvery color, with a white belly.

Sand lance favor habitats conducive to burrowing—sand, for example, or fine gravel, but not usually deeper mud bottom; they are seldom seen off rocky coasts. Sand lance congregate in dense schools, ranging from hundreds to tens of thousands of individuals.

OFFSHORE SAND LANCE / *Ammodytes dubius* Reinhardt 1837 / Northern Sand Lance, Sand

Figure 259. Offshore sand lance *Ammodytes dubius*. Nantucket. Drawn by H. L. Todd.

Bigelow & Schroder, 2002

Offshore Sand lance (*Ammodytes dubius*)

Sand lance generally feed on small marine animals, notably copepods. Most researchers agree that sand lance also prey upon macroplankton, but where and when of sand eel dining are subject to ongoing controversy. Scott and Scott (1988) indicated that *Ammodytes dubius* leave the bottom to follow and feed upon plankton as it rises through the water column at night then return to the bottom at dawn.

Spawning has not been observed. However, based on maturity and fecundity observations, sand lance appear to spawn once a year, mid-autumn to early winter (Nelson and Ross, 1991). Most sand lance mature at the end of their second year of growth, but a small proportion of individuals mature sooner than that—around the end of their first year (Winters, 1989).

Blueback Herring Snapshot

Blueback herring or sea herring (*Alosa aestivilis*) are just one of nine species of herring that we find here in southern New England. Their color, when fresh, ranges from blue to steel blue on the back to silvery on the sides and abdomen, and average about ten inches in length. Olive black longitudinal lines above the midline are sometimes evident on adults and a dark or black spot posterior to gill cover at eye level. They are distinguished from Atlantic herring by the position of the dorsal fin, which is ahead of the midbody rather than at it.

This species can be classified as marine, coastal pelagic, occurring in shallow inshore areas. These are schooling fish, and strongly so, and demonstrate a behavior of strong vertical migrations; rising toward the surface at dusk and sinking toward the sea floor at dawn.

Regarding feeding, Atlantic herring are facultative, zooplanktivorous filter feeders during daylight and twilight hours.

Striper forage (Blueback Herring)
(Regurgitated)

Bigelow and Schroeder (2002) report they are important forage for a variety of predators, numbering eighteen species of marine fish including striped bass, bluefish, and weakfish. As regards spawning, they are reported to spawn in late afternoon in the Connecticut River.

Summer (Inshore) Squid Snapshot

The longfin inshore squid, *Loligo pealeii*, is a schooling species of the molluscan family Loliginidae. It is distributed in continental shelf and slope waters from Newfoundland to the Gulf of Venezuela and occurs in commercial abundance from southern Georges Bank to Cape Hatteras. Historically, the lifespan of longfin inshore squid was believed to be one to two years (Summers 1971; Lange 1982). However, Brodziak and Macy (1996), using statolith aging, demonstrated exponential growth and a lifespan of less than a year. Longfin inshore squid reach sizes greater than forty to fifty centimeters mantle length (ML), although most are less than thirty centimeters (eleven inches).

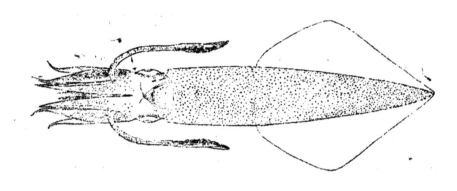

Longfin Inshore Squid, *Loligo pealeii*

Fish species preyed on by longfin inshore squid include silver hake, mackerel, herring, menhaden (Langton and Bowman, 1977), sand lance, bay anchovy, menhaden, weakfish, and silversides (Kier, 1982).

It's usually on a moon tide in the north rip when squid arrive, and when that happens, I know it's time for jigging the 'chutes and presenting monster squid flies. The reason for my excitement is that we can witness the smashing surface explosion that sizable stripers make. Nothing like that happens when jigging the wire.

V
ISLAND STRIPER STRUCTURES

DARK WATERS: HANK ALLEN ON THE ISLAND SURF

My biggest worry is that my wife (when I die) will sell my fishing gear for what I said I paid for it.

—Koos Brandt

Hank Allen does a tremendous amount of shore and surf fishing for stripers at the island, from April through December, most of which occur in late evening hours. Born in Flagstaff, Arizona, in 1961, he's worked in construction for thirty-five years, the last twenty-four of which have been on the island. During the busy summer months of July and August, he drives a taxi for the Littlefields, and his business card is labeled Snappy Cab. He lives with his wife Nelma on Beacon Hill, who keeps tight reins on him. His future plans are to start a full-time island guiding business, for those interested in fishing the island's shores.

Address mail to: Hank Allen, PO Box 889, Block Island, RI 02807, or by calling (401) 286-2906, or by e-mail to SIREG38@yahoo.com. He can also be contacted by calling either Twin Maples (401) 466-5547 or at BI Fishworks (401) 466-5391.

I thought it best to get right down to business, and over the course of an hour or so, I conducted the interview that follows. In the interest of clarity, the questions (with or without question marks) are bolded and italicized, while answers appear in traditional roman type. Obviously, the **AA** that precedes questions stands for "Al Anderson"—*me*—while the **HA** before each answer signifies the one and only "Hank Allen."

AA: Like me, years ago, I had a pair of Red Ball waders that served me exceptionally well. *Tell me about your waders and the equipment you carry when fishing the surf, boulders, or jetties at night.*

HA: I favor a pair of five mil, reinforced at the knee, neoprene waders, with separate felt-bottom spike boots. Neoprene is a must if you're serious about surf fishing, as are studded boots, otherwise stay off jetty walls and surf-washed boulders. I prefer Neoprene 'cause they're dry, warm, and comfortable. One other thing about jetties and rocks, be sure you look them over during daytime, preferably at low tide, so you get a better idea of what you're up against at night.

Hank Allen, After Dark Success

AA: *Who is the manufacturer of your waders?*
HA: Cabella's, they offer a variety of styles at various costs.

AA: *Tell me about the lights you use?*
HA: Lights are an absolute must, of course. I have two on my cap—one is a bill-mounted job that is strong (ten LEDs) and the other, smaller one, creates a green light that I use for "sneaking up" on the fish (I carry a spare in a special inside pocket made for my waders). This special, waterproof wader pocket, designed by me, has a zipper on it, is inside my waders, and contains not only my spare light, but my keys

and cell phone. The pocket provided by the manufacturer, on the front (outside) of the waders, contains a couple of lures, fishing license, and needle nose pliers, "which is easy to access."

AA: *Carry any other, easy to reach, equipment?*
HA: Yes. I also have a small backpack, and if using live eels, place them in a plastic bag, usually accompanied by either a bottle of soda or water. I also carry a short three-foot piece of 3/8-inch rope that is tied around my wader waist to prevent water from getting inside them. On the wader loop ring, I carry a small folding stainless knife (Leatherman) in the event I have to quickly cut my boots off.

Surf equipment waders rods reels

AA: *How about a gaff?*

HA: No gaff when I'm fishing the beach. But when fishing either the jetties or docks, I carry a short gaff with a small light taped to just below the grip so I can see the fish. If I have to gaff a fish, I make an effort to do so in its mouth so as not to kill it, as I release most of my fish.

Tackle

AA: *Tell me about your rods, reels, line, and lures.*

HA: For a number of years, I favored a Penn 704Z spinning reel, but that model was discontinued a few seasons ago. Today, I'm using a Daiwa XCaliber model, and it has held up well. I also have a Shimano 1000, that's OK. My Daiwa carries twenty-five-pound test Sea Strike/Billfisher Crystal Clear monofilament. I do not favor any spectra-style lines for my surf fishing.

Surf casting rods & reels

As for plugs, I only carry a few of them. My favorite is the seven-inch Long A Magnum Bomber model, black back, clear middle, chrome bottom. I also fish a five-inch Bomber Long-A model when anticipating smaller fish. These plugs are unweighted and have great action. To facilitate casting distance, I occasionally run off 100-150 feet of mono, securing one end to a tree or fence, and then stretching the line out to remove any memory. I then leave it and return up to several hours later. Those plugs I use have great action and seem to carry further.

Plug City up close

COMMENT: From my interview with Hank, it was obvious he knew how to fish these plugs like no one else. His success was obviously a result of years of experience fishing them.

AA: *Why are they (plugs) so good?*
HA: They catch fish . . .

AA: *Any idea why that is?*

HA: Their action, I guess. I've seen fish follow the plug's wake for extended distances before grabbing it, seems like they "tune in" on it before striking.

COMMENT: You're right. These fish can actually feel the movements of a plug, daytime or night, long before they see it, because of their ultrasensitive lateral line. Research has shown they can feel a small bait fish swimming nearby and react to it, despite it being unseen, and regardless of the background noise from any surf during total darkness.

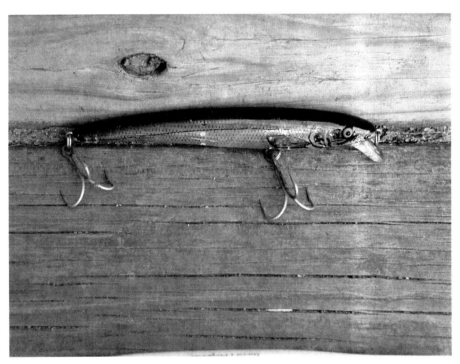

Favorite Bomber Plug

AA: *Why do you favor twenty-five-pound-test mono? Isn't it kind of heavy for the job?*

HA: Not really 'cause it usually allows me to retrieve a plug that hangs up on the many seaweed-fowled boulders. Sure, I might straighten a treble barb or two, but I'll get the plug back, and hooks can be easily straightened or replaced.

AA: *Is that why you attempt to remove the memory in your mono—to increase casting distance?*
HA: Yup.

AA: *How do you connect your line to the plug?*
HA: I use a small high-quality snap, not a snap-swivel. As for the connection, I use a Palomar knot. I have the utmost confidence in it and recommend it to others.

Conditions

AA: *What's the best way to find fish?*
HA: Not the way you might think. Islanders are pretty close-mouthed, so forget that. Besides, you'll never see an Internet report or read about a [legitimate] "hot spot" in our local paper.

It's simple, you just go out and look at spots during the daytime, and if one or two look promising, make a mental note on how to get there after dark. My favorite conditions are flat water, so any strikes on my swimmers or needlefish can be seen. These lures, to be effective, have to be clean and free of weed. I simply find a bright spot in the night sky and hold the rod tip and plug up against it to check it for weed. I like spots that offer "flat dark water" for my fishing.

AA: *I know you do some bait fishing, tell me a little about it.*
HA: Although I'll cast and drift large squid, my favorite is to fish small live eels, eels in the ten—to twelve-inch range (easier to cast), and I use large 7/0 Mustad hooks, fishing the eels on retrieve by keeping the rod tip high, and if I suspect a strike, simply drop the tip (drop-tip technique), followed by setting the hook. It's an effective technique for me.

AA: *What do you use for a leader?*
HA: I use surprisingly short leaders, ten to twelve inches of forty-pound test mono, using a small swivel, and not messing with the drag pressure, simply keeping it on the high side of moderate. The "drop-tip" technique works well for me.

AA: *Are bluefish an occasional problem?*
HA: Yes, they are, but if I still have a short section of eel on the hook, I'll cast again, letting it sink to the bottom, where I've occasionally hooked a feeding striper.

AA: *Where do most strikes occur when using eels for bass?*
HA: I retrieve them right up to my feet, as I've had strikes in the wash numerous times. I know your readers will marvel at this, but I see fish at night in the water often, I can hear them swirling and busting the surface on bait, especially when fishing quiet water, and I've learned to be quiet when fishing, so as not to spook them. Now, I don't know about your charter boat fishing at night, but I bet there are things you don't do, so as not to spook fish in the rip.

COMMENT: I took a minute to inform him that I believe low engine rpm, once the "sound" pervades a feeding zone, if it doesn't change, has little or no affect on their feeding behavior. Other boats, operated by "weekend warriors," speeding into or from a rip's shallow area, will cause them to relocate.

AA: *Tell me about your Old Harbor jetty fishing.*
HA: Timing is everything. Making a cast at the right time, based on a wave set, can be the difference between catching and not catching.

Hank Allen with a pair of Stripers

AA: *How about varying the speed of retrieve?*
HA: I'm not a fan of it. I prefer slow and steady, with either eels close to the surface or with plugs. With no one around at night, I can get away with casting nearly parallel to the beach or jetty, a technique that's worked surprisingly well for me.

AA: *How often do you see or find anyone else shore or surf fishing at night?*
HA: Rarely—if ever. I know of only one other fisherman that works the waters after dark, known as the "Phantom," who I've never seen, but I know him as Rick Hall, an accomplished local islander.

AA: *Rumor has it you've been a winner in several island sponsored striper contests, shore division, such as the one conducted by the Block Island Volunteer Fire Department, which uses donations to support them. The other is Chris Willi's Fishworks Tournament, with donations going to support the National Children's Cancer Society.*
HA: He told me he has placed in both of them and was a first place winner in those two events this past (2011) summer.

As we wrapped up the interview, Hank confirmed to me he's never seen or read an article about fishing Block Island waters, authored by an islander in any publication, and certainly not one about its shore or surf fishing. My hat is off to him for his generous contribution to *Island Stripers*.

(**Author's Note:** An interesting sidenote about my interview, Allen was a subtle undercurrent of the standoffishness most New England surfcasting island's seasoned casters reserve for "off-islanders," regardless of those outsiders' attitudes, intentions, or credentials.)

BI BY FLY: CHRIS WILLI SPEAKS

*A wise man told me once,
"It's not how many fish you catch,
it's where the fly-fishing takes you in life."*

—Michael L. Yelton

Early on in this book project, I contacted Block Island's Chris Willi, owner and operator of a fly fishing business on the island, and asked if he would be interested in making a few comments about it for the readers. He gladly consented, and here's what he had to say:

> Unlike other islands, Block Island waters offer the most diverse arena for fly fishing saltwater in New England, due to the sheer variety of conditions, structures, and environments. You can fish a rip current, rocky shore, sandy beach, deep hole, sand bar, point break, jetty, channel, or flat in one day. The best thing about it is that you don't need a large quiver of rods and gear. I've fished twenty years on Block Island, fifteen of it with a fly rod—the standard 9-weight, fast-action with a 10-weight intermediate line. There are occasions for a different rod or a sinking line or floater, but I am a firm K.I.S.S. (keep it simple, stupid) fisherman. The less crap I need to carry, the better—waders, stripping basket, needle nose pliers with cutter, and

my flies (usually six). The primary baits we encounter are sand eels, squid, silversides, and juvenile pollock. Occasionally, a school of baby bunker or butterfish will get lost and swing by. My top fly is the standard White Deceiver, preferably tied sparsely in a variety of lengths. Chartreuse, pink, lavender, black, olive, and tan variations are acceptable. Then we have the Clouser—same variations. I also like the "Striper Dragon" in white or black and just about any sand eel patterns. I list flies by the spot—you'll see many repeats.

NORTH END

Spots: Sandy Point (the North Rip, North Reef), **Cow Cove, Groves Point**

The west side of the bar is the deepest and the current can rip. Dead drifting or fast retrieves can both offer success, depending on conditions. The east side of the bar is shallower, but wading can be dangerous here, again due to the strong current—wading is not advised and also not necessary. Any moving tide is fishable. Clousers, deceivers, sand eel, and squid flies are recommended, one of a few places you can get a grand slam (stripers, blues, fluke, bonito) from the beach on Block Island. *Cow Cove* is a shallow cove with a cobble bottom. Floater with a popper (Gurgler) can produce on still nights. Fish either side of the high tide (high water best). *Groves Point*, located right at the parking lot, is wade-able rocky bottom; fish the point and westward, little current; best at the top of the incoming and outgoing (high water best); shallow as well as floater or slow sink recommended, snake flies and deceivers best.

Access: Via Corn Neck Road, parking at end. A beach permit (town hall) is required to drive out to Sandy Point.
Time: Dusk till dawn, can have midday blitzes at the rip. High water preferred.
Equipment: Fast 9-weight or 10-weight with intermediates at Sandy Point, Cow Cove, and Groves can be shallow, so floaters can be utilized as well. Wind and current are always a factor.
Flies: Deceivers, Clousers, Gurglers, squid, and sand eel models.
Warning: Sandy Point can be dangerous to fish—wade with caution.

NORTH RIP Chris Willi
(Image courtesy of Chris Willi)

CLAY HEAD

Spots: Isaiahs Gully (aka the Sisters) to Jerry's Point.

This area is one of the hardest to fish, as the entire beach is cobble and boulders, with a few sandy coves that offer the fantastic structure bass love. At high tide, there is little beach from Nicks Point to Balls Point. However, this area is best fished at high water—using intermediates and floaters. It is wade-able, but there are troughs and holes that can come and go. Best practice is to scout it out during the day before fishing at night.

Access: Corn Neck Road, Mansion Beach Road
Time: Day or night—High water preferred.
Equipment: Fast 9-weight or 10-weight with intermediates or floaters.
Flies: Deceivers, Clousers, Gurglers, sand eel models.
Notables: A bitch in a northeast wind as the bluffs can hinder back casts.

EAST BEACHES

Spots: Mansion Beach, Scotch Beach, Town Beach, Baby Beach, Crescent Beach.

This area is a classic New England beach facing the Atlantic Ocean with a sandy bottom. With a prevailing southwest wind most of the year, it offers sight fishing during the day and otherwise can be fished 24/7 regardless of tide. Sandbars, troughs, and holes come and go throughout the season. Some rocky outcroppings offer structure, but most fish are cruising the beach, feeding on small baitfish and crabs. This is the perfect beach for intermediate lines, and you can drop down to a 7—or 8-weight if there's no wind. Or you can get fancy and go up to an 11—or 12-weight, two-handed rod for more distance, but you can wade out pretty far along the entire stretch. Sand eel baitfish patterns are favorites with some flash. If a sinking line is used, then go to a mole crab pattern.

Access: All along Corn Neck Road.
Time: All day and night, tides not critical.
Equipment: 7—to 9-weight with intermediates or sinking lines.
Flies: Deceivers, Clousers, or sand eel models with a lot of flash or crab models.

Striper On A Fly
(image courtesy of Chris Willi)

OLD HARBOR

Spots: Old Harbor, Ballard's Beach, Pebbly Beach, Poop Chute, Old Harbor Point (O. H. Landing).

If you arrive by the Point Judith, Newport, or New London Ferry, this is where you will land—Old Harbor. It features a ten-acre harbor for ferries, town docks, and small anchorage. Two jetties surround it, and they offer a good vantage to cast whatever you like with stout rods. Landing a fish from these jetties can be challenging. The harbor itself offers fishing as well with shallows along virtually the entire shore area. The entrance channel banks have shoaled, making it a perfect beach to fish from. Every baitfish imaginable can be found in the harbor at some point during the season: squid, tinker mackerel, bunker, and juvenile pollock. I used to tie a fly called the "Bruised Banana" that imitated a small pollock and worked very well—four yellow hackles with black streaks in them, a touch of yellow/pearl flash, and a black EZ body head doubled back on itself. Ballard's Beach is south of the harbor entrance and is a short stretch of steep sandy beach followed by a stretch of rocky beach, until you arrive at the Poop Chute. This is the old outflow area from the sewer plant—which is a flat forty-yard stretch of rock jetty, perfect to cast from. It is awash at high tide, so studs on the boots are a plus (or just avoid it during the highest part of the tide. South of the chute is the picturesque Old Harbor Point, which is flanked to the south by a beautiful small cobbled cove called Green Hill Cove. The point has a few large boulders which are easy to wade to and stand on for casting.

Access: Water Street, O. H. Jetties, Ballard's Inn, Spring Street
Time: Mid-high tide to mid-low tide during low light or at night.
Equipment: 9—to 10-weight with Sink, Float, or Intermediate line, depending on location.
Flies: Any New England pattern: sand eel, silverside, tinker mackerel, squid, juvenile pollock.

Susanne's Fly Rod Striper

SOUTHEAST CORNER

Spots: Tilson Cove, Cat Rock Cove, Whale Rock, Southeast Point, Sand bank Cove, Lighthouse Cove.

This is the beginning of the infamous south side that has big rocky points with sandy coves, offering elevated spots for casting. This entire area is usually preferred at low light or at night, during incoming tide to the top of the outgoing, as fish cruise up into the rocky areas over the bottom. Newcomers should scout it out before trekking in for a night of fishing. Sinking lines should be avoided due to the rocky structure and 9-weight rods on up are recommended.

Access: Spring Street, Saint Ann's Church, Cat Rock Road, Mohegan Bluffs stairway.
Time: Low light or night, mid-high tide through mid-low tide.
Equipment: 9-weights and up—intermediates or sink tips with floating running line
Flies: Big flies—black, olive over white, chartreuse over white.

SOUTH SIDE

Spots: Mohegan Bluff Stairway, Great Point, Vail Beach, Barlow's, Snake Hole, Tom's Cove, and Black Rock.

This area is two miles of epic structure fishing, littered with rocks, boulders, and sandy coves, as well as troughs and sand bars, with one hundred feet bluffs behind you. Any fisherman coming to Block Island should at least see this side of the island, and if you fish it, scout it out with a bird's eye view from the bluffs, and then pick your spots. Generally home to bigger bass and blues, you can catch the occasional bonito or false albacore. Black Rock is probably the best known spot—it is difficult to get to, but usually worth it. Snake Hole Road has public access to Vail Beach—in the middle of the south side, so go left or right at the bottom and fish hard. Most fish caught here, that later make their way to the grill, have crabs in their bellies.

Access: Mohegan Bluff stairway, Second Bluffs, Snake Hole Road, Black Rock Road.
Time: Dusk till dawn
Equipment: 9-weight and up, Intermediate lines
Flies: Big half and halfs, Deceivers, and Clousers. Darker colors generally, crab and lobster patterns

Chris Willi
(Image courtesy of Michael Melford)

SOUTHWEST CORNER

Spots: Lewis Point, Dickens Point, Schooner Point, Southwest Point, Bluff Head, Cooneymus.

This may be the most fished stretch of beach by dedicated anglers on Block Island. Drop in at Conneymus Road and work south to Black Rock. Bluff Head offers a nice point where you cast northwest into a trough that regularly holds fish. It's fairly shallow, ten feet deep all along the point, with cobble bottom and fast moving tidal current on the flood. With the prevailing southwest wind, it can get tricky in a swell. You can get into some false albacore here with bass and blues. In the early season, this is usually my first stop by boat on my way to Block Rock.

Access: Conneymus Road
Time: Dusk till dawn
Equipment: 9-weight and up with intermediate or floater lines.
Flies: Deceivers, Clousers, sand eels—grey over white, black over white, all white, Gurglers, and sliders for top water.

WEST COVES

Spots: Steve's Cove, Dorie's Cove, Grace's Cove, Dead Man's Cove, Charlestown Beach.
Access: Cooneymus Road, Dories Cove Road, Graces Cove Road, Coast Guard Road (Champlin Road)
Time: Dusk till dawn
Equipment: 9-weight and up with intermediate or floater lines.
Flies: Deceivers, Clousers, sand eels, whitebaits—grey, olive, chartreuse, or black over white, and all white. Size 2 to 3/0. Gurglers and sliders for top water.

Gurgler Caught Striper
(image courtesy of Chris Willi)

WEST BEACH

Spots: Beane Point, Ball's, The Dump, Pounders, West Beach, Logwood Cove, Sandy Point
Access: West Beach Road
Time: Dusk till dawn.
Equipment: 9-weight and up with intermediate or floater lines.
Flies: Deceivers, Clousers, sand eels, Gurglers and sliders for top water, whitebaits—grey, olive, chartreuse, or black over white, and all white. Size 2 to 3/0.

Capt. Christopher Willi is a USCG licensed skipper and an IGFA certified captain. He's a Rhode Island native and a graduate of URI with a bachelor of science in wildlife biology and management. He has lived and fished on Block Island since 1992, began guiding the fantastic Block Island beaches in 1998, following which he opened a tackle store on Ocean Avenue in 2002. Chris is the only resident guide who specializes in light tackle and fly fishing and runs both inshore and offshore trips from New Harbor and Old Harbor in either his twenty-foot Aquasport, *Julia Ryan*, or a twenty-six-foot regulator center console model. He's fished up and down the East Coast, Colorado, Utah, Hawaii, Gulf of Mexico, and as far away as Japan. Chris cofounded the Block Island Inshore Fishing Tournament (BIIFT is in its eleventh year) and benefits both the National Children's Cancer Society and the Lions Club. Chris is an advocate of recreational fishing conservation and responsible commercial fishing practices. Chris welcomes all abilities and enjoys getting the "newcomer" hooked on the sport of fishing.

Block Island Fishworks opened in 2002 and is located on Ocean Avenue next to the bridge in New Harbor, offering charters, bait, tackle, surf, and fly gear to our dedicated customers. Open on May 15 to Columbus Day, (401) 742-3992, (401) 466-5392, www.bifishworks.com

Christopher Willi
Block Island Fishworks and Sandy Point Fly Leaders
www.bifishworks.com and www.sandypointco.com
PO Box 1373
1998 Ambrose Lane
Block Island, RI 02807
(401) 742-3992

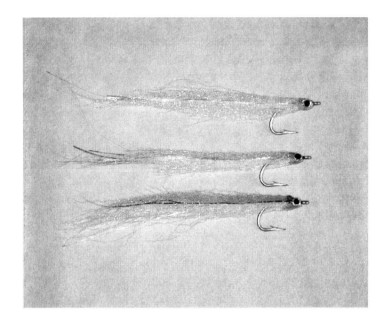

Whites Flies

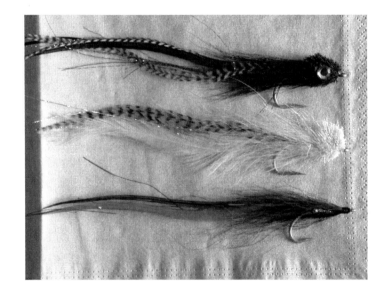

Willi's Eel flies

Sand Eel Flies (1)

Tubular sand eel flies

NORTH RIP PRIMER

When the wind is blowing from the North,
no fisherman should set forth,
When the wind is blowing from the East,
it's not fit for man or beast.
When the wind is blowing from the South,
it blows the bait into the fish's mouth,
But if the wind is blowing from the West,
that's when fishing's the best!

—Unknown

    I started charter fishing the North Rip for spring codfish back in the late 1960s with my nineteen-foot Aquasport propelled by a one hundred horse power Mercury outboard. These were strictly small-group ventures, during which we targeted cod using diamond jig/teaser rigs, with a small buck tail dropper rigged just ahead of (above) the chrome. While most charter boats bait-fished, we took our cod and pollock on artificial lures and relatively light tackle. And truth be told—despite what some bait-dunking purists thought—we seldom returned to our slip in a one-boat "groundfish crisis."

    We focused our activities in the island's outer rip, in depths from thirty-eight to sixty-five feet; as a rule, we preferred a flood tide to the ebb. Back then, I was vocal, letting my crew know, at the start of each drift, we were just up-tide of the well-known Double Hump and the fish it held. Once I'd set up a drift, I'd demonstrate the jigging technique that would be rewarded with a hookup, finishing with how to handle the tackle after boating a fish. Not only was that technique successful with cod, but as the season progressed, also with pollock in the twenty—to thirty-five-pound range—and then, as spring gave way to summer, with large-for-their-size stripers. I discovered that what worked for the cod and pollock prepared me nicely for the striper fishing that would soon follow. It was then I paid particular attention to the mono "dropper" connection, using a "special" loop knot instead of a three-way swivel. I still remember the early May morning when a pair of fifty-plus-pound stripers came aboard to the shock and delight of my two clients, the Fusco brothers from Providence.

It was about that time I discovered the Montauk charter fleet was striper fishing with the recently developed "spreader" or umbrella rig, designed by the Montauk skipper John Sekora. It utilized the then-popular Norwegian tube on a limerick-style (bent) hook, which nicely imitated the size, profile, and undulating movement (spinning) of a sand eel, due to its shape, when trolled through the water. This lure, sporting four single barrel swivel tubes off each arm, was absolutely deadly for stripers at Montauk and Block Island, home of the sand eel and elsewhere. Prior to that, most striped bass fishing was done jigging wire line using feathered or buck-tail dressed jigs. More about the "umbrella" lure later.

OFFSHORE SAND LANCE / *Ammodytes dubius* Reinhardt 1837 / Northern Sand Lance, Sand

Figure 259. Offshore sand lance *Ammodytes dubius*. Nantucket. Drawn by H. L. Todd.

Bigelow & Schroder, 2002

Offshore Sand Lance

Inner Rip

Block Island's North Rip was formed following the last glaciations, about fourteen thousand years ago, when sea levels rose to near present-day levels. Prior to that, a great inland embayment of freshwater, located between the island and mainland, collected sediments consisting of clay, sand, and gravel. These sediments were later "bulldozed" by a southbound glacial front to form Block Island. Millennia later, seawater invaded the area depleted of sediments, forming what is called Block Island Sound today. Research indicates there is still approximately four hundred feet of those freshwater sediments still in place over bedrock north of the island and upward of eight hundred feet in place over bedrock immediately south of the island.

Drifting over the inner bar at slack water, on a sunny, windfree day, one can easily view its composition from above, as depths range from only a fathom (six feet) to an average of nine to twelve feet, depending on the tidal stage. Further offshore, over what I call the Middle Rip, a depth sounder will reveal depths of eighteen to twenty-four feet, which hold stripers best on a flooding tide. Based on my experience, the northern end of the inner bar transitions into the middle bar at around 14524/43918 (Phantom LORAN) and has undergone considerable modification in shape.

Middle Rip

The Middle Rip begins at roughly 14524/43918 (Phantom LORAN) and extends to roughly 14524 / 43920 before the depths fall away to nearly forty feet. Further southward, just southeast of the 1BI Buoy, depths plunge to 120 feet.

Contrary to popular belief, the inner and middle bars are not composed of sand, for if they were, the ebb and flow of tidal currents would have deposited the sand elsewhere. Although it has a rather fragile composition, formed from prehistoric sediments of clay, gravel, and sand, it has been fairly stable for centuries and certainly for the forty or so years I've been fishing it. Reason being, it is a complex mussel bed of bivalves that create "strings" of byssal filaments, anchoring them to the sand, clay, and gravel seabed. Thus, it has been able to weather storm waves, which have modified its shape and face somewhat over the years. More importantly, it continues to attract not only sand eels and the stripers that feed on them, but mollusk-eating starfish as well.

Consistent Action Area

Several areas of the North Rip mussel bed have consistently held marauding stripers on both flood and ebb tides. It appears several inner rip areas have steep vertical fronts facing the oncoming tidal current, whereas other areas with more gradual slopes rarely do. Even in the wake of numerous hurricanes, these rip "holding areas" have remained, suggesting they possess some stability.

Seen for years by an old-timer like myself, the turbulence created during a running tide assumes a unique character, which is neither recognized nor understood by neophytes. However, simply due to the shape and size of the rip waves, I've learned where exactly in the rip fish frequently locate——day or night, foggy or clear. Much of this knowledge came about from my early experiences studying the interplay between bottom and currents in Montauk's rips.

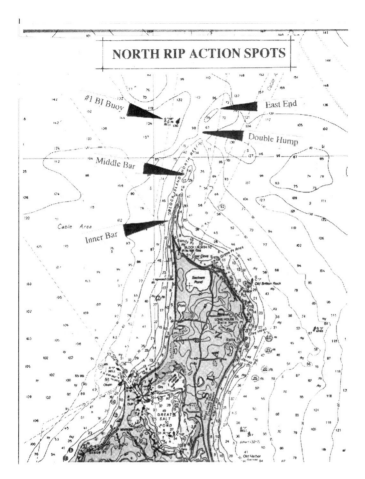

North Rip Action Spots

Because I'm familiar with the depth, structure, and shape of the inner bar, I have come to believe it was once emergent and extended much further offshore of Sandy Point than it presently is. In her book, author E. C. Ritchie (1975—eighth printing) states, "Sandy Point, at the extreme northern end of the Island, was a decoy for ships in early sailing days. In the course of the past two centuries nearly half of the eleven hundred or more shipwrecks occurring on the southern New England coast came to grief on the shores of the small Island of New Shoreham, otherwise known as Block Island."

On the inner cover of her book is a map of the island, which depicts a section of the inner bar that was above sea level for nearly a quarter mile. The terminus of the bar shows a widened area called the "Hummock" and southward connects with the "causeway" or narrow bar, upon which the first lighthouse once stood. That wooden structure only lasted for several years before being consumed by fire.

In stormy weather, the seas met over the causeway, making it impassable; and the survivors of many shipwrecks often perished attempting to reach the shore—so near and yet so far. This submerged (sand)bar extends over a mile and a half out under the ocean waters and the bell buoy.

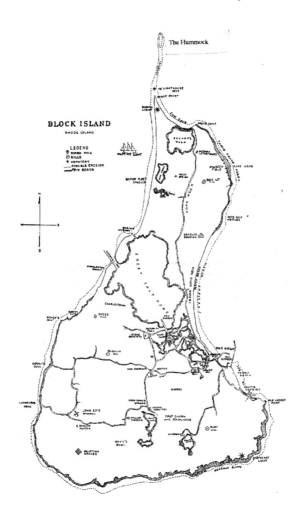

North Bar Hummock

Outer Rip

For as long as anyone can remember, the outer rip area, just east-southeast of the no. 1BI Buoy (14524.7 /43928.5), has a compact fifty-yard bottom area called the "double hump," which I can only surmise was created by the last glacier thousands of years ago. This steep-sided "double-hump" area finds the ebbing tide running toward the east-northeast (060 degrees), while the flooding tide runs west-northwest (290 degrees) over it. I'm forced to assume, because of their abundance, that stripers prefer its orientation to the ebbing tide over the flooding tide. These two near-vertical-sided "humps," which probably offer a certain hydrodynamic benefit to feeding fish, are located at roughly 14522.4 and 43921.6 (Phantom LORAN), as numbers of bluefish join them in this spot come late summer and fall.

East End

The outermost portion of the North Rip runs northeast and ends at roughly 14523.0 and 43921.6 (Phantom LORAN). I refer to it as the East End, and here, depths plummet from sixty to sixty-five feet to over 120. Since the ebbing current runs nearly parallel to the bar, there's little turbulence. As a result, the area, except during certain times of the year, holds few fish and can be difficult to locate. The time to be there is on the start of the flood, which occurs about an hour later than its start at Sandy Point. Tidal changes at the island headlands typically occur sixty to ninety minutes prior to those a mile or more offshore. On the flood tide, striped bass will come out of ninety to ninety-five feet of water into sixty to sixty-five feet of water, and should bait be present, take advantage of the turbulence.

NORTH RIP RIOT

Fish bite least on wind from the east.

—Unknown

Approaching Block Island's North Bar this late May afternoon, squadrons of terns and small gulls could be seen working over the growing ebb-tide rip. As we approached the rip's building face, we observed telltale swirls throughout the calm water up-tide of the rip. Turning into the running tide and engaging the troll valves, I stemmed the current and held the boat nearly stationary over the bottom. While doing so, I directed my fly rod equipped clients to present their offerings. With my elevated vantage point, and only yards up-tide of the rip face, numerous large-for-their-size striped bass could be seen pursuing bait in the first wave of the rip. Above, excited birds were screeching, jinxing, and diving, and I joined in with them, jumping and hollering like a schoolboy. Finally, after what seemed like an eternity, first one, then a second, and finally a third fly rod arched, followed by excited shouts of "Fish on!"

Regrettably, these hooked fish, now surging away, began destroying tackle. One looped and tangled fly line, stripped back only moments earlier, came off the deck and exploded several guides from the rod before parting. A second line simply disappeared, leaving only backing, while the spool of another reel (manufacturer's name withheld), fell to the deck, bounced and twisted like a Mexican jumping bean, then smashed back into the reel frame, parting the leader. Judging from the tackle destruction, it was obvious a "riot" had just occurred. Score three for the fish, zip for the anglers.

If you've never experienced rip fishing for hungry, early season moon-tide striped bass gorging on squid, sand eels or Atlantic saury, like those frequently found at Block Island's North Bar, chances are you're in for quite a surprise, not to mention possibly being totally unprepared.

North Bar Notes

Seen from the air, Block Island's shape resembles that of a pork chop, with its North Bar agitating the bait rich waters of Rhode Island Sound as they course into and out of Block Island Sound (NOAA Chart 13215). Extending northward for nearly half a mile from Sandy Point, North Bar is a relatively shallow, cobble-strewn mussel bed lying between both sounds. In the spring, cooler Rhode Island Sound waters flood over the bar to the northwest, while warmer Block Island Sound waters ebb to the northeast. The reverse is true in the fall, but that's a story for another time.

The eastern side faces Rhode Island Sound, and an unprotected fetch extends to the vineyard. Strong northeast, east, and southeast winds generate swells that can create dangerous inner bar conditions. On the other hand, prevailing winds out of the southwest, especially on an ebbing tide, create relatively calm surface conditions.

North Rip Twi-Light Striper

North Bar, or North Rip, as it's frequently called, is divided into a relatively shallow portion (inner bar) and a longer deeper portion extending out past the 1BI Buoy. Fly rod efforts are concentrated along the inner bar in depths ranging from four to fifteen feet, usually up-tide of the rip, out to what is commonly called "the break." This is a breach between the inner and outer bar, with the outer bar extending another one hundred yards or so northward. From there, curving to the northeast, the peak of the bar averages fifty to sixty feet below the surface. The "double hump" next to the buoy offers super fishing, but that too is another story.

At times, bait will concentrate in near-slack waters at Sandy Point, where depths push twenty feet, frequently with "feathers" over it. Early in an ebb tide, this bait can be carried north and over the bar, out of reach of a surfcaster, but within the reach of a boater's fly. Be careful not to stray into shallow water chasing breaking fish, as an errant wave could fall into the boat. Take it from me, only a few places like this in Southern New England offer such challenging, but highly rewarding, springtime striped bass fishing.

Know the Flow

Many are confused about tidal info when consulting a Newport tide chart. Instead, check when the current turns at The Race, Long Island Sound, along with predicted current strength. Ebb over North Bar (inner) begins about an hour before The Race, while flood begins about fifteen minutes prior. Flood current runs to the north-northwest (320 degrees magnetic), while ebb over the inner bar runs north-northeast (060 degrees magnetic).

Steph Cramer & Capt. Al
(photo by John Crowe)

Unfortunately, many anglers have ignored this area due to confusion regarding timing of the tidal currents. For example, anglers at Point Judith, Rhode Island, might note flood-tide waters till 6:46 a.m., whereas at North Rip, only a few miles across the sound, waters here flood till 9:40 a.m., nearly a three-hour difference. Best source of local tidal info is published annually in the yellow-covered *Eldridge Tide and Pilot Book*, available for $14 at many tackle and marine supply shops.

For what it's worth, I schedule four—to six-hour "twilight" charter trips only on those days immediately before and after both new and full moons from May-July, ensuring ideal tidal conditions and the action they create.

Measured Approach

There are three approaches to fishing this area: (1) Either anchor up ahead of the rip and cast parallel to it, allowing offerings to sweep down into the turbulence, (2) Stem the boat into the current and cast, again allowing the fly to sweep into the turbulence, or (3) Troll the fly along the rip face. On a moon tide, I prefer the latter, as experience has shown bait will quickly move back and forth along the bar when hungry linesiders appear. Once located, I can then stem up-tide of the action. Often, I've quickly anchored when concentrations of fish were high, making this effort well worthwhile. However, there is no better way to locate fish than to troll along the rip face, unless of course squadrons of terns or gulls do it for you.

Tidal strength will affect the numbers of fish holding station in a given spot. Several areas of the bar consistently hold fish, regardless of tidal strength due to the bar's orientation in the current, while other spots gather fish only during very specific—and short-lived—parts of a tide. I cherish this understanding, but freely admit it was no overnight study.

Jim Zien Fooled Another Striper

Unlike other stretches of high ground along North Rip which slope gently away into the deep, the inner bar's near-vertical faces—ten—to fifteen-foot cliffs really create ideal attack zones for foraging.

Watching the sounder closely as you cross the area around the 1BI Buoy or the famed Double Hump, your fishfinder will reveal several similarly near-vertical humps or peak areas that consistently hold fish. Nearly forty years ago, I discovered similar inner-bar edges existed, and under the cover of darkness, confirmed these frequently provided exceptional striper action. Although these zones stay fairly consistent, time of day, weather, tides, and sea conditions all influence success.

The secret to success, if trolling the fly, is to present the fly close to the rip "face" or line of breaking waves. Several inner bar areas demonstrate near vertical faces, that when light intensity starts to decline (afternoons, cloud cover, etc.) due to a dropping sun, gather fish.

SC & XPO with a T/R striper

'Chuting By Fly

Several years back, Capt. Ron Murphy, who runs the charter boat *Stray Cat* out of Falmouth, Massachusetts, offered me one of his specialized flies for our efforts at North Bar. A simple fly, it's tied on a 4/0 stainless hook, dressed with Polar Bear Super Hair and Polar Flash, and carries 3/8-inch holographic eyes. It matches the action of a squid when stripped back, much like a worked parachute jig. Check out www.straycatfishing.com for directions on tying Capt. Ron's Parachute Fly.

Murphy's Squid Fly

Although designed basically for trolling due to its bulky shape, this fly can be hot when squid crowd the rip. One need only cast fifteen to twenty-five feet behind the boat into a rip's strike zone.

On moon tides, current velocity can approach 2.5 knots over the inner bar, with action best early and late in the tides. Off the moon, currents max out around 1.3 to 1.8 knots. For this reason, fast sink lines such as a Teeny 475-grain or Cortland's LC-13 (lead core) work well. If you're interested in trolling the fly, I've found that a thirty-five-foot shot of LC-13 looped at both ends, for connecting to running line and leader, does a great job. Trolling at ¾ to a full knot, all thirty-five feet of LC-13 is run aft, and a rhythmic, sharp jigging action is imparted to the line. It's important to remember both jigging and striking are done by hand, following which the rod tip is raised and backing allowed to run against a moderate drag. Anchored or stemming the tide, a Teeny 250-grain or Scientific Anglers Uniform Sink Type 4 will carry offerings into rip face strike zones. Fluorocarbon leader material of twenty-pound test is a must with forty-pound shock tippet.

I advise my anglers to consider bringing several outfits, rigged and ready to go. Rods ranging from 10—to 14-weight, depending on conditions, serve best. Keep in mind, a twenty—to thirty-pound striper in a two—to three-knot current will cause you to lose up to one hundred or more yards of backing quickly, unless you apply maximum pressure.

Reels should be large-arbor models, capable of holding a hundred yards or more of backing, with composite—not cork—drags. Since we want to avoid extended fight times that exhaust the fish, stout rods are best to ensure survival.

Bill Krueger's Island striper

Additional Wisdom

Keep in mind that flat calm sea conditions without a white water rip typically offers less action than one with tide against the wind. With prevailing southwest winds, the best tide to fish the bar is flood. If a late afternoon or early ebb tide is in progress and winds are light northeast, east, or southeast, the rip will offer lots of white water and action to go with it. Be sure to stay in calm water up-tide of the rip, but if you have to fall down into it, return over some location other than directly over fish holding station. I've seen too many anglers ruin fishing with their wakes. If you have a fish on, idle across the current up-tide of the strike zone before drifting back.

On the ride home that late May evening, thanks to my providing several 10—to 14-weight outfits, we managed to tally several dozen stripers up to twenty-eight pounds, of which most were tagged and released for science in the name of conservation.

NORTH RIP AFTER DARK

There are only three things in life that matter—good friends, good food, and, oh dear, now I remember . . . big fish . . .

—Author Unknown

In 1970, with the advent of one of Dick Lema's first twenty-six-foot fiberglass, Bonito bass boats, my night fishing at Block Island's North Rip began in earnest. The trips started around 7:00 p.m., and if the weather permitted, ran through false dawn the next morning. Early on, I installed a TI LORAN-C receiver, followed by a Furuno Radar a year later. I'd initially refused to install such equipment, but soon gave in. Fishing in full dark, along with the inevitable problems with heavy fog during key parts of the season, mandated it. After installing that equipment—much as my stubbornness wanted *not to see its value*—I soon found it indispensable.

If a party faced high, late-afternoon humidity, and southeast wind, I knew fog would inevitably roll in. So to avoid frustration, I focused many nights' fishing efforts on the North Rip. There were simply too many problems associated with fishing on the Southwest Ledge at night in fog—lobster-trawl buoys not least. Besides, I was just more familiar with the North Rip at night in the fog, and with the LORAN-C aboard, it became a piece of cake.

Trolling Plugs After Dark

Years ago, at night with parties, trolling Danny Plugs on wire, during moon-tide periods, at both the "double hump" and the East End, found us taking high numbers of jumbo bass. With nearly a dozen stripers in the fifty—to sixty-pound range from mainland waters already to my credit, our "jumbo" tally peaked in 1975 and 1976. Naturally, word of our success got out, despite attempts to hide it. In June alone, each year, eight stripers (sixteen total) measured well in excess of the fifty-three inches (fork length), estimated to be fifty pounds or more, and over forty fish each of those months measured between forty-four and fifty inches (FL), estimated at better than forty pounds. I didn't bother to count the smaller fish, and there were many of them. The same was going on at Cuttyhunk, Massachusetts, at night and at Wasque, southwest of the vineyard during daytime. I know because Frank Sabatowski, skipper of the *June Bug*, and I were good friends at the time. Truth be known, I was catching a few more fish than he was, but he told of fish averaging greater size.

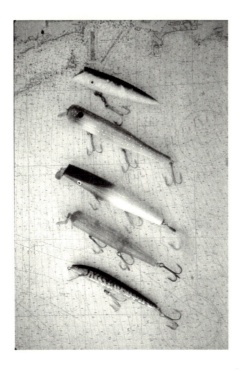

Plug Assortment; j-Plug. G00 Goo Eyes. Danny. Atom 40, Rebel

Tim Coleman, then-editor of *The Fisherman*, New England edition, began pestering me for reports to support his fledgling magazine endeavors. By then, my business was well established, and the rest is history.

Fishing the east end for stripers at night had other rewards, few of which my clients took advantage of. This included good numbers of pollock in the twenty—to thirty-pound range, and there were times when totes of large pollock joined totes of stripers the next morning at the Point Judith Fisherman's Co-op in Galilee. That's right, those pollock were large enough to grab a Danny or Goo-Goo Eyes plug, but they were nowhere near as strong as the bass.

"What, You Here Again"

It was in the early eighties that I penned a story for *The Fisherman* entitled "What, You Here Again?" Inspired by an emergency room physician, it briefly told of my repeated visits to South County Hospital (SCH), where several of my painful late night misfortunes were attended to. Large nighttime stripers that came into my bass boat on short wires hadn't fully completed their struggles; so to be safe, they were dispatched with a "Billy-club" to quiet them. After destroying several wooden (oak) models, I received a heavy duty, weighted, composite version from a law-enforcement client, which I still have to this day.

Fishing relatively short wires necessitated boating large, thrashing stripers, bearing HD multihook plugs, which had to be quieted before safe hook removal could occur—lest I suffer ugly consequences. Trust me, I speak from experience. Several times, while leaning down to dispatch a fish, just as its final efforts catapulted it off the deck, I found 3X hooks embedded in either a gloved hand or forearm. Several nights, when the tide quit early, with help from clients following return and cleanup, I could then leave for the SCH Emergency Room. However, one night, with a brand new 3X 7/0 Mustad treble hook simultaneously embedded in my right hand thumb *and* a thrashing fish, I instinctively lay down over the fish to quiet it. Despite a heavy-duty foul-weather jacket over a thick wool sweater, I soon wound up with a second very sharp 7/0 hook in my chest. I soon made an attempt to continue with the fishing.

Come to find out, I wasn't as tough as I thought I was; the resulting shock and blood loss found me puking. After a weak argument, my party suggested I return them to Snug Harbor Marina. My predicament that night later required one of the hospital staff to hunt down a large wire-cutting tool from their basement shop before the painful hooks could be removed. I was later told never to come back to South County Hospital again.

Bruce Mayer's North Rip T/R Striper

From the Ledge to the Rip

    The following is the second part of a *Fisherman* story about fishing the ledge first for stripers, then fishing the North Rip.

    Despite the ledge offering "super" action with large bass this afternoon, I was determined to check out the North Rip on the remaining flood tide before heading home. After nearly a dozen stripers fell to our twi-light trolled jigs, a second dozen fell to our after-dark plugs, now all fish are swimming away with tags. Because of steadily growing ledge-navigation lights, creating considerable congestion, my party surprisingly suggested we relocate. Heading northward, the concealed gunwale cockpit lights cast a crimson glow over my happy anglers as we sped away.

    Upon reaching the North Rip, with only an occasional "flick" of white, the flooding moon tide continued to surge over the North Rip's inner bar. Only moments later, once our wire-line "marks" reached their respective rod tips, a pair of hefty, keeper-sized bass "locked on." If there was any inhibiting "fire," or what is called phosphorescence in the water, it was totally disguised by the moonlight. Those two plugs that once throbbed below the surface on short-wire lines were now attached to the "explosive" muscle and sinew energy of surging stripers.

For the next ninety minutes, netted large-for-their-size stripers continued to swim away with American Littoral Society (ALS) tags. Just prior to the end of the tide, on the way back to Point Judith, a total of forty-one tag cards were counted for both the ledge and the rip tagged bass. Not bad for a two-stop, eight-hour, dock-to-dock trolling venture night.

Inner Bar

Contrary to what many authors state, the North Rip is not a sandbar, but instead is an elongated clay, gravel, and cobble-strewn mussel bed, similar to several mainland areas. Back in the early 1700s, this bar was reportedly a narrow, emergent peninsula, covered with small trees, shrubs, and berry bushes on its northern end, where island inhabitants picnicked. It was called the "Hummock" by some historians.

Night Time Rip Striper

Because of its composition, this mussel bed has several hard edges that create ideal attack zones for nocturnal-feeding stripers—fish that long ago, inherited a genetic disposition to prowl shoal areas in the darkness.

If you're familiar with the Double Hump area, your fishfinder shows several similar near-vertical areas that consistently hold fish. Nearly forty years ago, I discovered similar edges along the inner bar that frequently provided exceptional striper action—mainly at night.

Troll Valves

Years ago, a Cuttyhunk charter skipper told me I'd never catch a striper from a diesel-powered boat. Only a gas engine, he said, could present plugs slow enough to catch bass. That skipper was wrong about many things, most notably diesel-powered vessels. For over thirty years, I've used twin-disc gear troll valves, whose console-mounted controls readily slow in-gear trolling speed via reduced propeller-shaft revolutions. Better yet, I can stem into a strong tidal current, remaining stationary over the bottom, while anglers cast plugs into a rip face or retrieve fly-rod offerings. When I mark deep-water stripers on the troll, I can change the depth of our offerings simply by reducing prop-shaft speed. It's my opinion—and I may be as wrong about this as an aforementioned Cuttyhunk skipper once was about diesels and big bass—that taking an engine out of gear or changing rpm's, particularly in shallow water, negatively affects quarry behavior, thanks to noise change.

Strike Zones

On this particular night, the bluefish reportedly became thick on the ledge, but we encountered only a few. Our focus was to plug-troll one small area and see if we could enjoy some success. To my delight, we netted and released fifteen heavyweight bass, two at a time, on several passes, along with several bluefish. Although the "hump" we were fishing had twenty-eight to thirty-two feet of water over it, our plugs probably fished less than half that depth. A flurry of fish confirmed that these favored plugs created a much larger strike zone after dark than during daylight hours.

Super Plug

Back in the seventies, a client of mine gifted me a number of salmon plugs used by several Cuttyhunk stripermen, who'd caught loads of big fish on them. Over the years, I've come to favor one particular plug, the Luhr-Jensen original J-Plug, size 5 model, in silver/blue Top.

J-Plugs

Unlike other plugs, this J-Plug performs exceptionally well in strong rip-tide currents without spinning. More importantly, I believe this herring-dupe's action creates sonic vibrations that not only alert fish to its presence, but suggest injury. On the troll, rod tips beat a rapid cadence (loss of that rod-tip action typically signals fouling by weed). There is *no doubt*, in my mind, a striper's lateral line senses this plug long before it sees it.

Unlike other fixed-hook plugs, the J-Plug does not carry hooks that can be leveraged open or straightened by fish-jaw pressure. Instead, the fishing line passes through the plug, allowing it to travel up the line, while the free-swinging hook stays embedded in jaw tissue. This lure comes with a five-bead metal chain that attaches to two 2/0 treble hooks. Although they can be straightened, there are other reasons I choose not to use them. For one thing, we like to tag and release large fish quickly. Double hooks, besides threatening significant injury to fish or fisherman, require considerable time to dislodge, extending on-deck handling time—fine for fish you'll retain, but not for tag and release. Instead, I replace them with a single 4/0 3X Mustad treble—one that can be more readily dislodged. If fish take only a single barb of this heavy-wire treble, they stay hooked all the way to the net.

If you ever thought of getting away from the cost and trouble of live eeling and regard yourself a competent after-dark troller, consider giving these plugs a try on some future moon tide. If the snakes are more your speed, read on.

Eeling the Double Hump

The eastern sky was showing first light on this Block Island night trip as our drift approached North Rip's "double hump." It was early in the new moon flood tide, and suddenly our live eels became nervous, signaling pending strikes. Moments later, my three anglers had heavyweight stripers "thumping" rods and running off line. But that was soon to end, as our drift speed in the tide had now nearly doubled, confirmed by declining numbers of fish marking on my fishfinder. Experience told me our quarry would soon vacate this spot once current velocities peaked and light intensity increased.

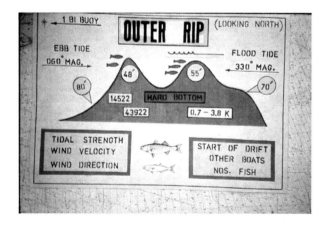

Double Hump

As daylight broke, a "rookie" skipper appeared alongside with his party, curious as to why we were headed home, contrary to what his Newport Tide Chart indicated. Stunned to learn about our late night success, even returning a few tagged keeper-size bass, and that he was still three to four hours away from the popular ebb tide, he disgustedly left for parts unknown.

Timing Block's moon tides played a major role in my charter fishing success, and the following is some of what I know about that.

On the Drift

In the spring, I'm at the island almost daily and/or nightly, so I have a good idea just where the action is. I typically fish parachute jigs prior to dark, then either live line eels or troll plugs at night (frequently both). Here are some strategies.

Several preps for drifting live eels include a few dry rags or cotton work gloves to grab the eels with when hooking them. I suggest anglers hook them in the lower jaw, bringing the point of the hook out one of the eye sockets, which is a natural hole in the skull and less easily split by the hook, helping prevent eel loss.

Another trick is to place your eels in a bucket filled with ice so their metabolism is slowed, making them a lot easier to handle. If unsure that the eel is still alive, simply watch it hanging from the hook to see if it curls its tail. If so, it's alive.

Watch'n that eel

Thin wire hooks made by Gamakatsu are my favorite; they won't spit the jaw of a small eel, even in size 7/O, and they are sharp right out of the package, unlike many other hooks. I also like a Mustad no. 92553BL, size 5/0 or 6/0, an octopus-style hook I snell to the sixty-pound-test fluorocarbon leader on a fishfinder setup. The idea of a fishfinder rig is to prevent missed strikes, dropped eels, and spit-outs when a striking fish feels the weight of a sinker. Allow a moment's hesitation, so as to give a bass time to take the eel into its maw, before you react. Simply raise the rod-tip to set the hook. The fish does the rest, as our success of connection is good. Be sure to hang the sinker about eighteen to twenty-four inches away from the nylon fishfinder sleeve or barrel swivel.

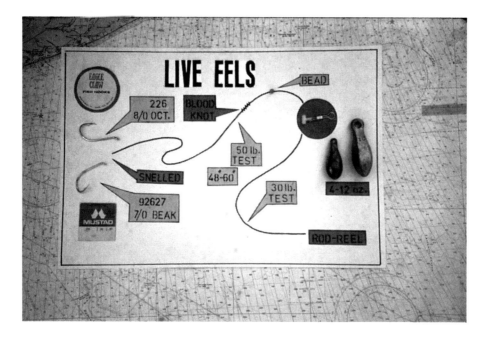

Eeling Fish-Finder Rig

Now, those of you who successfully fish circle hooks have to realize, not all of my clients are adept at using them properly. Once they master the drop-back technique with J hooks, they are challenged with using circle hooks. I prefer that clients use mono line (forty—to fifty-pound test), rather than spectra lines. Not paying attention to wind and sea conditions can create wind-wrapped guides that sabotage strikes.

On the drift with eels, I watch my Sitex Chromoscope (fishfinder) closely for presence or absence of fish. Knowing the tidal drift direction and approximate speed, I choose a predetermined spot to begin a test drift, figuring in tidal strength and wind direction. I mark the starting point of the drift, so I can either return to it or adjust it on the next pass, depending on success or lack thereof. When drifting through a rip, I note the hook-up spot, and then use it to modify, if necessary, our next drift. I orient the boat the same way for each drift, so my anglers become familiar with their situation. I use cockpit lights only when necessary, and both the mate and I quietly (and constantly) coach anglers to avoid common disasters.

How do you know if you had a bite, and then a spit-out following the strike? The answer is easy: If you see a light-colored mark near the head of the eel, it indicates the sandpaper-like teeth of the bass have removed some of the dark pigmented scales off the eel.

Small AA battery lights with neck lanyards are readily accessible, as are spare outfits, rigged and ready to go. Since we tag and release, teamwork is required to net them, then tag them before the run back up-tide. Be aware that other vessels may not show any lights when on the drift, so pay close attention to other "traffic."

In Review: The Drifting Drill

1. Note starting point of the drift.
2. Check tide set and direction.
3. Note wind direction and speed.
4. Note depth at which drift started.
5. Observe track of drift on plotter.
6. Mark lat/lon's where strikes occurred.
7. Keep rods/anglers spread out to prevent tangles.
8. Minimize noise, lights, and withhold camera flashes until the run back up-tide.

More on Moon Tides

Anglers who pay attention to detail know that in the course of a week (seven days), the tides are roughly the reverse of the previous week. If on a Sunday, it's low tide around noon, the following Sunday will show high tide around noon.

How much ocean tides rise and fall depends on three variables. First, when the sun and moon are in a line with the earth, their gravitational forces combine to produce a greater tidal range than usual. This occurs at both full and new moons, but don't blame your buddy for thinking they're equal. For several months of the year, new moon tides are higher, and then the same becomes true for full moon tides, a result of what you're about to read. Check it if you don't believe me.

Second, the moon's orbit around the earth is elliptical, ranging from about 252,000 miles at apogee down to 221,000 miles at perigee. Hence, the position of the moon in its elliptical orbit is very important to tidal heights and current velocity.

Third, the plane of the moon's orbit about the earth is inclined to the plane of the earth's equator. The moon, therefore, travels north and south of the equator, and only twice a month is it directly above the equator, resulting in the day's two high tides being nearly equal. When the moon has northern declination and is over the U.S., this high tide will be the greater of our two daily high tides. As a result, tidal currents will be the stronger of the two, frequently attracting larger fish for a longer period of time.

In summary, the height of the tides is influenced most by (1) the moon's phase, with full and new moon tides creating the highest tides and strongest tidal currents; (2) the moon's distance from the Earth in its elliptical orbit (tides being highest when it is closest—apogee vs. perigee); and (3) its declination, north or south of the equator, creating tides of different heights on the same day.

PARACHUTING THE LEDGE

*There are two types of fishermen—
those who fish for sport and those who fish for fish.*

—*Author Unknown*

Sunset was less than an hour away as winds diminished and a gentle swell crept over Block Island's Southwest Ledge. In the slack tide, lobster trawl buoys that had floated aimlessly were now beginning to strain against the nudge of a west-northwest flood current. In the boulder-strewn depths, pods of striped bass, recently arrived from their offshore migration, began searching out different feeding stations, as celestial forces were now at work, creating a tidal current that could deliver ample forage to these fish. Just above the swaying kelp, pods of squid darted along in the strengthening current.

High above, moving against this flow, anglers aboard the Prowler worked highly visible chartreuse parachute jigs on wire line, jigs that probed the dimly lit depths forty feet below the surface, just west-northwest of the "Peanut." Beneath, dozens of lateral lines perceived a rhythmic cadence, and out of the darkness, silhouetted against surface light, appeared an injured squid. As these surreal squids invaded a number of strike zones, several fish surged upward to inhale them. On the surface, shouts of "Fish on!" carried across the early evening waters.

If you've got plans to tangle with a few stripers come June, here's a peak at what goes on over the shoals, boulders, and rips of Southwest Ledge, Block Island, Rhode Island.

SUPER SW Ledge Striper

The Ledge

Check NOAA Chart no. 13215, Block Island Sound, for info on Southwest Ledge, a boulder shoal extending over 3.5 nautical miles seaward from the corner of Block Island, Rhode Island. This shoal area, one that breaks in heavy weather, is marked with a RACON Buoy at 14589.5/43867.5 (Phantom LORAN, 9960 Rate).

Be aware that vessels in possession of striped bass outside the three-mile Exclusive Economic Zone (EEZ) are in violation of federal law, and both state and federal enforcement agencies have the right to search and seize property from those not in compliance. If one catches a striped bass in federal waters, it must be released, as anglers are prohibited from having stripers in their possession.

Tidal Currents

Many agree the preferred tide to fish is flood, which runs 320 degrees (mag.) with an average maximum current of 1.5 kts. Ebb is a different story, running 140 degrees (mag.) with an average maximum current of 2.1 knots. Keep in mind, wind direction and velocity can influence both strength and duration of the tidal flow, not only on the ledge, but elsewhere as well.

Based on tides for The Race, flood tide for the ledge is concurrent, but the ebb starts about twenty minutes earlier. Just off Lewis Point, Block Island, tidal change times are considerably different, with flood starting about ninety-five minutes prior to The Race and the ebb about thirty-five minutes prior.

On the Troll

Come spring, lobster trawl gear invades the ledge, posing significant headaches for the unwary. For those trolling, care must be taken not to do so across the tide, as trawl buoys usually suck under in the strong current and become invisible. Forget trying to pull any gear up to untangle or free your lines. Once the current runs hard, those who know troll directly up-current to spots entered into memory on their DGPS plotters, minimizing potential contact with troublesome buoy lines. Constant vigilance is the key to avoiding trawl gear, up-and-down lines, and buoys.

Block Island SW Ledge striper 2011

Action on the ledge typically occurs early and late in a tide when currents moderate and occasionally on the slack. Those trolling tube and worm combos or larger "salami" hoses fare best at this time.

Anglers preferring wire typically deploy about two hundred feet of line when working two—or three-ounce lead-head jigs in thirty to thirty-five feet depths, and take care to shorten them to 150 feet when working lumps that come within twenty-three or twenty-five feet of the surface. When trolling forty—to fifty-foot depths, you may need three hundred feet of wire or more, depending on vessel speed, to score. Timing the tides here is very important if you want to reduce frustration and maximize success. (For additional thoughts on moons, tides, and their collective effect on striped bass feeding behavior, refer to the previous chapter "Moons and Tides.")

Mike Blank's T/R Striper

West-northwest of the "Peanut"

On this particular late afternoon, after watching my Sitex fishfinder as we turned south toward the ledge buoy, but well inside the EEZ line, an area just to the west-northwest of the "Peanut" (Phantom LORAN-C, 9960 Rate, 14578/43873) again marked good numbers of fish, but no resulting strikes occurred. Quickly checking our wire lines, we discovered several strands of eelgrass on each of our Uncle Josh pork-rind-dressed three-ounce Andrus parachute jigs. On our next pass, the marked area was vacant of fish, but as we turned across the current, all three rods again surged under the strain of heavyweight stripers. Fear of snagged lobster gear dissolved as bouncing rods signaled striper headshakes. Quickly relocating several anglers and straightening the course of the boat helped avoid tangles as we worked on gaining line. Shortly, two thirty-plus-pound stripers swam away sporting ALS tags, while the third fish, approaching forty pounds, entered the fish well.

As darkness approached and the fish evaporated, we ceased jigging the 'chutes. Shortly, we set out three wires with swimming plugs, and almost immediately, we had 'em on again. (For thoughts on plug-trolling, refer to the chapter "North Rip after Dark.")

AFTER DARK AT THE SW CORNER

*It is good to have an end to journey toward;
But in the end it is the journey that matters.*

—Ursula Le Guin

(**Author's Note:** The following is a modified version of a piece Don Smith, who fishes close to seventy nights per year at the island with longtime fishing partner and twice-over state-record-breaker for stripers in Rhode Island waters. The latter part of the entry is part of an interview I conducted to flush out some of the additional relevant details. For some thoughts on productive starting points along the Southwest Ledge to the three-mile "Fence," check out the chart reproductions, interspersed through this chapter, complete with Phantom LORAN coordinates for a few of the more popular and productive drifting areas.)

Don Smith on Block Island's Nighttime Cows

Block Island has long been recognized as a mecca of striper fishing. Every day during striped bass season, there are numerous charter boats and recreational fishermen trolling, jigging, and drifting for stripers. It's not unusual to see a hundred boats near the Southwest Ledge at one time. After dark, however, there are relatively few boats searching for bass.

My fishing partner, Peter Vican, and I fish Block Island approximately seventy nights a year. As Peter jokingly puts it, he doesn't want to go home to his wife, and I have no life, so we go fishing. The truth is we share a passion for striper fishing and get out every opportunity we have.

Our trips have yielded plenty of large bass each season, including some monster-size fish. Last July, Peter landed a seventy-six-pound fourteen-ounce striper. It's the largest striper on record caught by rod and reel from a boat and presently the Rhode Island state record.

For us, an excellent night of fishing is one where we catch and release thirty bass each over twenty-five pounds. An average trip is one that yields eighteen to twenty "linesiders" apiece over twenty-five pounds.

Is it easy to fish Block Island at night? It's not exactly a Sunday walk-in-the-park, but with the right equipment, it's certainly doable. By right equipment, I'm not referring to the equipment mandated by the Coast Guard, like flares, a first-aid kit, personal floatation devices (those things my generation calls life jackets), etc. that every boat must carry. I'm referring to gear that, in addition to GPS and a good fish-finder, makes night fishing safer for everyone on board.

I consider radar a must-have item for night fishing. Not only is it dark out there, but as weather fronts move across the area, fog can develop very quickly, making you totally blind. Radar serves as your eyes in the dark and fog. In addition to picking up any boat traffic, it will show you navigation aids and even lobster pot buoys, so you can avoid any entangling situation. Radar will also pick up thunderclouds from any sudden squalls that develop, providing you with distance to the storm and its direction. It can tell you if and when it might be time to quit fishing and head for the safety of Old or New Harbor until the storm passes. Pay attention to commercial boat traffic. There are a lot of tugs towing barges through the area at night. Almost needless to say, getting between the tug and barge can be fatal.

A good bow spotlight, preferably one with a remote control, lets you see what lies in front of the boat as you travel along. It can prevent you from ramming floating debris or running down lobster pots. A floodlight for the cockpit and stern area of the boat will help when landing fish. If you happen to drift over a lobster pot buoy and find the rope wrapped on your prop, it helps to see it clearly to free the boat.

Don Smith with a night-caught heavy

Keep your radio on. If you keep it on scan mode, you'll pick up some interesting chatter. Some nights, we hear boats as far out as the canyons talking about the tuna bite. Most important, however, is that the U.S. Coast Guard broadcasts notices to mariners about navigation obstacles and accidents. It's actually amazing how busy the Coast Guard can be at night with overdue and missing boats, capsizes, and other accidents.

New England weather changes can occur rapidly. The Coast Guard also broadcasts the location, speed, and direction of quickly forming thunderstorms, or squalls, along with wind velocity.

Many striper fishermen like to fish in the dark. They feel that any light spooks the bass. Never, I repeat, never, turn off your navigation lights. Some nights on the water are foggy or so black you can't pick out the silhouette of any boats drifting in the area, until they get on top of you. Distance is hard to judge at night, so the lights are the only way to keep track of where other drifting boats lie. Besides, there's always the unlikely chance that some idiot, without radar, will come zipping along at top speed and not see you until it's too late. Being sunk out there at night doesn't make my top-ten list of exciting things to do.

I recommend wearing a PFD at night. The vest types are comfortable and won't interfere with your fishing. Either manual or auto inflating types are fine, but I feel that auto inflating ones are just a bit safer. I also recommend that you attach a knife with a serrated blade to the vest. If you happen to accidentally tangle the prop in a rope, getting it wrapped up so you have to go overboard to free it, that knife can be a lifesaver. A serrated knife, like the one sold by Plante's Buoy Sticks, will make short work of any rope, including polypropylene. Go to the Internet and type in plantebuoysticks.

Equip the boat with a swim ladder. Even with a PFD to keep you afloat, you will find it just about impossible to lift yourself over the side of the boat wearing wet clothes. Having a swim ladder makes it a lot easier.

Have a good flashlight. We wear waterproof LED headlamps on our boat. They are great for landing fish, and in the unlikely event that you go overboard, they can help your fishing buddies find you. At times, the current moves pretty fast around Block Island, so you could be separated from the boat quickly.

Don't be deceived by the weather reports for Block Island, they are notoriously unreliable. We always joke with our fishing buddies that, seemingly the rule is if NOAA reports the wind at five to fifteen miles per hour, just add the two numbers together, and you'll come close to the actual wind conditions at the island. The weather reports for the island are truly unreliable for both wind speed and direction.

Pay attention to wave heights and their frequency in the forecast. Waves at a height of three to four feet, with a frequency of eight seconds or less, can toss a boat and make fishing very unpleasant—if not impossible. However, the same wave height at a frequency of thirty seconds is something you won't even notice and will seem like a very slight roll when you're drifting.

Finally, if you've never fished Block Island at all, I'd recommend that you try fishing days first, just to get the feel of the area and learn the spots before you head out for night fishing. Does it sound like I'm trying to scare you off? Really, I'm not. I'm just trying to point out extreme circumstances that, with a little common sense, can be totally avoided. Safety on the water is important at all times, and when we take it for granted, accidents happen. At night, there can be diminished visibility, so it's important to be alert to prevent accidents.

You should be aware of the current direction around the island. It varies greatly with location. This will have an impact on your drift and can become a little confusing, if you're not aware of it. This information is part of the tide charts available at the NOAA website: http://tidesandcurrents.noaa.gov/currents09/tab2ac3.html#18.

Almost all striper fishermen have preferred conditions for fishing. Such variables as moon phase, wind direction, and water conditions, all factor into it. Depending on whom you talk to, you will hear things like "Fish on either an outgoing or incoming tide." "Bioluminescence in the water spooks the bass," "Don't fish on a full moon," "Don't fish on a new moon," and above all, "Don't fish on your wedding anniversary or wife's birthday." While these things may be true for fishing from shore or fishing in the bay, they hardly pertain to Block Island. I can tell you from experience, that no matter what the conditions are, as long as there is bait around the island, the stripers will be there. It's just a matter of finding them.

We've fished Block Island in virtually every weather condition and moon phase, and it's made no difference. What does happen during a full or new moon is that the current runs stronger and you might have to compensate for it with more weight on your line or even power drift to slow down the drift speed, but the fish will still be feeding.

Another thing we've moved to the myth category is that bioluminescence in the water spooks stripers, and they won't bite. There's bioluminescence in the water at the island most nights.

The best night of fishing we ever had at the island occurred on an August night four years ago. We were fishing off Black Rock in twenty feet of water. The water was very clean and clear, and there was so much bioluminescence in the water that we could see a silver streak behind the eel as it swam to the bottom. Then there would be a big swirl of silver as the bass hit the eel, and we could follow the trail of light as the bass swam off. When we brought a bass to the boat, there would be two or three other bass swimming with it, and when they saw the boat they darted off in different directions, leaving a bright luminous trail behind them. We'd unhook the bass and watch the "light show" in the water as the bass swam down. Then we repeated the scene all over again with another eel.

Between 8:30 p.m. and 6:00 a.m., Peter caught fifty-eight bass over twenty-five pounds, and I caught fifty-three over twenty-five pounds, under these conditions. We fished both the incoming and outgoing tide in the same location. The fish just moved from one end of the structure to the other when the tide changed.

Wind direction may make it difficult to fish on one side of the island. All you need to do is head to the leeward side, and fish there in comfort. There are bass all around the island.

Trolling at night at the island is not something I'd recommend if you are inexperienced. The bottom structure and the number of lobster pots make it impractical. Perhaps the only exception is the North Rip. I know one charter captain (not this author) who will troll an umbrella rig after he marks fish at the rip, so as to find out what they are. If they are stripers, he switches over to drifting eels; but if they're blues, he moves off to pursue stripers at another location on the rip.

The best way to fish at night is to use live eels or chunk baits. Our preferred method of fishing is to use live eels rigged to Gamakatsu 6/0 Octopus Circle Hooks, on a forty-eight-inch long, fifty-pound fluorocarbon leader. We use fluorocarbon leaders because the material is highly abrasion resistant. Of course, that doesn't mean squat when the bluefish move in and cut off your rig with one swift bite of their razor teeth. At night, monofilament, fluorocarbon, or wire leaders work equally well. The bass won't shy away from the wire leaders at night, and the wire will keep you from getting cut off by bluefish.

For depths under thirty feet, we don't use sinkers unless the current is cranking. For depths over thirty feet, we normally use two-ounce egg sinkers. If the current is running strong, then heavier sinkers might be needed. We've used egg sinkers up to six ounces to get to keep an eel down at the bottom in a strong current. With a little experience, you'll quickly learn what works.

During the day, bass are on the move, looking for food and chasing bait. They can be found at all depths in the water column. At night, the bass gather around structures or mussel beds where the bait congregates. After dark, they move into the shallows or to the top of humps and ledge outcrops.

Fishing structure is important. Fish the rock piles, and when you move within an area, move along the contour lines that define the shape of the bottom—that's what the fish do.

Look for current lines (rips). Rips often form where the current meets a change in bottom elevation or a large structure and carries the bait along; the bass will also be there.

Put in waypoints when you find fish, and note the difference between an incoming and outgoing tide relative to that recorded point. That will help you to learn which side of the structure the fish are on for each tide condition.

Up to now, I've covered everything, but the most important part—where to locate the fish. One of the most popular areas to fish, both days and nights, is the Southwest Ledge. Some of the ledge lies in the EEZ outside the three-mile limit of the state waters. It is illegal to fish for striped bass in the EEZ. (Actually, the law is worded that you cannot have a striped bass in your possession. If fishing for other species, and a striped bass is caught, you are required to promptly release it.) That means you can't have a bass on board and have a fishing line in the water. You can, however, transport bass through the EEZ between Block Island and Point Judith—thanks to a recent easement that tightened up a long-standing loophole—provided you don't stop to fish, and all bass in your possession are of legal size and meet possession limits. How will the Coast Guard know if you stop in the EEZ? They have really great radar, and they do patrol out there. (Actually, the radar does not leave "tracks," but DGPS does, and this evidence, if confiscated, has been used to convict those conducting illegal activity.)

When asked about their boat and how it's set up, this is what Don had to say, "We have four red LED lights under the hard top that we have on at night. We leave the navigation and anchor light on (they are also LED). We have a rear floodlight that is an LED, and we use it about 70% of the time. We also have 2 suction mounted LED flashlights that we fasten to the side of the boat and use as landing net lights, and we have LED headlamps. It depends on the moon phase and the weather conditions as to how many lights we use, but the red LED and the suction cup lights are used 100% of the time."

He went on to say, "When the boat had halogen lamps, we left the motor running about 75% of the time, because with the fishfinder, GPS, radio, navigation lights and radar, would drain both batteries and we never wanted to be stranded. I would also cook on board using a 1100 watt inverter. This year we installed two 31 glass pack deep cell batteries, that are just super. The way the boat is configured now, we do not have to run the motor when drifting, so we will not drain the batteries."

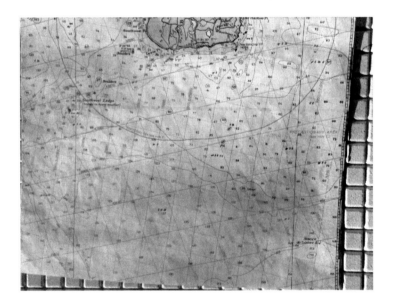

Block Island EEZ Line

Asked about their schedule, he replied, "We usually leave the dock between 6 and 7 p.m., sometimes earlier, and head to the Island. We typically fish until the bite dies after sunup—usually 8 a.m. or so, and then head back to Pt. Judith. When fishing in a tournament, we've been known to fish between 24 and 36 hours, nonstop. We do this in order to catch a fish that qualifies for first or second place. We do pay the price for it, though."

How crowded does it get? "Depending on the night. We can have 12 to 20 boats around the area, or as few as one. Some nights we are out there alone. It depends on whether it is a weekend or weeknight, and what the wind, wave and weather conditions are like. There is definitely less boats out there after dark."

The boat has radar, correct? "We have a color radar system on the boat which is used pretty heavily. Many of the boats out there at night fish without their lights on, so we always like to be sure we know where they're at, so we can avoid them, particularly when moving to begin another drift. Radar can also pick up storm clouds, so when we get a message about a storm cell that has formed and is moving rapidly, we can track it and know if we need to head for the safety of New Harbor. I would not advise anyone to fish out there at night without radar, simply because the weather can be hazardous and fog moves in quickly."

Does the boat have underwater lights? "We have no underwater lights on the boat. Just to give you an idea of how much time we spend out there, we retired our 225 HP Mercury Optimax after 5 years, when the warranty ran out, and replaced it with a new one of the same type and size. The motor had 2660 hrs. on it, so we averaged a little more than 500 hours per year. According to Mercury, the average boater/fisherman puts 75 to 100 hours per year on their motor."

What's the eel story? "We can never tell how many eels we will use in a nights fishing. We buy our eels by the pound and usually get 8 or 10 pounds at a time. If there aren't many bluefish around, we will use fewer eels. It's possible to catch 6 or 8 bass on one eel, and then again we could lose 10 eels to bluefish or dogfish before we find an area where the bass outnumber the pests. We usually go through about 25 eels apiece per trip. We also use 8 to 10 bar rags per trip to handle the eels."

"And before you ask, I'll also tell you that we burn an average of 60 gallons of gas per every two trips to Block Island. That's one weekend of fishing for us. If we go to the East Grounds for monster bluefish, or run out to the Dump, that amount increases. We spend just about every weekend on the water, from the beginning of May until the end of November. After Labor Day the weather goes downhill and our trips are usually only one per weekend. Last year the weather was really bad, with high winds and rainstorms every weekend, so we only got out on weekends twice during October and twice in November. It was the worst fall season we ever experienced in the 12 years we've fished together."

Then Don asked, "Have you ever seen the show *Taboo?* Peter and I could probably qualify for one segment. Fortunately Peter's wife of 36 years is very understanding. He was fishing like this when they started dating. My girlfriend is a nurse, and has to work every other weekend and every other holiday, so that takes a lot of the pressure off me."

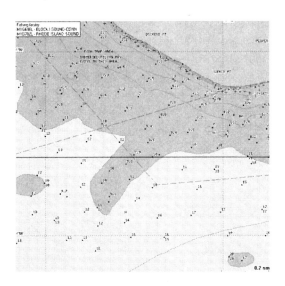

The Finger Thumb

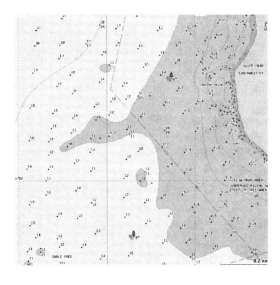

The Duck Head

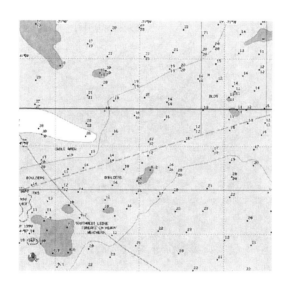

The Peanut & Boulders

SOME ISLAND STRIPER HAUNTS

Gone Fishin' . . . be back around dark thirty!

—Unknown

Tired of facing the weekend crowd on Block Island's Southwest Ledge? Interested in learning a new spot or two if weather forces a change in plans? Grab a chart of same, find a copy of *Eldridge's Tide and Pilot book* to scope out the tides around this pork chop-shaped piece of real estate, and get ready to jot down a few numbers for some different spots. Who knows, you just may find a new world of successful experiences.

North Bar (Inner)

This area starts at Sandy Point, just north of the automated light, and extends seaward for nearly a quarter mile. A very impressive rip forms here, thanks to strong currents running over North Bar, where water depths shoal up to within a lone fathom of the surface, then drop away eighteen to twenty-four feet immediately down-tide. Although trolling routinely takes some percentage of quality bass, certain conditions—as when birds take to the air, announcing swirling and breaking bass beneath, routine success can be had here trolling, but casting does well when birds are working over breaking and swirling fish, typically early or late in day around the end of May, June, or early July. Fish here are frequently under twenty pounds, but fish over fifty pounds have been taken by "sharpies" under the cover of darkness. Short wire lines with tubes, jigs, spoons, and plugs all work well, particularly under reduced light (foggy) conditions. Try keeping the boat just up-current of the rip in the calm water, while trolled offerings probe the rip's turbulence astern. Strong southeast and south winds offer relatively calm conditions in tight to the exposed sand spit where land meets all kinds of water.

Outer Rip, Double Hump

The "double hump" is located just east of the 1BI Buoy, with action best typically on the ebbing tide. Drifters score using both live bait and diamond jigs, with starting points well up-tide of the rip. Action comes typically in the fifty—to fifty-five-foot depth zone, look for fathometer markings on either of the twin humps. Be sure to mark your starting point so you can return to it on the next drift when action develops. Anglers who troll using 'chutes on long wires score as well, being careful not to interfere with those fishing vertically. New and full moon night tides can be quite productive, so much so that one or more Point Judith party boats can be found here on weekends just before dark after Memorial Day.

The outer rip extends to the northeast for another quarter mile from the 1BI Buoy area and holds fish on both ebb and flood tides, with this author favoring the early flood tide. Small boat owners should be aware of northeast winds on moon ebb tides usually create rough conditions.

Logwood Cove

On Block's west side just south of Logwood Cove is a rocky area that frequently holds bait and bass come June and early July. Mornings, at first light, have seen us trolling 'chutes or tubes under screeching gulls and terns toward wash tub-sized boils made by sizeable stripers. Several lobster trawl buoys typically mark the high spots, but pose little threat to those who pay attention.

Action here can easily continue into midmorning, depending on the amount of bait present. Trolling scores best, with casters a close second. A few years back, we did a Fuzzy Zeller Fishing Show here, the guest was Mark "The Bird" Fidreich, former pitcher for the Red Sox, and casting under the birds produced fish into the mid-teens. Then, as now, skiffs intent on going to Southwest Ledge zoomed by, totally oblivious to our arched rods.

Grace Point

Just south of the New Harbor Breakwater, this rocky bottom area offshore, in twenty to forty-five feet of water, attracts loads of springtime bait (sand eels) and those stripers preying on it. Daybreak in June and early July are best times, with action continuing into midmorning when winds are light. Trolling plugs, jigs, and tubes work best, with casting a close second. Give any lobster trawl buoys a wide berth, but don't hesitate to work into the deeper water as birds move that way as the sun climbs.

High water drop is my choice of time to be here, and in some mornings, bait, birds, and fish extend as far south as the southwest point bell buoy. However, there will be days when fog shrouds the seascape, making success more difficult, so best to check reports for the morning before heading out.

Southwest Corner (Inner Ledge)

Timing the tides is critical for this area, so try using *Eldridge Tide and Pilot Book*. Keep in mind, the flooding tide here starts about an hour before the outer ledge, so you have some time to check several spots out before moving further south toward the Southwest Ledge buoy. Best time to check out Lewis Point reef occurs when a flooding tide begins before daylight. Numerous rocky areas around the Hooter Buoy will hold fish in the early tide, and my favorite spot is the one just west-southwest of the Bell Buoy.

Trolling seemingly does best here in early season, using tube and worm or parachute jigs early in a tide. Live bait fishers, whether using herring, mackerel, or eels, make a point of staying off slack water, as pesky dogfish can mar attempts at success. Moon-tide currents typically find action tailing off when velocities increase. Keep in mind, any lobster trawl buoys here will suck under in the tide, posing problems for unwary trollers. Best to troll *into* the current—not *across* it—when probing potential action areas.

Southwest Ledge (Outer)

At times, Block Island's most popular striper area, action starts here the first or second week in May and continues through November. Trolling, diamond jigging, and live-bait fishing, all produce outstanding catches. Edges around the Boulders and Peanut, Duck's Head and just northwest of the southwest Corner bell Buoy have produced on both flood or ebb, best early or late in the tide if on the moon. Be sure to punch the memory button on your GPS unit when you hook up, as strong current flows can easily carry you a hundred or more yards away during the battle. Come July, bluefish abound typically into November.

On windfree days around either moon, both an ebb and flood tide rip forms on the outer portion, which trollers and live-bait anglers take advantage of, careful to watch for telltale signs of subsurface trawl buoys that can ruin your day, if snagged. Be aware the flood tide at peak runs to the north-northwest (320 degrees), while the ebbs run east-southeast (140 degrees). Fish that have taken up station on one tide are frequently elsewhere on the next. One other point, vessels in possession of striped bass outside the EEZ (three-mile limit) are in violation of federal law and risk prosecution.

Black Rock

Long a traditional area for anchoring and chumming in a westward running flood tide targeting large-for-their-size nighttime stripers, boats here can pull fish from it to their location well up-tide. Menhaden chunks have been the ticket, but the recent development of abundant dogfish has "cooled" such attempts. Trolled offerings such as tube and worm or eels have scored well at times just south and west of this high tide-awash boulder.

The twenty-four-foot edge just yards to the south, inside the buoy, has offered excellent success with school—and medium-sized stripers on the daytime troll. Target an early flood tide and be aware moderate sea conditions can improve one's success. Flat calm in gin-clear water is typically not ideal conditions for success on the oceanside of the island.

Southeast Light

Years ago, I spent a great deal of time here up tight in Light House Cove and in front of the rocky area just to the east. Recently, I promised my wife I would no longer take the not-so-new forty-two-foot *Prowler* in there, as the risk for disaster would be quite costly. Time to fish this area is during a moderate running sea, when waters darken, and stripers push closer toward shore. For those who prefer to remain cautious, drifting eels and trolling wire outside the twenty-eight-foot edge are two popular techniques, best on a flooding (westward) running tide. There are several rocky areas just south and west over which fish will hold, with early morning action starting in mid-May and lasting till early September. Be aware bluefish show in numbers after the

Fourth of July and can quickly obliterate your live bait supply. This area can have a few lobster trawl buoys marking rough bottom, so pay attention to your drift direction.

Old Whale Rock

This smooth-faced granite boulder hasn't claimed anywhere near the number of wrecks as Black Rock, but both inside and outside, you'll mark a rocky zone frequented by sizeable stripers. The current here runs to the southwest on both tides, harder on the flood than the ebb. Live bait and trolling will score in the rocky area just south of the boulder in eighteen—to twenty-five-foot depths, frequently marked on the deepwater side by lobster trawl gear. Best action on the troll is into the southwest running current, being sure to watch your fishfinder as you do so. Striper action starts here anytime in mid-May and runs through October, typically best at first light. Years ago, I could make the day here trolling springtime cod, pollock, and stripers, especially when rough sea conditions south of the island became impossible.

Old Harbor Point

Try slinging Atom 40 plugs just behind the breaking waves in Green Hill Cove at first light, best on high water when sea is building over the reef. Keep in mind, fish will move off into deeper water as the sun climbs and can be taken trolling or with live-bait fishing the eastern edge in thirty to fifty feet of water. The entire seaward edge of this reef has produced many sizeable fish to those who work it, with perhaps the best fishing coming after a northeast blow with a moderate sea running.

The Farm

Just south of Jerry's Point is a farm pasture that may show sheep, horses, or cows, and the surf fronting it has offered great action casting plugs, best at high water at first light. Later in the morning, try trolling or live-bait fishing the rocky areas and boulders further offshore. Be prepared for some sizeable fish any time come June, with bluefish becoming pesky in mid—to late July. If you're up for it, light southwest breezes after dark can produce some jumbo bass drifting and casting eels just outside the surf zone.

SOME NUMBERS
Phantom LORAN numbers (LORAN-C, 9960 Rate)
Positions meant to be starting points for fishing only

North Bar Inner Rip
14524.5 x 43917.7

North Rip Double Hump
14522.2 x 43922.3

Logwood Cove Area
14535.4 x 43906.2

Grace Point
14554.1 x 43893.5

Southwest Ledge (inner)
14564.9 x 43874.7

Southwest Ledge (outer)
14585.4 x 43868.7

Black Rock area
14453.0 x 43873.5

Southeast Light
14540.2 x 43869.7

Old Whale Rock
14534.1 x 43873.0

Old Harbor Point
14530.1 x 43880.3

The Farm
14527.7 x 43897.0

Unfortunately, NOAA Chart no. 13217 of Block Island provides no overlay of Loran LOP. Captain Segull's Chart of Block Island identifies many popular areas.

VI
FISH TAGGING

WHY TAG FISH?

*Because we don't think about future generations,
they will never forget us.*

—Henrik Tikkanen

You might wonder why I tag and release loads of striped bass. First off, they've been readily accessible; second, I do it because they're a very popular game fish; and lastly, because of my respect for the resource. In fact, today, I cherish it because angling creates a challenge, launches anticipation, and generates excitement. I think tagging is one of the better reasons for my going fishing. Crazy, huh?

In recent years, thanks to numerous clients, I've been able to mark over of five thousand stripers in one year (2006), both in-season across Southern New England coastal areas, as well as in estuarine overwintering zones, notably the Thames and Connecticut Rivers. If you find this behavior strange, let me assure you I practice tagging in the hopes it will improve our scientific knowledge of one or more popular fish resources—knowledge that will, if politics doesn't get in the way, generate improvement in our so-called management decisions regarding several species.

Tagging is a cooperative venture, but unfortunately, many who recapture tagged fish have no clue as to what's going on. Most who recapture a marked fish fail miserably to provide valuable info about it or the circumstances under which it was recaptured. Many I talk to about it site lack of reward for providing recap info—as with the ALS. Yes, I know both the USFWS and the HRF offer rewards, the funds for which come from federal tax monies, where ALS efforts are privately funded. Times have changed, of course, but back in the sixties when the ALS started up, those in charge believed anyone catching a tagged fish would recognize there was a reason—a dire need for better stock data—to report it. Sad to say, but failure to do so in today's world suggests apathy, ignorance, and disrespect.

Over the years, I've assisted the scientific community in other ways besides tagging. For a number of years, Brad Chase and Greg Skomal, along with their team from for the Massachusetts Division of Marine Fisheries (MA DMF), were aboard my vessel catching, tagging, taking blood samples, and then releasing various tuna and shark species. Simply put, in an attempt to better understand stress physiology of the catch-and-release event, and contrary to what critics postulated, their research proved catching a tuna on rod and reel would not result in its death, unless a prolonged, undue fight time produced a severe case of CO_2 poisoning called lactic acidosis.

On another occasion, crews from the NMFS Southeast Fisheries Science Center in Miami, Florida, were aboard to validate the use of circle hooks for tuna fishing in preventing the tissue damage frequently resulting from the use of conventional J hooks. Bottom line: Circle hook success depended on the talents of the angler using it.

For several years now, hundreds of my bluefin tuna finlet tissue samples were made available to John Graves and his research team at the Virginia Institute of Marine Science (VIMS) in an attempt to determine the origin (Mediterranean vs. Gulf of Mexico) of our Atlantic school bluefin tuna. Recent tag-recapture data and DNA analysis suggest this side of the Atlantic has been hosting Mediterranean and mid-Atlantic spawned bluefin tuna for some time. (John Graves was also a winner in *Sport Fishing Magazine's* Making A Difference Award, 2011).

Allow me several more comments from atop my soapbox. Another activity that became commonplace, and irritates me to no end, is when anglers attempt to catch as many Thames River overwintering fish as possible, for bragging purposes, with no thought as to how many fish might be injured in the catch-and-release event—injured as a result of quickly ripping hooks out of a fish in their haste to make another cast. Those who stood in the bow of their high-powered bass boats, guiding it with a bow-mounted electric-powered motor, unhooked their fish, and simply dropped them on the deck, and if they don't flop back into the water, gave 'em a swift kick overboard. That type of behavior really bothered me, and it's simply no way to handle one of New England's most valuable, if not premier, game fish. Not that I haven't injured some striped bass in the catch, tag, and release event, but I've made it a point for years to handle all tagged fish as quickly and carefully as possible, prior to release.

Yeah, I can hear the groans, and moans, and whistles now . . . Believe me, I get considerable satisfaction from knowing what I'm doing; something that can help the resource while enjoying the challenge of trying to catch them. Not that I'm hoping to convince you to try tagging, there are enough fish taggers out there now. What is needed are more anglers responsible enough to report a tag recapture to the tagging program agency, whether it's the CCA, the ALS, the USFWS, the HRF, the NMFS, or any other agency.

Gals Catch & Tag'em Too

Some T/R Critics Silenced

For decades, I've heard critics tell me fish tagging is painful to fish and increases stress levels due to fear that amplifies the mortality rate in the catch, tag, and release event. Well, the day has finally arrived when I can inform PETA (People for the Ethical Treatment of Animals) this is *patently untrue*.

In a recent paper, James D. Rose, PhD of the Department of Zoology and Physiology at the University of Wyoming, indicated fish are incapable of feeling pain. Research has shown fish do not possess higher centers of the brain that allow them to feel pain. Pain is a conscious experience, which in vertebrate animals are associated with the neocortex—which fish do not possess. Those who claim fish tagging is painful probably don't possess higher centers of the brain either . . .

A critique of the paper "Do fish have nociceptors: Evidence for the evolution of a vertebrate sensory system," published in Proceedings of the Royal Society, 2003 by Sneddon, Braithwaite, and Gentle.

James D. Rose, PhD
Department of Zoology and Physiology
University of Wyoming
Laramie, WY 82071
USA trout@uwyo.edu

The paper by Sneddon et al. is flawed and does not provide any legitimate evidence that trout are capable of feeling pain. There are numerous problems with methods and data interpretation in this paper, but this critique will focus only on those of greatest significance. First, an explanation of the invalid claims for evidence of pain will be presented, followed by an account of the misinterpretations of the behavioral results.

Flaws in the argument for a demonstration of pain

1. The authors' definitions of pain and nociception are invalid. Consequently, this paper does not actually deal with pain (a conscious experience), it deals only with nociception (unconscious responses to noxious stimuli). The behavioral results allegedly showing evidence of pain were misinterpreted. For the sizes of the fish used, these injections of liquid would have been equivalent to injecting one hundred milliliters (more than three ounces) of solution into the lip of a human.

In spite of the large dose of venom or acid, the activity level of these fish was not affected. They did not hide under a shelter in the tank, and they resumed feeding in less than three hours.

To summarize, the most impressive thing about the acid and venom injections was the relative absence of behavioral effects, given the magnitude of the toxic injections.

The bottom line of this critique is that any attempt to show pain in fish must use valid criteria, including proof of conscious awareness, particularly a kind of awareness that is meaningfully like ours.

I wish to emphasize that the improbability that fish can experience pain in no way diminishes our responsibility for concern about their welfare. Fish are capable of robust, unconscious, behavioral, physiological, and hormonal responses to stressors, which if sufficiently intense or sustained, can be detrimental to their health.

Cited reference: Rose, J. D. 2002. The neurobehavioral nature of fishes and the question of awareness and pain. *Reviews in Fisheries Science*, 10: 1-38. This paper can be obtained in electronic form from the author by visiting:

http://uwadmnweb.uwyo.edu/Zoology/faculty/Rose/default.htm

A recent paper published in *Reviews in Fisheries Science, 10 (1): 1-38 (2002)*, authored by James D. Rose, Department of Zoology and Physiology, University of Wyoming, entitled "The Neurobehavioral Nature of Fishes and the Question of Awareness and Pain," examines the neurobehavioral nature of fishes and addresses the question of whether fishes are capable of experiencing pain and suffering. Literature on the neural basis of consciousness and pain is reviewed and shows that

> "(1) Behavioral responses to noxious (harmful) stimuli are separate from the psychological experience of pain. (2) Awareness of pain in humans depends on functions of specific regions of cerebral cortex, and (3) (Since) fishes lack these essential brain regions or any functional equivalent, it makes it untenable that they can experience pain.
>
> Because the experience of fear, similar to pain, depends on cerebral cortical structures that are absent from fish brains, it is concluded that awareness of fear is (also) impossible for fishes.

Active ALS and NMFS fish taggers like myself, who have long been suspicious of such anthropomorphic accusations, based on our personal observations and records, applaud and welcome this news. I feel very confident now in saying "I told you so." Members of PETA, please take note!

Investigators have used tagging as a method to monitor various wildlife species for decades. The marking and tagging of fish by scientists started on a large scale between 1890 and 1900 (Jones, 1968). Leg bands on birds have documented geographic ranges, while radio transmitters on sea turtles and both Atlantic and Pacific bluefin tuna have identified migration routes and breeding areas. Thanks to advances in microtechnology, vinyl conventional (point-to-point) tags are now giving way to archival (recording) tags, a result of their becoming smaller, less expensive, with much greater battery life.

Fisheries biologists tag fish to obtain information about both short—and long-term movements, individual growth rates, mortality, migration, spawning areas, longevity, stock structure and abundance, geographic range, commercial exploitation, fish passage, abundance estimates, and habitat utilization. Now, more than ever before, fish-stock reduction due to intense fishing pressure necessitates better information. Valid up-to-date information provided by cooperator-assisted efforts is badly needed by federal, state, and private-agency fisheries managers to develop appropriate regulatory and conservation measures, politics notwithstanding.

Two Good-look'n Females

Over a decade ago, I authored a volume entitled *Game Fish Tag and Release*, published by The Fisherman Library, Point Pleasant, New Jersey. At that time, only several dozen private, state, and federal fish-tagging agencies along the Atlantic and Gulf Coasts were in place.

Today, that scene has changed dramatically, as various conservation agencies have threatened lawsuits if management decisions are not based on scientific evidence. Data evidence that can be obtained rather quickly through a tag, release, and recapture program, now instituted by an explosive number of state agencies. Would it surprise you to learn there are now over 225 fish-tagging programs along the Atlantic and Gulf Coast, many of which involve striped bass? Today, state and federal agencies are hard-pressed to base decisions on facts, at the risk of pending lawsuits, and consequently are turning to short-term tagging projects to provide the necessary information.

Why Tag?

Short—and Long-Term Movements

For example, a change in striped bass population dynamics, such as competition for habitat, could well be the cause for greater geographic ranges in short-term movement recaptures. This behavior could foretell future long-term movements within a population. Both Hudson and Chesapeake origin subadult striped bass and have been recaptured from as far away as New Brunswick, Canada, along with rivers and waters of the Bay of Fundy, Nova Scotia, Canada.

Individual Growth Rates

Growth rates for various age groups of striped bass can vary, and below normal ranges for female fish could follow weather pattern changes, habitat or forage reduction, and/or intraspecies competition. Years ago, I had the opportunity to determine the age of an eighty-five-pound striped bass taken by a net from Chesapeake Bay. My inspection of growth ring annuli on a series of scales off this female fish indicated her age between twenty-eight and thirty-two years.

Mortality

Tag-recapture software models can be used to predict mortality rates, such as what might occur in the catch-and-release event. The time of year, seawater temperatures, hook design, and fight time are but a few factors influencing striper fatality. Some studies suggest a striper mortality rate resulting from the catch-and-release event might be as great as 24 percent or as low as 8 percent. The HRF conducts their tagging activities during the winter when water temperatures in the lower river and around Manhattan are their lowest, reducing mortality rates. Studies have shown elevated water temperatures can raise mortality rates in striped bass substantially. During my overwinter (o-w) striper-tagging project, I feel confident knowing my tagging occurred during an optimal stress-reduced cold-water period.

Migration

Migratory distances can be correlated to both the season and age of a fish. How far a fish moves gives biologists a better understanding of possible causative factors for this behavior. Migratory behavior is inherent in female stripers, probably arising from their energy needs to meet egg production. Studies have shown most male stripers fail to migrate far from home waters at any time during their life history.

Happy Angler - Lucky Fish

Spawning Areas

Tag recaptures can profile not only the range exhibited by spawning fish, age of maturation, but time period of season as well. Today, advances in DNA studies allow scientists to identify chromosomal "markers," identifying not only the region, but also a fish's precise river of origin.

Longevity

Tag recaptures can give an indication of age-class size within a population, as well as profiling maximum age of a fish in a known population. For example, a high abundance of older age classes suggests only minimum mortality rates, whereas reduced numbers of age-group recaptures may suggest a greater one.

Stock Structure and Abundance

Should high numbers of age two and three fish be available for tagging by agency technicians or members, this suggests an abundance of that age class. Should numerous fish age six or seven be available for tagging, it demonstrates a strong year class. Should few or no age-ten fish be available, it suggests a lack of numbers of that year class. At the present time, there is little threat of a small spawning age class, instead one lies with recruitment of young fish.

Geographic Range

Tagging studies have shown that striped bass that originate in areas of Canada's St. Lawrence waterways do not range south into U.S. waters. Adult striped bass that overwinter off the Virginia and North Carolina capes are a mix of Chesapeake, Delaware, and Hudson River origin-fish. Studies show subadult Hudson River origin females are more apt to range further east than adults.

Commercial Exploitation

Recent tagging studies show the commercial catches of larger size, hence older, striped bass are in decline, a result of present ASMFC-adopted regulations, compounded by a lack of subadult fish, due to a lack of recent strong year classes. However, a recent (2011) young-of-the-year (YOY) index survey for Chesapeake Bay fish indicates the possibility of a potentially strong year class.

Abundance Estimates

Recent studies have shown striped bass stocks are on the decline, with nearly 42 million fish of all ages in coastal waters. However, a recent decline in the abundance of Hudson River stocks has been reported, despite a 2007 strong YOY index, greatest ever in nearly thirty years.

Fish Ladder Passage

Pacific Coast states have long electronically marked various river-origin fish (salmon) in an attempt to monitor abundance of returning fish to estimate spawning-stock biomass.

Habitat Utilization

Recapture areas for various size and age class fish can demonstrate how well various estuarine habitats are meeting the needs of a particular stock and age group of fish.

Foxes Guarding the Henhouse

Allow me to digress for a moment. Now, I'm not trying to sell the readership on becoming fish taggers, but a recent article of mine appeared in *The Fisherman* magazine about the success of the Northeast Regional Cod Tagging Program. For years, members of the New England Fisheries Management Council (NEFMC) argued that rod and reel fishing by the recreational sector, during the wintertime in the Gulf of Maine, were responsible for decimating the northeast spawning cod stocks. Right. (Would you dare to travel offshore in the winter, beyond the GOM cod demarcation line, in a twenty-one—to twenty-four-foot outboard?)

After individuals from several agencies marked better than one hundred thousand cod over a three-year period, many of which were by the commercial sector (read: groundfish draggers), it was discovered about 91 percent of the tagged cod were caught again by those same draggers within four months. Not wanting to admit guilt, dragger captains and crews refrained from reporting tag recaptures. As a result, upward of 40 percent were reported by "lumpers," processors, and observers. Despite the previous NEFMC claim, cod stocks were restored. The council is now considering a two-month cod season, two-fish bag limit, with closure to ground fishing by draggers in the Gulf of Maine. Seems dragging for northeast multispecies ground fish ranks third as this country's worst by-catch fisheries, but it took the science of fish tagging to identify the real problem.

CATCH A TAGGED STRIPER?

*I am a great believer in luck.
The harder I work, the more I have of it.*

—Pres. Thomas Jefferson

Authored by yours truly, a portion of this article appeared in *The Fisherman* magazine, New England edition, in 2008.

Funny, lots of anglers approach me wanting to learn about getting involved with tagging. I tell them they already are because numerous clubs and conservation-minded individual fishermen, as well as private, state, and federal agencies, are counting on them to report the recapture of *any* agency-tagged fish, whether or not the tag in question offers a reward.

Catching a tagged striper is a rarity, even as numerous agencies mark and liberate literally thousands of them annually. Most anglers gladly report a tag recapture, out of respect for the resource, intrigue about a fish's history, sometimes a reward—a cool fishing hat or a little eel money. If you're not quite sure what to do with a tagged striper, this chapter should get you up to speed.

Counting On You

Striped bass are the most commonly tag-recaptured fish on the Atlantic Coast. If you fancy light tackle and do considerable school striped bass fishing, your chances of recapturing one is statistically greater. Recapture rates for all marine game fish are low—a shore or boat-fishing focus makes little difference. If none of your buddies ever recaptured a tagged striper, consider passing this info along to them.

Federal—and state-funded agencies are marking more fish today than ever before in an effort to learn more about stock movements, growth rates, year classes, post-release mortality, among countless other behavioral and biological matters. No matter what the specific research interest(s) of the person hooking, landing, tagging, and liberating the fish, his or her root objective is the same—to furnish scientists, statisticians, and regulators richer, more abundant, and more reliable data, in hopes our beloved striper resource will flourish under a smarter, more nimble management regime.

Whether or not you elect to join one of the conservation-oriented organizations like the American Littoral Society (ALS), many of whose members actively participate in ongoing private sector striper tagging projects, you can do your part by simply reporting your recap!

Over a decade ago, when I authored *Game Fish Tag and Release*, there were just over three dozen tagging agencies from Maine to Texas. Under the provisions of the Magnuson-Stevens Fishery Conservation Act—the main piece of federal legislation guiding domestic fisheries management policy—as well as similar state-level documents, regulators are charged with grounding all decision-making in sound science (or at least "best available science"). This statutory mandate has led to dramatic expansion of fish-tagging efforts, and today, more than 225 organizations are marking various saltwater species in the name of science.

IGFA Fly Fish'n Trip

What to Do?

How do you know a fish is tagged? Easy, just look for the presence of a tag streamer, either in the dorsal (back) or belly areas. Although all tags are brightly colored to catch your eye, however, time and algae growth may change their appearance, turning it to green or brown.

If you spot a tag, quickly unhook the fish, and if you can, cover its eyes with either a wet towel or rag—a trick that quiets even unruly critters to avoid injury to them or you during their deck time. Carefully remove the plastic streamer without destroying the data number, zip code, or phone number, and place it deep in your pocket. Before you release the fish—be quick if it's undersize!—lay it alongside your rod and note its total length. Later, the fish safe back in the drink, you can measure that length on the rod then follow up with an estimate of its weight taken from a length-to-weight chart, such as the one for striped bass in this book.

Later at home, carefully remove any algae with your thumbnail under warm running tap water and read the tag message. If possible, use a magnifying glass to double-check the printed information. Don't mistake the agency zip code for the tag data number (the latter's typically a six-digit number), rendering recapture details worthless. Take a few minutes to record the information in your log, and then report it, either by mail, phone, or e-mail, depending on the agency.

Whichever tagging agency is involved, they want to know the kind of fish, your name and address, the date and place of recapture, total length and estimated weight of the fish, general health and/or appearance, whether the fish was released, tag removed or not, and angling method. As Pam Carlsen, former ALS Tagging Director was fond of saying, tagged fish are "scientific messengers," and what they have to tell may well be very important to their future.

Following notification of your recapture, the tagging agency will send you a report revealing who initially tagged it, when and where the fish was recaptured, plus length and weight details. Some agencies issue small monetary rewards, a recapture report suitable for framing, as well as the chance to win big ticket lottery-style cash drawing.

Tag-Recapture Events

Extensive research has proven that water temperature during the catch-and-release event significantly affects post-release mortality. Summertime water temps of 70F or more amplify the stress caused by fight, handling, and out-of-water time. Small fish endure ensuing blood chemistry changes better than larger fish can. If you plan to release your fish, minimize fight times, and if possible, avoid risk of injury to fish or fisherman by sticking to single hooks.

Protracted fights cause toxic carbon dioxide buildup, which in turn creates a deadly blood-gas change called *lactic acidosis*. Although the fish swims away at release, development of this condition can be lethal up to seventy-two hours later.

In a boat, release a large fish from above the water "head first" to initiate swimming and ram gill ventilation. If fishing shore-bound, grip the lower jaw of a smaller fish between your thumb and forefinger, then glide it back and forth to work water across the gills until you note signs of recovery; release it with some forward swimming momentum.

I've watched sharp surf men tote tagging gear in a five-gallon bucket; a small board temporarily fastened to the lid will keep the fish off any beach sand during tag deployment.

Some Problems

Occasionally, I receive e-mails, phone calls, or letters requesting info about the identification of, or address of, a tag recovered from a striped bass. Some tags, exposed to long periods of UV light, lose either their printed address or phone number. Internal anchor tag streamers that extend from the fish's belly—the Hudson River Foundation (HRF) and U.S. Fish and Wildlife Service (USFWS) both favor this tag type—lose part of the printed message to abrasion with coarse bottom sediments. Some tags accumulate so much marine growth it's nearly impossible to read the message prior to careful cleaning. If, despite best efforts to the contrary, you get stumped, best bet may be to send it back to the tagging agency for identification.

Unfortunately, not all recapture reports are valid. Several years ago, the ALS received a recap notice from a commercial fisherman whose less-than-accurate memory indicated my fish was grossly larger than when it was tagged.

To compound matters, the reported recapture date occurred long before the fish had ever been tagged! Another angler carried a tag from one of my fish around in his tackle box for nearly three years before notifying ALS. Better late than never, I guess!

What Becomes of Recapture Data?

Striped bass recapture data is presently being used by the Atlantic States Marine Fisheries Commission (ASMFC) Striped Bass Technical Committee to better understand—among other things—population dynamics, catch-and-release mortality, movements by year classes, as well as age and growth relationships.

Once their year-long recapture data is finalized, agencies like the ALS transfer it to the Northeast Fishery Science Center (NEFSC) computers in Woods Hole, Massachusetts, where fish scientists nationwide can access it. The ALS also publishes striped bass tagging returns in their annual *Underwater Naturalist*, listing species length, tagger's name, place tagged, date, who recaptured it, location, and date. Today, anglers recapturing a tagged fish can go online to retrieve valuable data. For further information, go to www.littoralsociety.org.

Underwater Naturalist

ASMFC's Sea of Approval

In 2009, the Atlantic States Marine Fisheries Commission (ASMFC) released a news item about its Interstate Tagging Committee (ITC) and certification process: "The first program to be reviewed and certified was the angler-based fish tagging program conducted by the American Littoral Society (ALS)." It further stated, "Tag return data collected by the ALS have been used by Commission Technical Committees to characterize migration patterns of bluefish and striped bass along the Atlantic Coast. In addition, ALS data have been used to help identify individual stocks and to characterize recreational discards for striped bass, bluefish and tautog."

Jeff Dement, fish tagging program director at ALS, has begun to implement several ITC-recommended procedural changes. ALS certification renewal through ASMFC is five years away.

Want to Tag Fish?

If you're interested in becoming a fish tagger, consider joining the ALS. Only members are eligible to tag fish; those who wish to participate can purchase them in lots of ten tags ($5), each of which has a corresponding index card requiring completion once its tag is deployed. Information on the card includes a tag number stamped on the card by the manufacturer, along with space for species of fish, date of tagging, location of release, name and address of the tagger, and size of the fish in length (inches) and estimated weight (pounds). For this project, as with all my tagged coastal game fish, if length is better than a half-inch increment, I'll indicate the next full inch (i.e., 15.75 inches is recorded on the card as sixteen inches. If those recapturing a tagged fish aren't sure whether to remove a tag, it frequently goes unreported. If the tag is removed, one should send it along with the recapture notice, which in the case of the ALS, requires a written note posted with the U.S. mail. The ALS does not presently recognize phone calls reporting a recapture. No reward is paid for the tag. Recapture information—the name of the person who recaptured the fish, the date, and location—is published in *Underwater Naturalist*.

TAG FISH Brochures

During my tagging, the only information immediately recorded is the length of the fish—an effort to reduce time out of water. Later, the date, species, location, and estimated weight are religiously entered. On all my tag cards, the initials of the angler are included in the comments section for my records. Over the years, Carlsen and Dement have been kind enough to indicate those initials on the recapture notice.

Finally, in an attempt to streamline my tagging, I fabricated a tagging board with a clear Plexiglas surface that allows me to see, at a glance, the underlying paper ruler showing fish length. This measuring board also conveniently holds pencil, tag needles, and tag data cards. Long ago, when windy conditions threatened loss of tags and cards, I punched a second hole in the data card to accept the opposite end of the tag, which then holds it secure to the card, and then secured all around with a rubber band. I then created a makeshift slot on the outer wall to hold them securely, but allow ready access. If this project sounds like a lot of effort, suffice to say that you were not there to witness one of the all-time great games of the "Fifty-Two Pickup," a veritable ballet of spastic incompetence, sodden tag cards, gusty winds, and airborne expletives.

Some Tagging Guidelines

The following recommendations (in part) were taken from a letter by Tom Lake to Pam Carlsen over two decades ago. They are as applicable today as they were then.

Tag Responsibly to Ensure Maximum Survival

1. Minimum time out of water increases probability of survival.
2. Low spring and fall water temperatures improve survival rates.
3. Should fish be a "bleeder," survival is questionable at best.
4. Use a wet cloth to handle or hold fish while tagging.
5. Avoid tagging live—or cut-bait-caught fish unless using circle hooks.
6. Avoid fish stress when tagging by covering the eyes in bright sunlight.
7. From a boat, fish should be released in a head-first manner, so as to initiate swimming motion.
8. From shore, be sure to gently "work" a fish prior to release to ensure survival.
9. Minimize tag card data recording to reduce out-of-water time.

B. Learn From Tagging and Recovery Data Collection

1. Keep a record of interesting tag recaptures.
2. Monthly and annual record keeping may indicate a trend.

Other Tags You May Find
Hudson River Foundation (HRF)

The Hudson River Foundation (HRF) began a tagging program in 1984 and since then has marked nearly 450,000 striped bass, mainly in the lower Hudson, off Manhattan. Tagging occurs chiefly between November and April and is basically confined to age one to two fish. HRF tagged striped bass are caught in trawl nets by professional biologists and tagged with an internal anchor tag, the streamer of which extends from the fish's belly. This multiyear study of Hudson River striped bass, which make up a significant portion of our seasonal striper population in New England, has about a 7 percent recapture rate, due to the incentive of tag return rewards. Since 1987, due to increased numbers of female striped bass, results indicate the number of bass that survive to become juveniles has remained high and constant, indicating the Hudson River has reached carrying capacity for this stock.

To report a tag recapture, call and/or write:

Hudson River Foundation
PO Box 1731
New York, NY 10163
(212) 924-8290

HRF Reward Flyer

U.S. Fish and Wildlife Service (USFWS)

The USFWS striped bass tagging program began in 1985 with the marking of hatchery-reared fish. Now, federal and state biologists from Massachusetts to North Carolina are interested in expanding its database to serve as one of the primary sources of tag-study information for the ASMFC. Scientists, managers, and administrators depend on program information to make smart management decisions for the future. Today, biologists and fisheries managers from the USFWS, National Fish and Wildlife Foundation, NMFS, and state agencies from Massachusetts to North Carolina are participating in a coast-wide tagging program.

To report a tag recapture, call:

USFWS
1825 Virginia St.
Annapolis, MD 21401
1-800-448-8322

USFWS Flyer

GAME FISH TAG & RELEASE

For Further Reading . . .

The author's third book, *Game Fish Tag and Release*, describes the techniques for tagging a variety of game fish from sharks, billfish, and tuna to striped bass, snook, bluefish, and redfish. Major tagging programs are profiled with tips, tricks, and insights revealed in interviews with top East Coast taggers explaining the challenge, value, and enjoyment of tagging. From the sale of each book, $2 will be donated annually to four major programs. Paperback, *The Fisherman* Library, 196 pages, autographed for only $18.95.

IF YOU RECAPTURE A TAGGED STRIPER,

RECORD:

1. The tag number
2. The date fish was caught
3. The fish's total length and estimated weight
4. The location of recapture
5. Whether it was released with tag intact.
6. Any other pertinent comments such as fish condition.

SOME AGENCY CONTACT INFO

American Littoral Society
18 Hartshorne Dr., Suite 1
Highlands, NJ 07732
(732) 291-0055
www.littoralsociety.org

Hudson River Foundation
PO Box 1731, GCS
New York, NY 10163
(212) 924-8290
www.hudsonriver.org

U.S. Fish and Wildlife Service
1825 Virginia St.
Annapolis, MD 2140
1-800-448-8322
www.fws.gov

SOME TAGGING AGENCIES

Today's mighty oak is just yesterday's nut that held its ground.

—Anonymous

AMERICAN LITTORAL SOCIETY

The littoral society's fish-tagging program was started in 1965 by Graham Macmillan, then a society vice president and an avid sport fisherman. After consulting with fisheries biologists, he set up a program that, with only a few refinements, has served well since.

The basic premise of the program was and is that many fishermen release much of what they catch, especially those fish with a legal minimum size—striped bass and fluke, for example. Why not encourage fishermen to tag those fish before they release them? And beyond that, why not develop a whole new breed of angler, one who fishes and releases routinely? This tagging program would be appropriate for all the marine game fishes of the coast and for those that run up coastal rivers.

ALS LOGO

Further, it was decided to make the program self-supporting (i.e., the fishermen would pay the cost of the program) and to make it as easy as possible. Finally, it was decided that all data produced were to be published and made available to the fisheries scientists who would use it, and that all directly involved would learn about the fish they had either released or recaptured. Participation in the tagging program is limited to society members, individually or through club membership.

The program has maintained these principles, has occasionally been referred to as the "underwater Audubon Society," and has grown to be the largest voluntary fish-tagging program in the nation. All data are published in their *Underwater Naturalist* and is available online.

Author's Recent ALS Striper Recaps

In April 18, 2011, John Altson's ALS tagged striper from the May 27, 2010, season, T/R at twenty-four inches, 5.5 pounds, in the North Rip, was recaptured by the NJ DEP. Recovered in Delaware Bay, at Reeds Beach, in a net survey, it measured twenty-seven inches TL (three inches of growth). It was retagged with a USFWS tag (no. 557794) and released. No further information has been forthcoming.

Altson's Striper, 2010

AMERICAN LITTORAL SOCIETY

SANDY HOOK, HIGHLANDS, NJ 07732

May 11, 2011

Dear Al,

Congratulations. A fish that you tagged has been recaptured. We have the information, and it will be published in the UNDERWATER NATURALIST.

Our records show that this is your 2056th fish return to date. I hope you get many more. The enclosed "goldfish" patch denotes the recapture of your fish.

Tag: 786728
Date Released: 05/27/10
Measurements: Length: 24 inches (FL)
Weight: 5 lbs. 8 oz.

Species of Fish: Striped Bass
Date Recaptured: 04/18/11
Measurements: Length: 27 inches (TL)
Weight: 6 lbs. 4 oz.

Released at:
North Rip, Block Island, RI

Recaptured at:
Delaware Bay, Reeds Beach, NJ

Tagger: Al Anderson

Recapturer: NJDEP Net Survey

Thanks for your interest in the Society and for working with other volunteer taggers to help scientists learn more about fish migrations and growth rates. Your participation is important to us, and we apppreciate your help.

Sincerely,

John Altson
Enclosures

Jeff Dement
ALS Tagging Director

ALS Tag removed, fish re-Tagged w/ USFWS Tag # 557794

P.S. Remember, tag kits are now $6.00 with needles ($5.00 without) for a set of 10 tags. Society membership dues and tag kit costs are tax deductible.

Phone: 732-291-0055 • WWW.LITTORALSOCIETY.ORG • Fax: 732-291-3551

Altson's ALS Recap Letter 2011

A striped bass caught by Vincent Minchillo in July 13, 2007, measuring twenty-four inches, 5.5 pounds, released at Block Island, was recaptured by Jeff Mayer in Delaware Bay, New Jersey, on April 10, 2011, near the Maurice River, nearly four years later, measuring thirty-two inches TL (eight inches of growth) and weighed fifteen pounds (est.).

Capt. AL ANDERSON

AMERICAN LITTORAL SOCIETY

SANDY HOOK, HIGHLANDS, NJ 07732

April 14, 2011

Dear Al,

Congratulations. A fish that you tagged has been recaptured. We have the information, and it will be published in the UNDERWATER NATURALIST.

Our records show that this is your 2054th fish return to date. I hope you get many more. The enclosed "goldfish" patch denotes the recapture of your fish.

Tag: 728036   Species of Fish: Striped Bass

Date Released: 07/13/07 (FL)   Date Recaptured: 04/10/11 (TL)

Measurements: Length: 24 inches   Measurements: Length: 32 inches
              Weight: 5 lbs. 8 oz.   Weight: 15 lbs.

Released at: Recaptured at:
Block Is., RI   Delaware Bay, NJ
                                             — near the Maurice River

Tagger: Al Anderson   Recapturer: Jeffrey Mayer

Thanks for your interest in the Society and for working with other volunteer taggers to help scientists learn more about fish migrations and growth rates. Your participation is important to us, and we apppreciate your help.

Sincerely,

Vinny Minchillo
Enclosures
                                             ALS Tagging Director

Fish keys

P.S. Remember, tag kits are now $6.00 with needles ($5.00 without) for a set of 10 tags. Society membership dues and tag kit costs are tax deductible.

Phone: 732-291-0055 • WWW.LITTORALSOCIETY.ORG • Fax: 732-291-3551

Minchillo's ALS Recap Letter

On July 15, 2011, while fly fishing in the North Rip, Bill Krueger recaptured an ALS striper initially tagged for Arthur Adamski, who was fishing with me the previous season on October 9, 2010. Not surprisingly, this fish was recaptured back in the same spot seven months later, measuring approximately an inch greater and about a pound heavier (twenty-seven inches, eight pounds). Some critics might say this fish never left the area, but we know better. This fish was retagged for the ALS (tag no. 799369) and released. Initial tagging data was provided about three weeks later following receipt of the tag-data card.

ADAM's Oct. 2010 Striper

Regarding Krueger's recapture and the seasonality, one could assume, because it carried specimens of *C. elongatus*, that it was either a member of that school of fish that o-w offshore or had recently joined those schooling fish that did, resulting in transfer of the fish lice.

Krueger's Recap; July 2011 (showing Striper fish lice)

This recap marked the twenty-sixth time I recaptured one of my tagged stripers in the same spot I'd initially tagged it (dozens of stripers have been recaptured by numerous other anglers in the same areas they were tagged by me). I believe these facts prove that these fish, along with many other species, have memory and are genetically programmed (encoded) to return to those forage areas that favored their predecessors. How do they do that? You may ask. I will offer a theory on that shortly.

ISLAND STRIPERS

AMERICAN LITTORAL SOCIETY
SANDY HOOK, HIGHLANDS, NJ 07732

August 11, 2010

Dear Al,

    Congratulations. A fish that you tagged has been recaptured. We have the information, and it will be published in the UNDERWATER NATURALIST.

    Our records show that this is your 2000th fish return to date. I hope you get many more. The enclosed "goldfish" patch denotes the recapture of your fish.

Tag: 747125

Species of Fish: Striped Bass

Date Released: 04/10/08

Date Recaptured: 06/26/10

Measurements: Length: 18 inches (FL)
    Weight: 2 lbs. 8 oz.

Measurements: Length: 23 inches (TL)
    Weight:

Released at:
Thames River, CT

Recaptured at:
Kittery, ME

Tagger: Al Anderson

Recapturer: Joshua Rockwell

    Thanks for your interest in the Society and for working with other volunteer taggers to help scientists learn more about fish migrations and growth rates. Your participation is important to us, and we appreciate help.

Sincerely,

Jeff Dement
ALS Tagging Director

P.S. Remember, tag kits are now $6.00 with needles ($5.00 without) for a set of 10 tags. Society membership dues and tag kit costs are tax deductible.

Phone: 732-291-0055 • WWW.LITTORALSOCIETY.ORG • Fax: 732-291-3551

ALS Tag Recapture Letter copy
(No. 2000—Striper)

In a report prepared by former Tagging Director Pam Carlsen, which was published in the *Underwater Naturalist*, "The total fish tagged in 2006 was 29,756, that's 3,870 more fish tagged than in 2005. We had 1,326 recaptures, 76 more than in 2005. Our number one species tagged is still the striped bass: 22,775 (5,139 or nearly a quarter of those [23%] were tagged by this author); number two was summer flounder (fluke), 3,174; moving into third place was tautog (blackfish) with 1,636. Bluefish dropped to fourth place, with 1,308 tagged (390 or 30% were tagged by this author). The balance is a variety of species from Maine to the Gulf of Mexico. In April of this year (2007), all of our data were sent to the National Marine Fisheries Service, Woods Hole, MA, where it has been dispersed to the scientific community." In a private communication, Carlsen indicated, "We will probably have over 30,000 fish tagged in 2007. I am in the process of putting the tag cards in the computer right now."

Underwater Naturalist

According to Jeff Dement, here's how 2007 and 2008 turned out:

— Tags sold in 2007: 13,540 regular "spaghetti" tags and 16,610 "lock-on" style tags, for a total of 30,150 tags sold. There were 840 fewer tags sold than in 2006.
— Number of fish tagged in 2007 (all species) had 25,390 tags implanted, 4,366 fewer tagged fish in 2007 compared to 2006 (29,756).
— Fish reported recaptured in 2007 totaled to 1,264, which were sixty-two fewer than recaptured in 2006 (1,326). A total of twelve of the 2007 recaptures were "at sea" for five years or more.
— The number one species tagged is still striped bass at 16,729 (of these, 3,061 or 18 percent were courtesy of my anglers), fluke came in second with 4,123 tagged, bluefish ranked third with 1,617 tagged (501 or 31 percent of these were courtesy of my anglers). Right behind them were blackfish with 1,547 tagged. Of the 497 Atlantic cod tagged, 411 or 83 percent of these were courtesy of my anglers. Black sea bass rose in popularity with anglers with 234 tagged. Following up were weakfish, speckled sea trout, red drum, winter flounder, scup, and Atlantic croaker, in that order.

For comparison's sake, let's look at the latest ALS tagging data for the year ending 2008, which is as follows:

— Total fish tags installed in all species: 20,155. (Note: 2006 has been one of the best years ever for member tagging with 29,756 fish marked). The number of reported recaptures for fish tagged grew to 1,336, which is the most ever (ten more than reported in 2006).
— The number one species tagged in 2008 was striped bass with 10,818 marked, followed by fluke with 5,383 fish marked (the most ever), followed by tautog with 1,344 fish marked, with bluefish tailing behind with only 890 fish marked (334 or 38 percent of these courtesy of the author's clients). Atlantic cod were next in line with 271 fish tagged (244 of these were courtesy of my anglers), followed by 203 black sea bass, then 67 weakfish, followed by 23 winter flounder (50 percent of which were due to Jeff Dement's efforts).

ALS Tagged Bass about to be released

Turning our attention to 2009, here's some selected data Jeff Dement related to Gary Shepard, NMFS scientist with the NEFSC:

- This year, the program has again experienced a reduction in the number of fish tagged, with that overall number being approximately 16,370 individual fish tagged. The following is for only some selected species: striped bass, 8,896; summer flounder (fluke), 4,974; bluefish, 765; tautog, 634; black sea bass, 419; Atlantic cod, 215; weakfish, 28; scup, 23; and grey triggerfish, 124.
- Although the total numbers of fish marked by ALS members has fallen off within recent years, the numbers of fluke tagged have continued to rise. This is most likely due to the rekindled popularity of the resource along with a resurgence of the stock. It's possible the decline in numbers of striped bass marked were due to a decline in the stocks. Without any doubt, the changing economic climate has led to a decline in saltwater fishing related activities.

In 2010, Jeff Dement reported:

— American Littoral Society Fish Tagging Program ended with a total number of tag events (all species) of 15,990. Tag event numbers for selected species include: striped bass, 6,508; summer flounder, 6,488; tautog, 1,255; bluefish, 931; black sea bass, 252; winter flounder, 158; Atlantic cod, 109; red drum, 42; scup, 36; red grouper, 28; gray triggerfish, 18; and weakfish, 14.

For the ALS Tagging season in 2011, only preliminary numbers are available, as tag data cards were still coming in as this headed to the presses. Nevertheless, Dement offered Shephard some opinion regarding the society's tagging activity.

I strongly believe that the recent reduction in ALS tag events can be strongly attributed to our country's present economic condition, resulting in fewer angling trips, and less extraneous angling expenditure (tags). In both 2010 and 2011, the numbers of striped bass tagged, compared to 2006, declined by over 70%, a sure sign of decline in recent numbers of "school-size" fish available for tagging . . .

ALS TAGGED STRIPED BASS

	All Members	Anderson
2006	22,775	5,139 *(23%)
2007	16,729	3,061 *(18%)
2008	10,818	1,888 *(17%)
2009	8,896	1,683 *(19%)
2010	6,508	805 *(12%)
2011	4,000 *(Est.)	285 *(> .05%)

* The bulk of the striped bass traditionally T/R by ALS members have been primarily juvenile (subadult) size fish. Over the last five years, there has been a tremendous decrease in the numbers of these stripers T/R by its members (80 percent decline), including numbers T/R by this author (> 99 percent decline). Where are this fishery's recruits? The answer is unsettling; they don't exist in northeast waters!

HUDSON RIVER FOUNDATION

The Hudson River Foundation (HRF) was established in 1981 under the terms of an agreement among environmental groups, government regulatory agencies, and utility companies seeking the constructive resolution of a long series of legal controversies concerning the environmental impacts of power plants on the Hudson River.

The purpose of the Hudson River Foundation is to make science integral to decision making with regard to the Hudson River and its watershed and to support competent stewardship of this extraordinary resource. This purpose will be pursued through support of scientific research; communication to expand knowledge about the river among the scientific community, policy makers, and the public at large; initiatives to enhance management of the Hudson ecosystem; and education about the river and physical improvements to the riverfront.

The majority of HRF's funds are used to support independent, objective research that will inform policy making concerning a broad range of scientific and public policy areas affecting the Hudson.

The Hudson River Fund was created in recognition of the critical need for an independent institution to sponsor scientific research and education programs that would contribute to the development of sound public policy concerning the river's ecological system. The Hudson River Fund received its initial endowment of $12 million in 1982. The fund, which has since tripled in value, has enabled the foundation to award more than seven hundred grants totaling approximately $35 million through 2008.

To complement the grant program of the Hudson River Fund, HRF has a significant internal program designed to bring scientific understanding to bear on public policy. Most of the internal program is linked to three major well-established management initiatives, the federally sponsored New York/New Jersey Harbor Estuary Program (HEP), the New York/New Jersey Harbor Estuary Program (HEP), and the Contamination Assessment and Reduction Program (CARP).

HRF Tagging Program

The Hudson River Foundation (HRF) began a tagging program in 1984, and since then has marked over 450,000 striped bass, mainly in the lower Hudson, off Manhattan. Tagging occurs chiefly between November and April and is basically confined to age one to two fish. These wintertime stripers are caught in trawl nets by professional biologists and tagged with an internal anchor tag, the streamer of which extends from the fish's belly. This multiyear study of Hudson River striped bass, which make up a significant portion of our seasonal striper population, has about a 7 percent recapture rate, due to the incentive of tag return rewards. Since 1987, due to increased numbers of female striped bass, results indicate the number of bass that survive to become juveniles has remained high and constant, indicating the Hudson River has reached carrying capacity for this stock.

In addition, anglers are sent a certificate of participation, informing them of when and where the fish was originally tagged to thank them for their participation in the program.

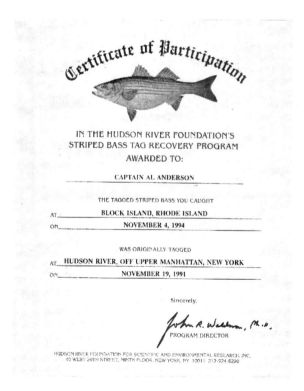

HRF Recapture Certificate

The HRF's Striped Bass Tag Recovery Program was set up in 1984 under an agreement among regulators, environmentalists, and the Hudson River electrical utility companies. As part of this agreement, the utilities conduct biological monitoring of Hudson River fish stocks, including striped bass. The role of the Hudson River Foundation is to coordinate the recovery of the tags and to record and analyze the data they provide.

In accordance with this settlement, each winter striped bass are tagged in the Hudson River off Manhattan. Anglers who catch these tagged fish cut off the tags and send them to HRF. In return, HRF will send them a $5 or $10 check and a questionnaire. A check will be issued *only* if the exterior section of the tag is returned.

When an angler returns a completed questionnaire, his or her name is entered into an annual drawing for nine prizes: two $1,000 prizes; two $500 prizes; and five $100 prizes.

In addition, each angler is sent a certificate of participation, stating when and where the fish was originally tagged.

Caught a Tagged HRF Striper?

When you catch a striped bass with an HRF tag, regardless of whether you intend to keep the fish or not, please cut off the tag and make a record of the date, location, total length of the fish (the distance from the tip of the upper jaw to the tip of the tail), and the condition of the tag insertion site. Then send the tag to the:

> Hudson River Foundation
> Box 1731
> Grand Central Station
> New York, NY 10163

Common Questions about Tag Recovery

Q: *Why are fish tagged?*
A: Fish are tagged to get answers to a wide variety of questions concerning their abundance and behavior. Much has been learned about the migration patterns of Hudson River striped bass through this program.

Q: *Where are tagged fish released?*
A: Tagged striped bass are released at several sites located in the lower Hudson River and New York Harbor. See map at right.

Q: *How many fish are tagged?*
A: Each winter, from November to April, approximately ten thousand to twenty-five thousand striped bass are tagged in the Hudson River. Over 450,000 fish have been tagged through 2007.

Q: *How long are the fish when they are tagged?*
A: In the HRF program, most striped bass are between seven and twelve inches when tagged.

Q: *How are the fish tagged?*
A: The tag is placed into a small incision made in the area of the fish's belly. The wound is treated with a disinfectant and the fish is quickly placed back into the river.

Q: *Can I tag fish for the Hudson River Foundation?*
A: HRF does not have a tagging kit for recreational anglers. Anglers can tag a wide variety of fishes through programs of the ALS.

Some HRF Striper Stats

— Each winter, from November to April, HRF technicians catch, tag, and release approximately ten thousand to twenty-five thousand striped bass in the Hudson.
— Almost five hundred thousand fish have been tagged through 2010. In the HRF Program, most striped bass are between seven to twelve inches in length when tagged.
— A tag called an internal anchor tag is placed into a small incision made in the area of the fish's belly. The wound is then treated with a disinfectant and the fish is quickly returned into the river.
— Striped bass eggs hatch in forty-eight hours and larvae grow to six inches in one year. Age two fish may reach twelve inches in length. On average, of the six hundred thousand eggs a young female may release, only six hundred will hatch, and of those, only three will reach age two.

Obstacles, Victories

Since the start of my interest in Thames River overwinter striper behavior, I've recaptured a number of HRF tagged fish. Recapture of HRF marked fish in this contingent of overwinter fish, and there are a number of them in Southern New England, has only provided information regarding initial tagging. Unfortunately, I have not been able to learn from HRF officials the magnitude of HRF fish that have been reported recaptured in the Thames. This would shed some light on the importance of this particular overwinter contingent, of which there appear to be at least nine others in Southern New England. Repeated requests for this information from the HRF have been politely denied. With a bit of diligence, however, I've been able to piece together some info from my recaptures. For example, here is one e-mail message to a companion angler:

Ahoy Steph:

CONGRATULATIONS! None of this would have been possible without your help . . . . Re: our Saturday's 12/6/08 HRF recap, it appears that tag #545755 (pretty sure of all the numbers despite intense algae fouling), which was re-tagged and released with ALS #758163, measured 17" (TL) and was estimated to weigh 2.25 lbs. A HRF fish you caught about a year earlier on 12/12/07, bearing tag #545570 (just 185 numbers shy), measured 14" and was estimated to weight 1.75 lbs., and was retagged with ALS #745607 and released. Here's how I see it. There is an excellent chance both fish were female and may have had the same female progenitor (rational for that statement comes from the fact that striper came to the Thames River to over-winter). At the end of their second year, both were netted and T/R with internal anchor tags while over-wintering in the Hudson by HRF. I suspect they may have been DNA programmed to venture to the Thames River for one or more years to continue over-wintering therein. Just how many HRF marked fish over-winter in the Thames we will never know, but those '07 recaptured fish that measured approximately 14", grew to approximately 17" a year later. In my mind this confirms at least a few returned again to the Thames for over-wintering. It was one of those tagged fish, perhaps from the same cohort (similar genetic over-winter message) you that you recaptured. Isn't it amazing what info we can piece together from the simple act of a tag recapture?

U.S. FISH AND WILDLIFE SERVICE

The USFWS striped bass tagging program began in 1985 with the marking of hatchery-reared fish. At the present time, federal and state biologists from Massachusetts to North Carolina are interested in expanding its database to serve as one of the primary sources of information for the ASMFC. Scientists, managers, and administrators are dependent on program information if they are to make smart management decisions for the future.

Today, biologists and fisheries managers from the USFWS, National Fish and Wildlife Foundation, NMFS, and state agencies from Massachusetts to North Carolina are participating in a coast-wide tagging program.

> The Cooperative Tagging Program is made up of both Federal and State agencies working together along the eastern seaboard toward the preservation and restoration of anadromous fisheries. Information gathered is used to identify causes of decline in fisheries resources, monitor the status of stocks, and to evaluate restoration of fish populations. The program's success is in part due to the cooperation of both recreational and commercial fishermen in reporting tagged fish.
>
> Severe declines of striped bass landings during the 1970's led to the passage of Section 7 of the Anadromous Fish Conservation Act in 1979, more commonly known as the Emergency Striped Bass Study. The Act instructed the Secretaries of Interior and Commerce to implement studies to determine the causes for the decline of migratory stocks of Atlantic striped bass.
>
> Toward that end, water quality conditions on spawning grounds were evaluated. Concurrently, the Services initiated a coast-wide striped bass tagging and hatchery programs to estimate rates of exploitation and natural mortality and to determine if hatchery-reared fish could supplement wild stocks in severely depleted rivers. During the same period emergency fishing restrictions were imposed by the coastal states from NC to ME to protect the remaining striped bass stocks.
>
> As a result, the Chesapeake Bay's migratory stock of striped bass was declared restored as of January 1, 1995. For the Fish & Wildlife Service, other Federal agencies, state agencies, research groups, and the users of the resource, the recovery of striped bass is a well-deserved reward for years of effort, research, and extreme sacrifice.

A central database, designed and managed by the USFWS stores coast-wide tagging information and dependent and independent survey data. This information is used to develop and implement appropriate management measures to maintain a viable and sustainable fishery.

Since 2005, nearly twelve million marked hatchery-reared striped bass fingerlings have been released into the wild. In 1988, hatchery fish comprised 50 percent of Maryland's young-of-the-year in some striped bass rivers. Today, as hoped, hatchery fish are far outnumbered by wild fish. The Maryland Department of Natural Resources reported that the 2011 young-of-the-year index was the 3rd highest since the survey began in 1954. (Note: the MD DNR YOY Index for 2009 was one of the lowest on record, raising questions about the resource's future. In 2011, the same YOY Index was one of the highest on record, leading many to suspect inaccurate data). While evaluation studies continue on the potential contribution of hatchery fish to wild stocks, hatchery-reared striped bass marked with coded wire tags are now used primarily to gather information on population dynamics and migration patterns to answer management questions.

USFWS Recapture Certificate

Migratory striped bass are found from the St. Lawrence River to North Carolina. Tag returns are providing better understanding of migratory patterns. The tagging program has confirmed that some 1-2 year old striped bass do leave bays and estuaries to forage along the coastline. Tag returns of three-year old hatchery fish released in the Chesapeake Bay have come back from as far north as New Brunswick, Canada—over 1,000 miles from its point of release, demonstrating that hatchery stripers can migrate as far as those born in the wild. Tag returns have also provided information on rates of migration. For example, one striper swam 500 miles at an average 16 miles per day before being recaptured.

Tagging data on striper mortality has shown that approximately 20 percent of adult wild stripers die each year from sources other than direct fishing for striped bass. Tagging data has also shown that both juvenile wild and hatchery stripers, during their first 1-3 years, suffer higher mortality than adults. Information on mortality rates obtained from the tagging program allows biologists to evaluate and adjust individual state and coastal management programs as needed.

More than 700,000 hatchery-reared and wild striped bass have been tagged with an external anchor or "belly" tag since 1985. Anglers returned more than 95,000 of these tags by the end of 2009. In addition, all hatchery-raised stripers—more than 11 million fish in all—are also tagged in the left cheek with a tiny micro-encoded piece of wire which anglers cannot see but researchers can detect with specialized equipment.

Caught A USFWS-Tagged Striper?

If you catch a tagged striped bass, please cut off the tag and record the date, location, and method of capture. Call the U.S. Fish and Wildlife Service at 1-800-448-8322 to report the information. Anyone reporting a tag will receive a certificate of participation and a reward.

WHAT'S BEEN LEARNED: TALE OF THE TAG

Observations always involve theory.

—Edwin Hubble

The term *contingent* is used to describe a group of fish that engages in a common pattern of seasonal migration between feeding areas, wintering areas, and spawning areas. It was only recently that researchers recognized various New England *contingents* of striped bass were composed of Hudson River—origin stripers. Historically, nearly every colonial-period northeast river supported overwinter striper populations; only when fish tagging came into existence could stock origin be documented. *Over-Winter Striper Secrets* confirmed the bulk of Thames River o-w stripers shared a Hudson River origin, basically a result of their tag-recapture movements.

Northeast Contingents

Tagging field studies have also confirmed sub-adult overwintering stripers become limited to a "saltwater wedge" environment. The reason being osmoregulation requires energy for maintenance of their tissue salt balance, critical to existence, and small fish carry only limited energy stores.

Historical documents and archeological research confirm striped bass overwintered at the head of Connecticut's Thames River for thousands of years and was a contributing factor in determining the location of the Pequot Indian winter campsite due to the abundance of overwintering striped bass.

Numerous studies have confirmed it's the females of the species that conduct spring, summer, and fall migrations for purposes of foraging. Not only do Hudson River—origin stripers conduct distant migrations as sub-adults, but Chesapeake Bay—origin fish do likewise, as this author had a summertime Bay of Fundy, Nova Scotia-tagged striper recaptured back in the Choptank River, Maryland, the following spring. Male striped bass do migrate, but research indicates approximately only 10 percent of a stock migrates.

The number of overwintering striped bass in the Thames has drastically declined in the last three years, for reasons that can only be due to a reduction of recruits coming into the Hudson River—origin stock.

Recent research suggests that the absence of obvious disease (mycobacteriosis) problems, together with low YOY survey counts, suggest spawning population concerns are responsible, along with high fishing pressure, decreased fisheries regulation enforcement, poaching, and other factors.

Tagging has also confirmed that once Hudson sub-adult fish appear to reach maturity, they join other stocks in overwintering offshore in mid-Atlantic waters. However, I found a significant percentage of immature females returned to the river for overwintering purposes, upward of 33 percent annually, which is suspected to be a result of "genetic memory" during pre-adult seasons. Only a small percent of Hudson River—origin fish appear to be *Thames contingent status* fish.

Once Thames o-w winter fish reach twenty-one inches and about four pounds, they rarely return the following season, suggesting that maturation (reproductive hormones) have made an appearance. Stripers in the twenty-three—to twenty-six-inch range, although sexually mature and capable of spawning, are not of productive spawning age. But at twenty-eight inches (minimum recreational possession length), they have spawned at least once, and hence present ASMFC regulations allow rod-and-reel harvest.

Over a period of ten years, not only have fish tagged by me been recaptured, but other agency-tagged fish have also been recaptured.

These include tagged fish by other ALS members, HRF tagged fish, and USFWS tagged fish. Although "schooling fidelity" has accounted for some recaptures, this author believes "genetic memory" is at the cause for this behavior.

Our tagging on the Thames suggests some clues as to why most sub-adult ALS striped bass are recaptured within three years of being marked. It is this author's opinion that since most sub-adult stripers are found in estuarine foraging areas, they are subject to considerably greater angling pressure than those occupying bay, sound, or ocean waters. The amount of angling pressure in estuaries (saltwater ponds, creeks, rivers) is considerably greater and does not require a boat in which to do it.

One of the primary reasons for *Over-Winter Striper Secrets* was to discover where overwintering fish migrated during the summer. Those from the Thames visited a total of forty-three other northeast river systems prior to the recapture event. The most popular river system and associated estuarine environments was that of the Merrimack River on the Massachusetts—New Hampshire border, including the Plum Island area. This zone has been historically mentioned by others and continues to support both Hudson-, Delaware-, and Chesapeake-origin stripers.

Three-year-old sub-adult stripers, averaging thirteen to fifteen inches in length, are incapable of storing much energy for overwintering. As a result, they are genetically programmed to go into *torpor* when triggered by wintertime environmental conditions. Consequently, they are less active, as a means to conserve energy, whereas larger older stripers remain active, as we could tag and release over a hundred fish that size daily in the month of January, depending on weather conditions. Their active behavior, although limited to the saltwater wedge, was the reason for our success.

It should be noted that active fish demonstrated no evidence of foraging. Once water temperatures fall below 40°F, little or no foraging occurred, as digestive enzymes fail to work below that temperature, as confirmed also by lack of "pooping" on my tagging board.

Curious as to whether there were other substantial *contingents* of New England overwintering stripers, it was discovered that nine others existed in southern New England. These included *contingents* in the Housatonic, Connecticut, Point Judith's Potter's Pond, Pettaquamscutt (Narrow River), Providence, Seekonk, Acushnet, and Charles and Mystic Rivers in Boston.

It was discovered that "schooling fidelity" begins at an early age, basically at or before age three in female stripers, with members of a school migrating as a small unit to other summertime estuaries. The fieldwork during this project indicated some stripers will migrate considerable distances when only in their second season, with some of the fish traveling into both Rhode Island and Massachusetts coastal waters at age two (ten inches) in length.

Island and Coastal Striper Migration

Based on my personal tagging records, our stripers here in southern New England have been recaptured from the following coastal areas: North Carolina, Virginia, Maryland, Delaware, Pennsylvania, New Jersey, New York, Rhode Island, Massachusetts, Vermont, and Maine.

For years, I've been asked why adult fish caught in the spring run, both on Long Island's ocean side and sound, seemingly fail to be seen in the fall.

Where do they go? And why? The answer is an easy one: these adult fish that made up the spring run undoubtedly came from spawning in the Hudson and then headed toward summertime foraging areas. In the fall, they do not return to the Hudson but instead return to the mid-Atlantic coastal and offshore overwintering areas, well away from any rod and reel efforts.

I'm asked why we don't catch any sub-adult stripers at the island, whereas they do at Martha's Vineyard and, occasionally, at Nantucket. I'm no expert, but I suspect these areas have some estuarine areas that contain forage species, unlike that at Block Island. I do not recall ever catching any number of sub-adult fish at Block Island.

Stripers I've T/R at Block Island in the spring have been reported recaptured at Nauset, on the Cape, as soon as seven days later. Is this more evidence of genetic "road signs" speeding coastal migration? Also, not surprisingly, Thames overwinter-tagged stripers were recaptured a week later in the Merrimack River area. Olfaction (smell) may have played an incidental role in this behavior once in close distance, but there had to be a genetically programmed reason.

Many of our early season island T/R stripers have been recaptured from coastal Connecticut areas, as well as Rhode Island and Massachusetts coastal areas. This suggests that the island is simply a foraging "waypoint" in their migration. I've recaptured my own T/R stripers from Block Island, Thames River, and Rhode Island coastal waters, all of which again support "genetic memory," or what used to be called "instinct."

Stripers that appear at the island, T/R by me, seemingly do so for just for a limited period of time before moving on. Thanks to the help of many clients, the numbers of bass T/R were considerable, yet only a few have been recaptured within a limited period following their marking. They visit, but could it be if there is little forage to hold them, they "boogie"?

As indicated elsewhere, many of my early season tagged arrivals were reported one or more years later from nearby coastal areas, including Delaware Bay, Delaware River, and its feeder estuarine spawning areas. Included also were recaptured fish from coastal Long Island and Long Island Sound waters the following spring, suggesting spawning Delaware and New York stock fish. Waves of later season T/R fish (i.e., late June and early July) are reported recaptured the following season or later from Maryland and Virginia waters. This timing (early summer) suggests the arrival of more distant spawning Chesapeake Bay fish.

Bioacoustics and Migration

For over forty years now, I've been tagging and releasing striped bass in the name of science, for the Sandy Hook, New Jersey-based ALS. I've been at it both part time, and now full time, as a charter boat skipper, with over sixty thousand game fish marked for science, forty-three thousand of which have been striped bass, resulting in my being recently recognized nationally for my conservation efforts.

This latest book deals primarily with adult striped bass (*Morone saxatilis*) and provides me an opportunity to advance a few ideas. My previous book dealt primarily with Hudson River—origin sub-adult stripers; and although it answered many questions, it also created many more. As a result, I'd like to outline several concepts for a theory I have regarding their ability to navigate through New England's coastal waters quickly and efficiently.

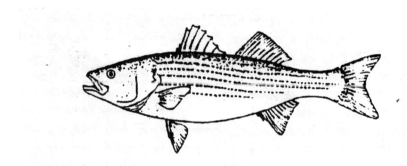

XL Striped Bass

Years ago, I spent some time working for Marie Fish at URI's Graduate School of Oceanography (GSO), monitoring and recording the sounds blackfish (tautog) made via several Narragansett Bay hydrophones. I soon discovered that the presence or absence of a hydrophone background noise depended heavily on tidal conditions. (Consider: Flood tide, little background noise; but ebb tide, most notably at several sites, created quite a ruckus.) I'm convinced that the shape, size, and orientation of the numerous ledges and other structures that dot the New England seabed create tidal-current "noise" ("sonic profiles" seems a more apt description), unique enough to possibly act as a "sign post" or "road sign" aiding striper navigation.

Since the lateral line of a striped bass is extremely sensitive, and because our New England area has many unique tidal current rips, I suspect each rip has its own distinct acoustic, or "sonic," qualities—to the extent that no two sounds are exactly alike and can likely be identified over considerable distances; not only identified, but possibly encoded in the very DNA of many Chesapeake—and Hudson River—origin striped bass. Just as when every new Soviet submarine launched, the U.S. Navy spent literally years electronically profiling, recording, and documenting its sonic "footprint."

I'm curious to know if you, the reader, think these sonic profiles or "melodies," undoubtedly unique on one tide, but different on the other, could be encoded in a striper's DNA and used as "sign posts" to aid in navigation.

Overwinter striped bass I've tagged in the Thames River, Connecticut, have been recaptured as little as seven days later in the Merrimack River, New Hampshire—easily 120 nautical miles distant as the crow flies. This could only be possible if "sign posts" or "road signs" were encoded. Research has shown school-size Hudson River—origin bass have utilized the Merrimack River and associated estuarine environs for decades as primary nursery areas. They are "programmed" to migrate to and from these specific areas, hence unlikely their speedy movements are haphazard, as many have suggested.

A recent study has shown that early in their life history, as larvae, striped bass have the ability to actively catch zooplankton (*Eurytemora affinis*) in complete darkness within seven days of postfertilization (DPF) after yolk sac formation (Sampson, 2011). Striped bass larvae, at this point, have an average size of 3.1 millimeters (1.25 inches), develop a mouth, and begin feeding on microscopic zooplankton. Soon, their diet changes to tiny copepods and cladocerans (water fleas). Juvenile stripers eat insect larvae, larval fish, mysids (shrimplike crustaceans), and amphipods (tiny scavenging crustaceans). In 1976, recruitment researchers, Heinle et al., found that an abundance of *Eurytemora affinis* during the spring led to a strong year class (four to five times greater) than during a poor year class. Also, his research suggested a close relationship between detritus (organic material) and copepod abundance, which rested upon the creation of winter estuarine ice. Evidence suggests that the colder the season, the greater the available detritus available to zooplankton populations, and thus a relationship to strong striped bass year classes.

All of that is interesting, but I'm straying from the point I'm trying to make: *if, within a twenty-four-hour period, a juvenile striped bass did not eat a zooplankton such as E. affinis, it would not survive*. Finding and eating zooplankton was paramount to becoming older. Their developing lateral line was critical to their life cycle existence.

Zooplankton; Copepod & Amphipod

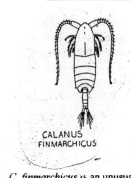

CALANUS FINMARCHICUS

C. finmarchicus is an unusually large Copepod (4 mm.) in length.

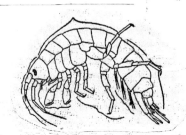

G. locusta, (Amphipod) common to tne New England coast, reaches up to 1"in length.

Zooplankton Members

A striper's lateral line is a row of pits containing sensitive hair cells (neuromasts). Together, these cells are used to detect motion, pressure waves, and vibrations in the surrounding water to locate prey or predators and help the fish orient itself. These cells, referred to as neuromast mechanoreceptors, are sensitive enough to detect the hydrodynamics of a nearby microscopic "water flea" (read zooplankton) in the turbid murk of an estuary. These neuromast cells are sensitive enough to detect frequencies in both the ten to sixty Hertz as well as the forty to two hundred Hertz range; and along with the swim bladder and inner ear (otolith), as they age, can detect sound pressure signals from distant sources. No one currently knows how well or how far striped bass adults can detect sound pressure, but anglers know they react (avoidance behavior) to frequencies below one thousand Hertz from a nearby vessel. Most striped bass anglers know full well striped bass can locate and engulf a live eel in fifty to sixty feet of silt-laden water, on a pitch black night, in a running tide, obviously without ever seeing it until the last moment. Striped bass can more easily detect a lively eel than an ailing eel—one reason they catch better.

It appears that the next step might be the examination of variable DNA "markers" unique to migration behavior of different populations of summertime migrating New England fish. Focus could center on sub-adult Hudson River—origin stripers, as their spring and fall coastal movements (1) tend to occur over shorter time spans and (2) have less variation in geographic distance and location, as many sub-adult fish utilize Merrimack River area estuaries.

Recent DNA studies found considerable inter-individual variation but relatively small levels of inter-population variation among samples from the lower western shore of the Chesapeake Bay. These results suggest stochastic genetic differentiation among these populations, but it is unlikely, and that relatively strong selection for locally adapted genotypes would be required for inter-population differentiation to occur.

Existence of unique genetic "markers" for river spawning habitat of striped bass is now known. We can identify a Hudson River—origin striper from a Chesapeake striper, moreover a Choptank River—origin striper from a York River striper, based on their unique "genetic markers." No two genetic markers for river origin are alike; these are now cataloged and can be used to identify a striper's river of origin. Betcha didn't know that! I am confident research will soon uncover those genetic markers for divergent migration behavior.

ALS TAGGING WEEKENDS, 2010-2011

Back in 2009, American Littoral Society (ALS) tagging director, Jeff Dement, raised the idea of offering members a spring weekend devoted to striper tagging. After much discussion, we decided to offer two weekends fishing Block Island waters. The society would provide tags, and I would provide the vessel and know-how. Here's how it went.

When Dement arrived on Friday, May 21, 2010, we had no idea what we'd find at Block Island; I suggested we scout out the Narrows in Upper Point Judith Salt Pond late that afternoon. We caught, tagged, and released a quick nine stripers and decided it would likely be wiser to start Saturday where we knew fish were rather than gambling on the island. Not until midmorning Saturday did an e-mail report that stripers had arrived at the island which we'd fish that afternoon. Previously, our Saturday morning group had a ball with light tackle schoolies, and then with larger fish on our Saturday evening's and Sunday's split-day ventures.

May 22-23, 2010

A total of a dozen members fished aboard the *Prowler* that weekend, a total of four four-hour trips over the two days. All members fished one morning and one evening trip. New Jersey's Ed Green, fishing the Narrows with his group Saturday morning, caught a nineteen-inch, three-pound bass that marked the fifty-five thousandth career T/R game fish to land in my cockpit. That fish was one of twenty-four school bass (fourteen to twenty-two inches) marked for science that morning.

55,000th Career TR—ALS Tagging Weekend

That Saturday afternoon, we trolled the North Rip in 51°F water, finding a few birds working some bait and some bass in deep water, tallying, by trip's end, fourteen fish in the twenty-three—to thirty-inch range.

The next morning, we worked the last of the flood at the southwest Corner under all manner of birds, tagging and freeing fifteen-inch fish up to thirty-four inches. The second trip, trolling the rip put another twenty-five stripers to a high of thirty-three inches in the boat; all went home sporting yellow ALS loop tags. The weekend tally was a respectable seventy-eight linesiders tagged and released for a dozen members.

To his credit, Jeff Dement, assisting as a mate, handled himself well with the landing net and at the tagging board. He kindly suggested I use my tag for the fifty-five thousandth T/R.

June 12-13, 2010

Another dozen ALS members joined us this second weekend, which ran on the same schedule as the previous session. On Saturday morning, in 56°F water in the North Rip, my crew stuck, fought, tagged, and liberated seven school bass and a lone blue. That afternoon, six members teamed up for ten quality fish to around twenty-eight inches—for a day-end total of eighteen fish T/R amid light winds and few raindrops.

On Sunday June 13, six members climbed aboard at 4:30 a.m. to head across. Four hours later, twenty fish had been T/R, sixteen bluefish from twenty to twenty-four inches and four stripers from twenty-four to twenty-five inches.

Later that afternoon, seventeen striped bass from twenty to twenty-nine inches and six bluefish to twenty-nine inches were marked and sent back, bringing Sunday's total to forty-three fish—and a weekend grand total of sixty-seven. Coupled to the earlier May weekend, during which we marked seventy-eight striped bass, ALS members had tagged a total of 145 fish.

Jeff & Betti Dement; 6/11 ALS T/R Weekend

> Following the compilation of 2010 ALS tagging data early in 2011, Dement sent it off to NMFS's Northeast Fisheries Science Center (NEFSC) in Woods Hole, which subsequently forwarded it to the ASMFC Striped Bass Technical Committee.

2010 Weekend Log

On both weekends of 2010, many of the seventy-eight tagged-and-released stripers were heavily infested with unknown parasitic copepods. Infestations were so severe that the cockpit wore an even coating of dislodged parasites. All the indications were that this body of fish had quite recently arrived from offshore—inside the last forty-eight hours certainly, given a collective skunking for those who'd fished the island two days prior.

Research indicates that these fish become densely schooled during the late winter and early spring, and that school migrated together from the mid-Atlantic to Block Island, Rhode Island waters. Our timing for this event couldn't have been more perfect to witness this host-parasite relationship.

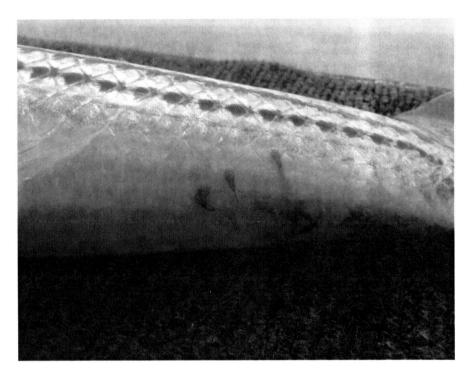

More Fish Lice, Island Striper

Many of these ectoparasites were readily visible, clustered on the rear of the fish in caudal areas; the infestations of the degree we observed are called *Caligulosis*. It turns out these copepods are all free swimmers until rising offshore water temps trigger mating. Following mating, females (which produce egg strings containing hundreds of fertilized ova) attach to the striper to feed on mucous, while males resume free swimming. I vowed to have these fish lice identified following our 2011 venture. In early July, a tag-recaptured striper demonstrated numerous fish lice.

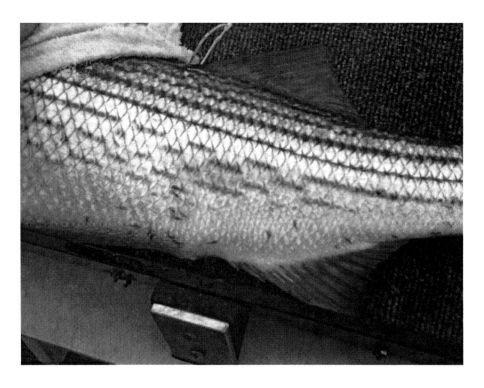

Krueger Recap; July 2011 (Striper fish lice)

June 4-5, 2011

Over two eight-hour sessions on Saturday, June 4 and Sunday, June 5, 2011, another half-dozen ALS members—specifically, Chris and Susan Downer, Russ and Judy Walters, Ed Nellis and Bette Dement—took advantage of superabundant sand eels scouring the North Rip with tube-rigged umbrellas. By late Sunday, they'd managed to implant lock-on style ALS tags in a total of thirty-two fish—eighteen bass and fourteen bluefish—before setting them free. The weekend's largest striper, a 32 ½-incher, was caught and subsequently T/R Saturday by Ed Nellis. A well-constructed tagging board was located at the stern, allowing Jeff Dement to quickly measure fish (FL) and apply the tag prior to release.

Jeff D. & Capt. Al; Helm shot

Prowler Dockside: Jeff & Betti Dement

Working Weekends . . .

With the help of many long-term ALS members during these ALS tagging weekends, we made several important discoveries. Prior to and following the ALS tagging weekends in 2011, charter parties that retained legal-sized stripers had their fish filleted at sea. The observations indicated roughly 10 percent of these fish were mature males, well in excess of the required twenty-eight-inch minimum length, confirming what has been reported in the literature. Also, the numerous female fish we examined were in a pre-spawning mode (ripe gonads), indicating they had not (and would not have) spawned.

We also noted—sometime later—that a significant percentage of the early season arrivals we tagged and released were recaptured in late season (2011) from Delaware Bay and New Jersey waters. (This trend was verified by colleagues who recaptured numerous fish in and around the North Rip that bore U.S. Fish and Wildlife tags attached in New Jersey/Delaware Bay.) We were thus able to conclude that a number of Block Island's early season fish are of Hudson River or Delaware River origin.

Again, in early 2012, once all the 2011 ALS tagging data has been compiled by Jeff Dement and others, it will be forwarded to the Northeast Fisheries Science Center in Woods Hole. Following Center review, the data will be forwarded to ASMFC's striped bass and bluefish technical committees to help guide future management decisions.

For more information about fish lice (*C. elongatus*), check out the chapter "Giving Something Back," and for those ALS member taggers that were unable to take advantage of our scheduled tagging weekends, an article about these particular striped bass fish lice is being considered for publication in an upcoming issue of our ALS *Underwater Naturalist*.

VII

SOME TRANSITIONS

2011: YEAR OF THE RECORD BREAKERS

*A great fortune depends on luck,
a small one on diligence.*

—Unknown

(**Author's Note:** The following pieces speak to one helluva year in big-bass fishing in New England waters. The first relays the details of Peter Vican's Rhode Island 77.4-pound record breaker caught at Block Island's Southwest Ledge on Father's Day, June 19, 2011. The subsequent four entries lay out the then-elusive bits of the puzzle surrounding Greg Myerson's now-confirmed All-Tackle World Record 81.88-pound monster striped bass, landed in Central Connecticut waters on August 5, 2011. All the latter have been cobbled together from several sources in the interest of providing a reasonably accurate account of the angler's momentous catch, which unseated Al McReynolds's famed and long-standing [twenty-nine years, in fact] "mark to beat"—a catch that has forever etched the number 78-8 in the brain of every striper sharpie of the last three decades. For those with dreams of topping the new mark, take heart. There are some very large bass around thanks to the fish that remain from some very strong year classes that came into the striper world in the waning years of the moratorium in the 1980s. Bottom line? There would be a great many seasoned bassmen not in the least surprised to see some other massive specimens come ashore in the coming seasons.)

Superbass: Peter Vican Shatters Own State Record With 77.4

by Zach Harvey

(from *The Fisherman* magazine, New England edition, July 7, 2011)

Sunday morning, Father's Day, June 19, Peter Vican and longtime fishing partner, Don Smith, shot northward toward the Rhode Island mainland, Vican's 24-foot WellCraft closing on the West Gap. Vican hailed Snug Harbor Marina on channel 66, calmly asked that the crew have a tote ready on the dock, told them he had a bass, probably over 70 pounds, to weigh in. Around 6 a.m., the boat tied up, Smith and Vican flopped two substantial bass up onto the dock. A few minutes later, one fish had received a final documented weight of 48 pounds, and the larger of the two fish read an impossible 77.4 pounds on the State-Certified scale. For the second time, Peter Vican had toppled Rhode Island's state record for striped bass.

The first time, back in 2008, a fish of 76 pounds, 14 ounces had unseated long-time record holder, Joe Szabo of Block Island, whose 70.5-pound benchmark had held since 1984. This second time, Vican would beat his own mark—upgrade it, you might say—and also come within 1.4 pounds of Al McReynolds' 1982 all-tackle world record 78.8. Don Smith, who was present for both of Vican's record catches, recalls Vican saying "It would be the worst thing to beat my own record and not beat the world record." That's of course, just what happened. But it in no way diminishes Vican's big-bass credentials. For one thing, Vican is now the first fisherman to officially crack 70 pounds more than once in one lifetime. For another, there's no arguing with the duo's track record: they've effectively locked up the top slots in several tournaments they've fished for years, and they release—legitimately—numerous fish between 40 pounds and the mid 50s each season.

Vican's 2008, 76 lb. 14 oz. striper

Theirs is a familiar story in trophy bass fishing: the guys who put in the time night after night—the wide-open fishing and the slow-picking—are the guys who catch big fish regularly. And not just for the obvious reasons, the finding and staying on a pile of bigger fish, tracking them easier to do fishing consecutive nights. Vican and Smith also have some sharp sources, Island regulars with whom they exchange information. You don't tap into such networks without proving yourself.

Asked how they came to be drifting where they were that fateful Saturday night/Sunday morning, Vican was quick to credit Capt. Matt King of Hula Dog Charters, who runs out of New Harbor on the Island. "I called him on the cell as we were leaving the dock—like I usually do," said Vican. "He told us he'd had some bigger fish in that general area during the day." Upon their arrival after 9 p.m. Saturday night, Vican and Smith worked a 42—to 52-foot drift north of the well-known "Peanut," a place they call the "Desert" because it's a generally nondescript patch of sandy bottom flanked on the ends by rocks. "It's a place that doesn't look like much," Vican said. "You never really mark much bait there—I have no idea why fish pile up there, but they do. I've actually had fish—big ones—come out of there with sand in their gills and scales."

Conditions were about ideal, according to Vican and Smith, seas two to three, long troughs, wind light and just a hint off the direction of the tide.

The two caught fish in their "Desert" right from the start, thanks to a fairly brisk drift that kept them moving fast enough to stay out of the dogfish. "We landed more than a dozen fish apiece over 25 pounds, doubling up on more than one drift," Smith recalled later, "Right around midnight, we doubled up on some large fish. I landed a 48-pounder and Peter's was only slightly smaller. On the very next drift, we duplicated the catch, both landing fish around 45 pounds." Since Smith had kept the 48, all others went back. The drift died right around 1 a.m. and the dogfish swarmed the place, forcing them back into recon mode.

Vican said they spent some time looking around, and eventually moved into the shoal water around Black Rock to hide from the dogfish and stay busy through the slack. After some uneventful drifting for a couple hours, Vican decided to return to the scene of the earlier activity, since that area had produced fish for him on both tides in the past. The tide was moving along pretty well when they arrived, their speed over ground over a knot and a half, and Vican was relieved to be clear of the dogfish.

The big fish inhaled Vican's eel just after 3:30 a.m. "It took some line out, but nowhere near the amount you'd expect from a fish that size—never made any really big runs, the way Peter's first fish did," reported Smith. (In contrast, Vican's 2008 record fish ran him down to within a few coils of the bare spool in what amounted to much more of a textbook light-tackle battle.) Smith continued: "[this fish] actually swam with the boat and kept diving. Peter would pry her up a couple feet and she'd lunge right back down to the bottom. After ten or twelve minutes, it surfaced maybe 25 or 30 feet behind the boat, and Peter started to reel it toward the stern. When the fish saw the boat, it rolled on its side and started running out off the rail." It was at that moment, the fish momentarily broadside, that Smith finally got a look at her, and he yelled to Vican that she was clearly a monster.

Vican applied pressure and got the fish turned around as Smith readied the landing net, an instrument Smith later described as "not all that big—maybe 22 inches by 24 inches at the opening." Moments later, Vican guided the exhausted cow bass head-first into the net, and Smith, charged up with adrenaline, simply flopped her into the cockpit. "It took both of us to lift the last record fish into the boat," admitted Smith. "This time, I was so hyped up I just grabbed the frame of the net and flipped the fish into the boat. I couldn't believe how small my 48-pounder looked next to this fish." The duo quickly grabbed the tape measure to get length and girth, then fed the numbers into the "800 Formula," which gave them an estimated weight of 79 pounds.

The fish measured 52 inches, with a girth—from collar all the way to the beginning of the tail's taper—of 35 inches. "It looked like a brick with a tail—not at all like the crescent shape most bass have across the belly," said Smith.

Asked about the gear he used, Vican explained that he uses the same approach basically all the time. AS luck would have it, he was using the exact same reel—same combo, in fact—that he was using when he landed the last record-breaker: a Penn 560 Slammer paired off to a 6'6" St. Croix Premiere rod rated for 12 to 25 pound test. That reel was spooled up with 50-pound Tuffline XL running line to a #75 Coastlock snap, connected to a small barrel swivel, and 48 inches of 50-pound fluorocarbon running to a snelled 6/0 Gamakatsu Octopus Circle hook. Contrary to one rumor circulating, the fish was very definitely caught on a live eel. Matt Conti at Snug Harbor Marina confirmed that the duo buys 100 or more eels for every outing. Vican noted he's seen very little difference between fluoro, mono—even wire, which he's used to subdue bass well in excess of 50 pounds over the years—in night eeling. "We use the fluoro because we have hundreds of rigs tied up ahead of time," he added. Smith said that as a rule they use no weight when drifting eels in 30 feet or under unless boiling current absolutely necessitates it. Where they fish that night, they needed to run a three-ounce egg sinker up above the leader to keep their baits in the zone.

The fish will be skin-mounted by Northeast Taxidermy Services. Vican noted that tissue samples will be provided to biologists at Woods Hole, who called to request them. "They said the fish was likely between 26 and 28 years old," reported Smith. "I gather they've never had a chance to test samples from a striped bass that old."

Vican's 2011 R. I. Record Striper
(Image courtesy of Don Smith)

New World Record Striped Bass Reported by Kevin Blinkoff

(from *onthewater.com*, August 5, 2011)

Here's the facts, reported to us by Connecticut-based *OTW* writer Kierran Broatch: This morning, Striper Cup angler Greg Myerson weighed in a striped bass that registered 81.88 pounds on the scale at Jack's Shoreline in Westbrook, Connecticut—almost 12 hours after it had been landed Thursday evening aboard a boat in Long Island Sound.

Myerson has not yet decided if he will submit an application to the IGFA for all-tackle world record certification. Here's a photo of the fish, taken earlier this morning.

Myerson's World Record Striper
(Image courtesy of Sherwood Lincoln)

Myerson's 81 Pound Striped Bass Update

by Zach Harvey

(from *The Fisherman* magazine, New England edition, August 11, 2011)

On Friday morning, August 5th, Greg Myerson, age 43, of North Branford, CT carried a massive striped bass into Jack's Shoreline Bait & Tackle in Westbrook, CT. On the shop's scale, which was certified by the State of CT two years ago—the massive cow bass weighed 81.88 lbs., "in the round" or whole.

Myerson landed the fish at approximately 8 PM on the evening of Thursday August 4th. The big fish laid in the cockpit of his 18 ft. outboard-powered center console, as he elected to fish the remaining tide, but conditions deteriorated, and he headed for the "barn." Myerson fishes with eels almost exclusively for stripers, basically around Southwest Reef, inner and outer, an area of boulders and broken bottom outside Clinton, CT. He did not indicate exactly where he was fishing, but did say he pulled his bass off a boulder that had given him countless heavyweights in recent seasons. By one account, he landed three fish over 60 lbs. last season, along with numerous fish over 50 lbs., so it's safe to say he knows what he's doing.

Greg says he uses heavy tackle—a necessity on the tight drifts he fishes, thanks to tight "knots" of lobster gear, whose up-and-down lines "eat" any hooked fish. He uses Quantum reels spooled with 50 lb. Gorilla Braid and light stand-up rods made by St. Croix, and fish's mostly homemade 3-way rigs of very heavy material.

He caught the fish on a slower part of the tide, when he feels big calorie-conscious fish tend to gorge themselves.

The battle lasted about 20 minutes from hookup to flopping the fish in the cockpit. Fortunately his problems with the landing net and the swim platform were short lived. The fish taped 54 inches before weighing 81.88 lbs. on the scale.

Greg was adamant about fishing from his 18 ft skiff; it gives him clear view of his electronics, the size of his marks, his exact position, drift speed, and view of his immediate area. "Bigger boats simply can't do that in spots I fish," he said. This author under-stands that very well, as he fished many a night from his 14 ft. skiff in lobster gear fowled waters, taking fish over 60 lbs.

Myerson's IGFA Application

81.88: CT's Myerson Eyes Queen Mother of All Word Records

by Zach Harvey

(from *The Fisherman* magazine, New England edition, August 18, 2011)

If the last few days have proven one thing about the striper fishing world, it's that collectively, those who live and die by the whims of seven-striped bass can generate wild rumors faster than the entire population of junior-high girls in the state of California. Since last Friday, August 5, every striper-minded internet forum, blog and so on has gone absolutely haywire as folks with an almost shocking lack of firm facts have typed out electronic reams of hot air about the recent catch. So, right here and now, we'd like to set the record—at least the first part of the record, the part we know for sure—straight. Here's what we know:

On Friday morning, June 5, Greg Myerson, age 43, of North Branford, CT carried a massive striped bass into Jack's Shoreline Bait and Tackle in Westbrook, CT. On the shop's scale (which was last certified by the State of Connecticut two years ago—a point that has fed the rumor mill), the massive cow bass weighed 81.88 pounds "in the round." A crowd gathered in the shop's parking lot as striper fanatics from across the region reacted to the first waves of rumors and speculation. Late-morning, Myerson loaded the fish back into a large cooler in the back of his truck and headed home with it.

Backing up now, I called Myerson late Friday afternoon to gather some details from a preliminary round of *Facebook* rumor control. Here's what he had to say . . .

Myerson landed the fish at approximately 8 p.m. on the evening of Thursday, August 5. The big fish lay in the cockpit of his 18-foot, outboard-powered center console while he elected to fish out the remaining push of the tide, but conditions deteriorated and he soon headed for the barn. Myerson fishes with eels—the largest he can find—almost exclusively, and said, in somewhat generic wording, that he fishes around Southwest Reef (inner and outer), an area of boulders and broken bottom outside Clinton, CT. He did not explicitly say that he was fishing Southwest Reef when he landed this fish. He did say that he pulled this bass off a boulder that has given him countless other heavy bass in recent seasons. (By one account, he landed three fish over 60 pounds last season, and numerous other fish over fifty, so it's safe to say the guy knows just what he's doing.) Myerson—and Myerson only, in all likelihood—knows where he was drifting when that "big girl" climbed on.

Greg said he uses gear that's very heavy—a necessity on the short drifts he fishes, thanks to tight little knots of lobster gear whose up-and-down lines eat hooked fish. He uses Quantum Reels and light tuna stand-up rods made by St. Croix, spools up with 50-pound Gorilla Braid and fishes mostly home-tied three-way rigs of very heavy material. He caught the fish on a slower part of the tide, when, he's observed, big, calorie-conscious fish, tend to feed.

The battle lasted roughly 20 minutes from hook-up to cockpit. Myerson noted he got the landing net hung up on the swim platform as he was trying to guide the fish in, then hung the fish up in the wheel briefly. Whatever he did in those critical seconds, he did it right.

One final note: Myerson's adamant about fishing in his 18-footer, the close quarters giving him clear view of his electronics—the size of the marks, his exact position, drift speed and so on. "Bigger boats, you just can't do that, can't fish the spots I fish properly," he said. We got cut off after a brief phone chat, but I'm hopeful we'll have reconnected by the time you're reading this.

The fish taped 54 inches, and once again, per the scale at Jack's Shoreline Bait and Tackle, registered a whopping 81.88 pounds. The doubts about the scale should be resolved soon. State Certification or no, Jack is a straight shooter, and there's no reason to think that the weight's off because a representative of the weights-and-measures bureaucracy hasn't put a fresh sticker on the unit.

Bottom line here is this: Everyone's a critic, and Greg Myerson's not a public-relations specialist. But he's one helluva bass fisherman, and this 81.88-pounder he just landed is only the latest in a pretty steady stream of heavies on his trophy bass rap—sheet. This fish is bigger than all of us—a gift—so let's give her and the guy who fooled her after umpteen migrations and time out of mind, their due. Stay tuned. To check out photos, visit us on *Facebook*.

Twenty-Nine Year Reign Ends with Approval of a New Striped Bass Record

(from an IGFA press release, on or around October 19, 2011)

Greg Myerson's 37.1 kg (81-pound, 14-ounce) striped bass record was approved on Wednesday, October 19, after the International Game Fish Association's (IGFA) Record Committee came to a consensus on the catch and its supporting documentation. Myerson's catch created a whirlwind of excitement in early August for striper anglers everywhere, but especially in the northeastern USA.

"After a 15 minute fight on my St. Croix rod and Quantum reel, I got the striped bass close enough to the boat for netting," Myerson shared in the testimony accompanying his world record application. "The fish was bigger than I thought. I slipped on eel slime and banged my ribs against the gunwale of the boat. But it didn't matter. The monster fish was mine. At this point it was about 8 pm, I put the fish into the hold and fished the rest of the tide. As I fished, I repeatedly peered into the hold and asked myself 'is this striper really that big?' The following morning, I brought the striped bass to Jack's Shoreline Bait and Tackle to be weighed. The fish measured 54 inches in length and tipped Jack's digital scale at 81.88 pounds. It really was that big."

The IGFA's approval of Myerson's catch marks the end of Albert McReynolds' 29-year reign as All-Tackle record holder for this prestigious saltwater species. In addition to now holding the All-Tackle record, Myerson's catch also landed him the new men's 37 kg (80 lb) line class record, which previously stood at 70 lb. Congratulations to Greg Myerson on this historical record catch—and good luck to you striper fishermen aiming to best it in the future!

GIVING SOMETHING BACK

*Each person should live their life as
a model for others.*

—Rosa Parks

Fish tagging is an opportunity to increase our knowledge about several resources, where much still needs to be learned, as well as an opportunity to conduct conservation in the name of science. If you must know, a way for me to assuage feelings of guilt that developed early in my career from not understanding the true value and importance of our fisheries resources.

I don't tag fish so I can talk or write about it per se, I do it in part so my clients can experience it and talk about it, letting others know about their involvement with marking fish for the sake of science. There is no immediate feedback from it—that takes time. Recaptures, if they occur, may take weeks, months, or years, but we can proudly say it not only makes fish available for others to catch, but tagged fish act as "scientific messengers." Following notification of a recapture, both clients and myself receive the satisfaction of knowing what we're doing is worthwhile.

Truth be known, along the way several miracles of medical science saved my "bacon," i.e., neurosurgery for removal of a brain tumor, and a decade later quadruple bypass surgery, which by the grace of God, allowed me to continue my fishing. But more importantly, these events compelled me to consider what I might give back, not just to the resource and the angling community, but to my family and friends as well. Other members of the recreational sector were "giving back" in one way or another, and I simply wanted to count myself among them.

Early Years

Fishing has played a major role in my life for as long as I can remember—and possibly back further than that. It all started when, during a lunch period in third grade, I visited a local park not far from my primary school (PS no. 7) in Fords, New Jersey. (In those days, students could leave school at lunch time.) It was there that I discovered a small pond loaded with sunfish, and with a bent pin, some thread, and dough balls made from my sandwich, that I caught my first few fish. I put 'em all back, of course—but rumors that I tagged them are entirely untrue. My love for the challenge of catching fish has persisted ever since, and the gear at my disposal has evolved quite a bit.

Shortly thereafter, I discovered golden shiners, hatchery-reared trout, and largemouth bass. I'd ride my bike to Roosevelt Park from my nearby Metuchen home and spend the day figuring out how to catch a few fish, and in the process, began to discover the world of aquatic nature. When I finished up my day's angling, I'd hide my crude tackle in lakeside bushes, and then ride home.

I clearly remember being haunted by a fish I later discovered was a largemouth bass—a fish I had absolutely no idea how to catch. Carefully watching others, I became obsessed with the idea of catching them. That plan would come to fruition years later, targeting them with surface plugs from twilight past dark at numerous lakes and ponds in New Jersey, New York, Rhode Island, and Massachusetts.

My uncle, Royal Anderson, a Normandy invasion survivor and trout-fishing enthusiast, further fueled my growing passion taking me along with him on New Jersey Opening Day trips to the Musconectcong River, one of central New Jersey's famous trout streams, during my junior high years. It was there I would become totally frustrated in any attempt to catch "opening day" trout. Lockwood Gorge, part of the North Branch of the Raritan, was shrouded in mystery as well, and despite all my ventures there, with either my father or uncle, I failed miserably. As a novice, I vowed one day to conquer the challenge of catching hatchery-reared trout and would finally enjoy some success against that goal later in high school.

Another uncle (on my mother's side), Harry Bernau, started a part-time rod building and lure-making business in the basement of his Perth Amboy residence basement, just for those who enjoyed surf casting for striped bass. Over the years, he befriended me and did his best to supply me with the necessary freshwater tackle to catch not only a trout, but largemouth bass. One fall afternoon, while I sat at home in Fords, New Jersey, Uncle Harry drove up in his new '49 Mercury and invited me to check its trunk. There, lying on some newspaper, were three of the largest fish I'd ever seen. Surf casting that morning at Sandy Hook, New Jersey, in a nor'easter, he'd caught several striped bass in the twenty—and thirty-pound range, the largest so far in his seven-year surf casting career. The memory of that afternoon was never forgotten, and years later, I dedicated my first book, *Game Fish Tag and Release*, to an aunt and uncle who, more than anyone else, fostered my love for fishing.

Working as a carrier, and then later as branch manager for the *Perth Amboy Evening News* in high school, I found little time for fishing. Bound for college, the *PA Evening News* offered me a scholarship in journalism—yikes, no thanks.

College Years

In the spring of my junior year at Fairleigh Dickinson University (FDU) in Teaneck, New Jersey, I vowed to take up springtime trout fishing with a vengeance. It so happened my new dormitory roommate, Dennis Sabo, a friend since childhood, had a passion for fishing that eclipsed my own. Together, we would head off to the headwaters of North Jersey's Hackensack River in early morning to catch a few stocked trout before biology electives. Imagine the looks we received arriving late for our laboratory session, still clad in waders and fishing vests, with a creel of trout we intended to dress out in a lab sink after class. Thankfully, our professor tolerated our unusual behavior.

Before my senior year ended, I had elected to go to summer school and earn additional credits necessary for graduation with a bachelor of science in biology. Despite this, we managed to spend a few successful days largemouth bass fishing in Farrington Lake outside New Brunswick, New Jersey—first, with popping bugs on the fly rod, then by casting surface plugs, then graduating to offering black rubber worms.

Later on, Dennis followed me on to graduate school, my studies taking me to Long Island, New York, and him to Cambridge, Massachusetts. We shared many freshwater and—later on—saltwater fishing experiences, and he felt as responsible toward the resource as I did. Many years later, Dennis, who wound up as an active charter captain out of Falmouth, Massachusetts, would lose a long struggle against alcohol. It was a sad time for me—and a reminder that anyone, myself included, could fall victim to the scourge of alcoholism. If he were still alive today, I am sure he would have made a significant contribution in the fight to make the striped bass a national game fish.

My first year in graduate school at the University of Buffalo introduced me to "lake effect snow," sleep deprivation, and my poor decision to continue in a specific field of endeavor (laboratory technician and daily protocol) for which I soon lost almost all interest. One bright spot on this otherwise forgettable stretch was the knowledge my trout fishing skills had been honed to near perfection. Those native trout that lived in the headwaters of the Susquehanna River, south of Buffalo, were simply overwhelmed by my skills. I left UB a cum laude graduate of wild brook trout fishing.

Graduate School

The following fall, I enrolled at Adelphi University on Long Island, where I'd work toward a master's degree in fisheries parasitology. My major professor, Richard Lacy, guided me through several intense study years, for which I will be forever grateful. These were some of the most challenging and also some of the best years of my life. To assist my studies—and help rationalize the "need" for each fishing excursion—my rod-and-reel catches provided numerous specimens for routine lab examination. During this period, I tagged and released my first fish, a largemouth bass, which I recaptured numerous times thereafter.

It was then I realized the tag-and-release event, conducted quickly and efficiently, would have little or no impact on a fish's well-being. In case you're wondering, there were no tagging programs available at the time for either fresh or saltwater recreational anglers. Fish tagging was certainly being conducted, but it was strictly by trained technicians with specific scientific interests and/or affiliations.

The spring of my second year of grad-school study took me to Florida for a few days largemouth fishing with another graduate student, Tom Burke, who routinely joined me on various ventures to ponds, lakes, and rivers on Long Island.

I was increasingly fascinated by fish behavior, and upon entering a post graduate zoology program at the University of Rhode Island, I discovered saltwater fishing for striped bass. One mentor by the name of Bob Pond introduced me to the American Littoral Society's tagging program. Pond who had developed the Atom swimmer, famous for catches of giant stripers by surf casters, also founded an organization called Stripers Unlimited. As my hunger to learn more about striped bass increased, and my fishing interests solidified into a legitimate life plan, I began tagging these game fish for the ALS. I was fascinated by their movements, so much so that I joined Chuck Meyer, a freelance photographer and writer for *Sport Fishing Magazine* on a trip to Nova Scotia. (Meyer was travelling on assignment for the Canadian Tourism and Travel Bureau.) During that trip, I was fortunate to tag and release numbers of subadult stripers in the Bay of Fundy, one of which was recaptured in Maryland's Choptank River—some nine hundred miles south and west, as the crow flies—the following spring. Research published years later by John Waldman and colleagues confirmed that the range dynamics of Hudson River schoolie striped bass extended north to the rivers of New Brunswick, Canada.

Early on, as a member of the ALS, I discovered the more I learned about striped bass movements, the more fascinated I became, and so the more I wanted to learn—a familiar cycle to anyone afflicted in earnest with *Morone saxatilis*.

Another mentor of mine was Jerry Sylvester, who, with help from his wife, Edna, ran a bait and tackle shop in Narragansett, Rhode Island. He was a highly talented surfcaster, and over many years of his generous advice, I developed considerable admiration and respect for the man. Jerry knew a great deal about striped bass behavior and impressed me from the beginning with tales about fishing with notables such as Vlad Evanoff and George Heinold, freelance and contributing editors for *Sports Afield* and *Outdoor Life*, who visited him each fall for action-packed surfcasting along the Narragansett oceanfront. The yarn—more a theory—that most intrigued me was his opinion about striper "memory." Sylvester was convinced that age classes of striped bass would return year after year to favored areas. In so doing, they would naturally return a bit bigger with each passing season to the network rocky ledges, boulders, and beaches for which Narragansett, Rhode Island, is famous.

Sylvester was convinced the stripers he caught at Frenchman's Reef off Fort Varnum (just north of the Narrow River mouth on Narragansett Bay's West Passage) returned year after year. Although these bass would be larger and stronger than the previous year, their numbers dwindled by degrees, until only a few very large fish from that school remained. I never forgot his admonitions about fishing that area, and several years later, in 1966, I boasted a sixty-one-pound striper there for my fishing companion Frank Jimmis. A year later, fishing the same spot, I caught what would become—and remain—my largest striper—a sixty-three-pounder. Who knows, several years prior that fish could have eyed one of my Atom Juniors or live eels, but for whatever reason, declined to strike.

Jerry was right about many things, several of which offered material for a number of stories published by *On the Water* and *The Fisherman* magazines. My favorite, entitled "Timing Is Everything," profiled a unique area behind the Coast Guard House along Gansett's seawall. The only way you could pull a striper out of the hole there was to cast beyond it, then retrieve a plug while the foaming water, following a breaking wave, covered it. Without the whitewater, which triggered fish into striking, most efforts would be fruitless.

Larry Tessier, a friend of Jerry's who owned a shoe store in Wickford, Rhode Island, accompanied me on numerous nighttime ventures. Since Larry could only get away during evenings, we did a lot of nighttime fishing at shoreline areas like River Rock, Frenchman's Cove, Matunuck's Deep Hole, and Carpenter's Bar, among others. Larry was with me the night I caught my first twenty-five-pound striper from what is now the Dunes Club side of the Narrow River mouth. Plug was an Atom Junior, offered on twelve-pound-test mono, on an eight-foot Hurricane spin rod sporting a Zebco Surflite 860 reel, which, incidentally, I still use today. Larry said I "hooted and hollered" so loudly after beaching the fish, you "could'a heard me a mile away."

Tagging Awards

A few years later, I became a small-boat charter skipper, specializing in striper fishing under the cover of darkness. This approach piqued the interest of several outdoor writers, among them New Jersey's Milt Rosko and George Heinold from Connecticut. Rosko profiled some of our nighttime eel fishing for jumbo stripers in his book, *Secrets of Striped Bass Fishing*.

Later, in the fall, my daytime fishing turned to school-sized bluefin tuna, which occupied much of my time on weekends. When asked to assist Frank Mather, I jumped at the chance. At the time, "Franko," as we called him, was engrossed in studying bluefin tuna biology at the Woods Hole Oceanographic Institute (WHOI) and using tagging to uncover more information about their movements and growth. One of my first reported Block Island bluefin tuna tag recaptures came from European waters, which absolutely astonished me. It was at this point in my fishing career that I decided to dedicate my efforts to learning more about several fish species.

I realize now, years later, just how fortunate I was to be involved with Mather and his research. Because of "Franko," who is now honored in the International Game Fish Association's Fishing Hall of Fame for developing a tagging program for Atlantic bluefin tuna, my tuna tagging activities resulted in my being appointed the IGFA's representative for Rhode Island. Back then, E. K. Harry, IGFA president, decided to invite me to be a representative for the simple fact I was tagging bluefin tuna, not selling them.

Bluefin tuna Tag & Release pennants

In 1995, thanks to years of help by serious charter clients and friends, I found myself being honored with the IGFA's Conservation Award for contributions to tuna science via substantial ongoing tagging efforts. Other honorees that year included George Barley (Florida everglades protector), Dr. Sylvia Earle (brilliant marine scientist), Scott Furman (environmental law advocate), Cong. Wayne T. Gilchrest (protector of coastal resources), Stanley Meltzoff (noted game fish artist), and Jack Samson (legendary editor of *Field and Stream*).

In 2003, the Rhode Island Saltwater Anglers Association (RISAA) honored me with their Marine Conservation Award for my outstanding game fish tagging achievements.

The Right Clientele

Don't for one minute think my fish-tagging success is mine alone. Most of it lies with the cultivation, beginning several decades ago, of a forward-thinking, conservation-minded clientele. An attitude that endorsed and championed the "conservation for science" ethic of tagging, which came about as a result of wide spread overfishing on several popular fish stocks by the commercial sector, has gained steam in the angling world. When the bottom fell out of the striped bass stocks in the late seventies and early eighties, following which the Atlantic States Marine Fisheries Commission (ASMFC) regulations established keeper-fish size limits slightly greater than the average size of adult spawning stripers, my clients, both new and repeat, took an active role in tagging efforts. Since the size of striped bass "keepers" was kept slightly greater than most available (to comply with federal law), many undersized fish had to be released. As a result, most of my wonderful clients adopted and supported my idea—"Why not let 'em go with a tag in 'em?"

Over the years, clients have helped create several outstanding tagging feats; namely, one in 1998, another in 2004, and again in 2006, involving the marking of a total of 15,474 game fish for science during those three seasons.

1998 TAGGING SEASON

4,649.... FISH TAGGED (15,830 Career)

3,221.....ALS Striped Bass T/R (10,238)
940...CGFTP Bluefin T/R (2,524)
302.....ALS Bluefish T/R (1,859)
96.........ALS Bluefin T/R (96)
50.....CSTP Sharks T/R (1,110)
36......CGFTP Albacore T/R
3......CGFTP Yellowfin T/R
1.....BF White Marlin T/R

Recaps.by PROWLER anglers.... (10)
ALS - 3, USFWS - 5, CSTP -1, GFTP - 1
*(8th ALS striper recap.back)

189 ... PROWLER tag recap. fish
were reported during '98 season
striped bass.........151
sharks................17
bluefish............14
tuna.................7

1998 Tagging Season

2004 TAGGING SEASON

5,157..... FISH TAGGED (36,180)

2,963 ....ALS Striped Bass T/R (25,522)
479 ......ALS Bluefish T/R (3,781)
625 .... ALS Codfish T/R (830)
4 .....ALS Haddock T/R (22)
4 ......CSTP Mako sharks T/R
17 ......CSTP Blue sharks T/R (1,345)
1,065 ....NMFS Bluefin tuna T/R (4,552)

Recaps by PROWLER anglers 13
(7 came from the PROWLER)
USFWS, 2, ALS - 7, HRF -1, BSC - 1
NMFS - 2

Fishing community reported the recap of
111 PROWLER tagged fish
striped bass.......... 87
sharks 11
bluefish 7
tuna 6

2004 Tagging Season

2006 TAGGING SEASON

5,668 ..... FISH TAGGED (46,097)

5,139..... ALS Striped bass (34,067)
390 ...... ALS Bluefish (4,507)
73....... ALS Codfish (1,323)
57 ..... ALS Haddock (65)
2 ..... CSTP Blue sharks (1,356)
6 ...... NMFS/CTC Bluefin tuna
1..... NMFS/CTC Yellowfin tuna (4,779)

Recaps by PROWLER anglers 6
6 ALS tagged stripers, two
T/R by my own hand

Fishing community reported the recap of
171 PROWLER tagged fish
striped bass 46
codfish 18
bluefish........ 5
haddock... 2

2006 Tagging Season

Unfortunately, few in the New England charter fishing industry have ever understood the advantages (immediate and longer range) to assuming their logical roles as stewards of the resource(s) on which their very livelihood depends. The conservation ethic—whether or not it involved tagging—has remained discouragingly foreign to some of the region's skippers, several of whom have so far over the years as to ridicule me not just for fish tagging, but for passing on the lucrative black market trade in undersize fish. Thanks to a few dissenters in the charter ranks, I've had to refuse to keep "short" bass with a number of parties, and as a result, lost their business. If that was their attitude—if, that is, they measure a day's fishing against its yield in dead meat (much of it destined for freezer burn and, ultimately, the landfill)—I wanted no part of it (or *them*).

I've been told that I've marked more fish for science than anyone else alive. I've authored numerous articles on fish tagging, along with several books that profiles this "conservation for science" ethic. Most importantly, I hope I've helped to generate an increased awareness of this activity in the northeast angling community. Although I've generated few followers, many have commented that if there ever is a legacy, mine might be one of not only supporting a better understanding of our fisheries resources, but fostering a greater responsibility toward those resources anglers pursue. If history bears all that out, it's a legacy I'd proudly embrace.

THE INTERNATIONAL GAME FISH ASSOCIATION

IGFA Cetified Captain Logo

MISSION

The International Game Fish Association is a not-for-profit organization committed to the conservation of game fish and the promotion of responsible, ethical angling practices through science, education, rule making, and record keeping.

BRIEF HISTORY

The IGFA was formerly launched in 1939 at a meeting hosted by the American Museum of Natural History in New York. Several months later, there were two associated scientific institutions, ten member clubs, and twelve overseas representatives. A decade later, there were ten scientific institutions, eighty member clubs, and eighty-one IGFA Representatives in forty-one areas of the world.

Today, there are approximately three hundred representatives from nearly ninety countries and territories on the international committee that help keep us apprised of fisheries issues and help influence local authorities to promote game fish conservation. These representatives are ambassadors of the IGFA—liaisons between angling interests in their area across the globe and IGFA headquarters in Florida. I think I can confidently say my respect for fisheries resources lay behind their decision to appoint me as one of their New England representatives.

IGFA representatives are asked to support the many goals and programs of the organization, with emphasis on encouraging anglers to become members and promoting the conservation goals of the organization.

IGFA Philosophy and Objectives

"IGFA's objectives are founded in the belief game fish species, related food fish, and their habitat are economic, social, recreational and aesthetic assets which must be maintained, widely used, and perpetuated; and that the sport of game fish angling is an important recreational, economic and social activity which the public must be educated to pursue in a manner consistent with sound sporting and conservation practices."

One of several major IGFA objectives is to develop and support game fish-tagging programs and other scientific data collection efforts, and to aid scientific and educational institutions, which provide vital instruction and research in ichthyology, the fisheries sciences, and related studies. It is in this realm that I've been honored to participate.

For more information, go to www.IGFA.org

2004 IGFA AFTCO Award; Most Bluefin & Yellowfin Tuna by a Capt.

SOME UNEXPECTED TAGGING RESULTS

*Life preys upon life.
This is biology's most fundamental fact.*

—Martin H. Fischer

Over the last two years, American Littoral Society (ALS) members fishing Block Island's waters participated in scheduled ALS Tagging Weekends for striped bass. In so doing, they witnessed an extraordinary increase in the number of fish lice being carried by adult island springtime stripers. During our May and June 2010 ALS Tagging Weekends, and especially during our weekend in June 2011, member-tagging efforts discovered nearly every sexually mature adult striped bass carried abundant fish lice. Several times, the cockpit deck of the boat was littered with shed ectoparasites. Those fish then traveled on to various Southern New England sounds, bays, rivers, and salt ponds; following which several fish were later recaptured by New York, Connecticut, Rhode Island, and Massachusetts anglers. It appears these fish do not readily shed all their ectoparasites, as many anglers mentioned and questioned both their occurrence and identification on their tag-recaptured stripers.

As a result of the high infestation of fish lice on tagging weekend stripers marked in 2011, this ALS member took it upon himself to track down the identification of these ectoparasites, sending collected specimens to several noted researchers.

Personal observations on the incidence of parasitic fish lice infestation on the first wave of early 2011 season Block Island stripers indicated a significant increase over several previous seasons. More than 90 percent of the initial wave of 2011 springtime stripers were tagged and released (T/R), or retained by later charter parties, were found to be moderately to heavily infested with this unknown copepod.

IDENTIFICATION

In an attempt to identify this parasitic copepod, vials containing the unknown specimens, placed in isopropyl alcohol, were sent to several researchers for identification. Unfortunately, species identification could not be easily made at that time, so I took the liberty to send additional specimens to Dr. William Poly, a noted Copepoda expert for identification. On August 21, 2011, here's what Bill Poly had to say in his latest e-mail:

> I've identified the parasitic copepods as *Caligus elongatus* (Caligidae), using both light and electron microscopy, which has been reported from captive reared striped bass by Hogans (1994) and quite a few other fish species in the Atlantic. Not sure they've been found on wild striper though. Additional literature will be consulted to double-check the ID and look for more host records for *C. elongatus*. Perhaps you will find some additional information too. Can you send the collection data for these specimens so a good label can be included in the vial? Locality
>
> (incl. county, state, and GPS coordinates, if available), date, collector(s), collection method (for host), and any other notes
>
> (e. g., depth) would be great.
>
> Thanks,
>
> Bill

Tag Recap'd. Bass With Fish Lice

Following my e-mail report of the host species collection data to Bill Poly, I was informed they had never been reported in the scientific literature on wild striped bass (*Morone saxatilis*). Surprised and intrigued by this statement, further research disclosed this fish lice species has been misidentified by other researchers on nine different occasions, beginning in 1840 (Kabata, 1979). The length (time) of its synonymy, accrued during more than a century of research publications, reflects also the ubiquity of *C. elongatus* and the extraordinary range of its known hosts. Under its incorrect name, *C. elongatus* has been recorded from most regions of the world's oceans. Its host list includes more than eight species of fish, both teleosts (bony fish) and elasmobranches (sharks), representing seventeen orders and forty-three families (Kabata, 1979).

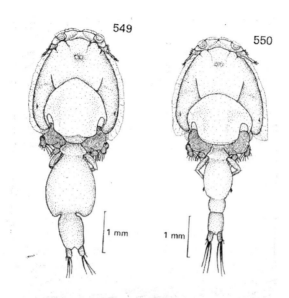

Caligus elongatus **Nordmann, 1832**

Fig. 549. Female, dorsal

Fig. 550. Male, dorsal

In an attempt to learn how and why so many early season fish, which we assumed became infected while overwintering in waters from New Jersey to North Carolina, it became necessary to review the life cycle of this ectoparasite. One conundrum faced was the fact closely related fish lice species succumb once their hosts enter freshwater to spawn. Either infestation occurred after spawning or those adult infested fish never spawned. There is evidence to support the latter statement, based on the female striped bass that were filleted for other early season parties.

STRIPER FISH LICE

Research indicates that striped bass have been reported to be the host of forty-five disease-causing ecto— and endoparasites. "The total number of copepod species parasitic on both freshwater and marine fish was recently estimated between 1600-1800 in number, of which about 90% are marine" (Kabata, 1979). Most mobile parasitic copepods cause minor or transient damage to gills or skin, unless they are present in overwhelming numbers.

Striper caudal area with fish lice

BIOLOGY of *Caligus elongatus* Nordmann 1832

At present, it appears the most numerous species of sea lice on striped bass is *Caligus elongatus*, belonging to the family Caligidae in North Atlantic waters, which, incidentally has become somewhat economically important to salmon farming (Boxaspen, 2006). The primary species infecting salmon is another Caligid called *Lepeophtheirus salmonis*, and has received considerable attention.

Sea lice can affect the growth, fecundity, and survival of their hosts because their feeding may cause skin lesions leading to osmotic problems and secondary infections, which can lead to mortality at sea. Sea lice have a relatively simple life cycle with *Caligus elongatus* having eight stages (Kabata, 1979). Gravid sea lice females produce a series of egg strings, and following hatching of the egg, the larval stages disperse immediately into the water and are planktonic drifting with the current.

Caligus elongatus normally infects its hosts at the copepodid stage. These lice subsequently develop in molts through four sessile (chalimus) stages that are anchored to the host skin before attaining adulthood, following which they can move freely around on the host surfaces (Piasecki, 1996). The adults are good swimmers, and although usually attached to their hosts by a long, thin feeding tube (hence the species name), they may also occur in the plankton. Free-swimming adults have been sampled from planktonic trawls (Boxshall, 1974) Wootten, Smith, and Needham, 1982).

Adult lice can readily change hosts, which imply hosts can be infected independently by both copepodids and adults. These freely swimming adults suggest a highly mobile parasite can survive without a host for long periods of time. This author noted dozens of these lice on the cockpit deck of the boat following capture of the fish, indicating successful escape from their host.

Caligus elongatus is less host-specific and has been reported on a variety of benthic and pelagic species of North Atlantic marine fish (Kabata, 1979). It is possibly the most common parasitic copepod on fish in the North Atlantic (Jackson, Deady, et. al, 2000). Due to its generalistic nature, *C. elongatus* might be such a good swimmer and have such a good chance of finding hosts in nature, that being unattached is relatively less of an advantage for this parasite compared with other parasitic copepods with narrower host ranges, such as the salmon louse (Kabata, 1979).

This discovery is believed to be the first time *Caligus elongatus* has been reported in the literature from wild, early season migrating striped bass (*Morone saxatilis*), caught, tagged, and then released back into Block Island, Rhode Island waters.

GENETIC RESEARCH

Early in the fall of 2011, I e-mailed Prof. Ted Durbin at the University of Rhode Island's (URI) Graduate School of Oceanography (GSO) and inquired if he would be kind enough to photograph several specimens of sea lice identified by Dr. William Poly. His associate Maria Casas, then assisted with several photos. In a later discussion, he inquired if he could sample the specimen's mitochondrial cytochrome C oxidase genotype and compare it to others. I agreed, and here's what he had to say in his latest e-mail:

Hi Al,

> We have sequenced the mitochondrial CO 1 gene. This gene shows considerable variability between species and has been used for the Bar Code of Life study and the Census of Marine Life study. There are some sequences of this gene for *C. elongatus* already on GenBank (a database of sequences of different DNA sequences submitted by scientists from around the world) submitted by a Norwegian, and attached is a link to his paper. The sequence of the *Caligus* you gave us is almost identical (only one base-pair difference out of 641 bp sequence we determined) to the genotype frequencies of *C. elongatus* on wild and coastal hosts, which varied significantly between spring and autumn. Lice from these fish show a large proportion of genotype 1 lice in March-June every year (Oines & Heuch 2007). This strongly suggests infestation commenced during the spring migration of striped bass from Mid-Atlantic waters to southern New England.

Ted went on to say . . .

> I am not sure where you want to take this but we could submit the sequence we obtained to GenBank with the three of our names on the submission. For this we would need details as to time and location of collection, and the species it was collected from. We could talk further once you have had a chance to digest the paper. You may wish to include it in your book.

SEASONALITY

Recent research offers the possibility recent infestations of *Caligus elongatus* are survivors from the previous year, or that in the absence of survival, it would be reasonable to assume migrating hosts become infected in late season at sea. Since other migratory fish such as herring inhabit much the same areas during the winter months, it is possible such hosts sustain the life cycle of this fish lice species.

Research conducted by Durbin strongly suggests (confirms) those Block Island bass were actively infested with genotype 1 fish lice during their spring migration. Furthermore, oceanic conditions of high salinity and low temperature enhance the chance for longevity of the adult female stage (Oines and Heuch, 2007), it is possible that the female can overwinter on a host in the open-ocean and return to coastal areas when the fish return to spawn. Chalmii of the related Caligid copepod *Lepoephtheirus salmonis* have also been recorded on Atlantic salmon from the open sea (Jacobsen and Gaard, 1997) so they may overwinter on the host at this stage. Currently, little is known about the reservoirs and routes of infection underlying the sudden spring-time increase in *Caligus elongatus* on coastal migrating striped bass.

Since all ALS Weekend caught striped bass were quickly T/R, it was impossible to discern if spawning had occurred. It is possible these migrating fish succumbed to infestation while en route to Block Island waters. However, initial observations indicated none of the filleted fish of later charter's that were examined demonstrated any obvious post-spawning conditions. Not until extensive fieldwork discloses other wintertime open-ocean hosts of *C. elongatus* will this picture become clearer.

A METAMORPHOSIS

A man and his boat do not need to be justified!

—Unknown

My charter fishing career at the island began over four decades ago from an outboard-powered nineteen-foot Aquasport, then progressed to a twenty-five-foot open bass boat, then to an enclosed thirty-five-foot center console vessel, and is finishing up with my present vessel, a forty-two-foot twin-Cummins diesel-powered North Carolina express-style Carolina sport fisherman—again configured as a center console enclosed with a tower. At present, I also own a Honda powered seventeen-foot Boston Whaler, now used for near-shore and overwinter striper fishing, but more about that shortly.

Prior to that, I started my Rhode Island saltwater fishing from a leaky fourteen-foot plywood Bristol skiff, then moved on to a sixteen-foot aluminum Starcraft, before jumping into the Aquasport.

Although my striper tagging began in the late 1960s, there were days only few bass were marked, for several reasons, either from my Bristol, Starcraft, or Bonito. It wasn't until the striper moratorium while fishing my thirty-five-foot Legnos that my serious striper tagging began. That resulted from an attitude transition about a resource that we collectively created. Instead of take, take, take, I decided it was time to start giving something back—by tagging.

Bristol Skiff Days

Early in my nighttime saltwater fishing ventures to catch sizeable stripers, I purchased a used fourteen-foot plywood Bristol skiff along with an eighteen-horse Evinrude outboard from Point Jude Boats, owned and operated by Paul Fitzgerald, back in 1965; I berthed it at Middlebridge on the Narrow River in Narragansett, Rhode Island. At the time, I was a new member of the Scituate Saltwater Anglers, which was competing in the annual R. J. Schaefer (beer) Saltwater Fishing Contest (club division). Our club became state champs three years in a row, thanks to the talents of a number of veteran anglers. Because of the limitations of my boat and equipment, I concentrated on drifting live eels at night with one of several club members, in and around the boulders and ledges of Fort Varnun, located on the western shore of Narragansett Bay's west passage—and not far from my Narrow River berth.

Cheating Death

To get to our stripers, we had but a short run from Middle Bridge to the mouth of Narrow River in Narragansett. At the time, the river had no lighted channel markers—only sticks with white plastic Clorox bottles inverted over their open ends. And the "channel" itself, a winding lane clear of the ubiquitous snarl-the-prop-and-stall-the-engine eelgrass, was no bargain, either. In it, depths ranged from two to four feet.

The rivermouth—then, just as now—was shallow. On an ebbing moon tide, the current was easily four knots in narrow channels, there was no breakwater on the windward side, and the sandbar guarding it shifted continuously amid wind and wave action. At the bottom of an ebbing tide, a phalanx of breakers stood between the river channel and the open water adjacent to Cormorant Rock.

I usually made it a point to navigate seaward before dark, when I could more clearly see what I was up against and maneuver accordingly. Suffice it to say I made more than one decision to turn around well short of the river mouth, so as not to tempt fate.

It was after dark, coming home—usually in a boat laden with oversized stripers whose total weight further increased risk of running hard aground—that the channel became downright hairy—particularly in my plywood skiff, which leaked like a sieve; the fact that the eighteen-horse outboard that powered it missed badly at full throttle did little for my sense of well-being. Fortunately, running the river mouth was at least *conceptually simple*—time the sequence of advancing breakers and whitewater to keep waves under or otherwise *outside*—as opposed to *in*—my skiff.

Nights when a flood tide and current aligned, running into the river, passage was usually easy enough. But on ebbing moon tides, a sea running out front, I knew better than to chance it, and waited out a tide change—daylight, even—tied to the bulkhead a short jog to the south'ard at Monahan's Dock.

Frank's Sixty-One

One of my fishing partners back then was Frank Jimmis, a tough, slightly built, excitable chap from Providence. His goal was to catch a sixty—to seventy-pound striper, and since I had a boat, he knew his chances would be better with me than fishing from the shore. We spent a great deal of time working the ledges and coves in front of Fort Varnum, a WWII installation just north of Narrow River. Varnum was (is) a boulder strewn, whitewater ledge area with deep-water channels that harbored numerous heavyweight fish, mostly between dusk and dawn. Here, Frank and I would cast and retrieve or drift live eels from my skiff—methods dictated by conditions. Usually. You know the story. We were young and took unbelievable chances.

61 lb Striper; Frank Jimmis, Capt. AL, 14' Bristol

Potential Disaster

As it was, every fifteen or twenty minutes, I had to start the engine, put it in gear, speed the boat up while pulling the transom plug to drain the rising bilgewater. One night in Varnum Cove, following this ritual, Frank hooked a fish that towed us around for a good while. We both knew it was a good one, and he fought it carefully, keenly aware of the mere twenty-pound mono tethering us to the fish; as the fight wore on, he became more and more excited. The boat continued to fill with water. I told Frank he'd better boat his fish before we sank beneath the waves. To buy time, I began bailing the boat by hand with a plastic jug, but made little or no headway.

Frank finally brought the fish boat-side, and I put my battery-powered neck light on it, finally seeing what he was hooked to. Frank immediately became hysterical. I managed to neatly gaff and lift it aboard, while our near empty six-gallon fuel tank, my tackle box, and other sundry items sloshed around in a badly wallowing boat. Had I not immediately started the engine and put it in gear, we would have sunk in that cove—not a nice thought, for sure!

On the scales, Frank's fish weighed a tad over sixty-one pounds—our largest so far that summer. Several nights later, I pulled one of fifty-three pounds out of the same spot, and several other fish that size were caught by other club members just a stone's throw away, before that summer ended.

Many of those members shook their heads at my after-dark boating nerve and ability, especially when it meant traversing the mouth of Narrow River at night under foggy, rough, ebb-tide conditions. I knowingly cheated death there numerous times, avoiding those breaking-wave conditions that could quickly broach an underpowered, mishandled skiff. Although that skiff leaked badly, there was no need for a bilge alarm; when either my six-gallon fuel tank or the dead bass underfoot started to float, that was the signal to pull the transom drain plug. That, maneuver in turn signaled the end of a drift. I'd start the engine and accelerate, letting quantities of bilge water to drain out astern.

It didn't take long for my after-dark striper ventures to produce contest-sized fish. Following weighing and measuring, those in the high teens and up went to the Fisherman's Co-op in Galilee, Rhode Island, the next morning. Best fish that season was Frank Jimmis's aforementioned sixty-one-pounder, taken on a live eel. The following season, I bested a sixty-three-pound jumbo striper from the same spot that had surrendered Frank's fish.

Man of Tin

Fast-forward to my second vessel, a sixteen-foot aluminum Starcraft Mariner model, sporting a thirty-three-horse Evinrude outboard—a rig I spent even more time in after-dark. After the first season, that Starcraft went back to the factory for repair, as it had developed numerous leaky rivet joints. That year and the year after, I also spent some weekday time as a mate aboard the party boat *Gail Frances,* skippered in those years by Capt. Ken Putnam, and also worked part-time for George Browning, aboard his *Swordfish II,* a day dragger out of Point Judith. Armed with ample sea time, I studied for and passed the USCG skippers license test in Providence, Rhode Island. All the while, I was a graduate student in URI's Zoology Department.

Milt Rosko, a noted outdoors writer from New Jersey, after learning about my success, came to Rhode Island to fish with me after dark for sizeable stripers using live eels. Later, he was kind enough to include my nighttime striper fishing in his book, *Fishing From Boats.* The following summer, Al Reinfelder and companion Lou Palma (Alou Eel fame) joined me in a number of successful nighttime Narrow River ventures, casting to stripers holding in the street-light shadows under Narragansett's Sprague Bridge. I too had previously fished under Long Island's Wantaugh and Meadowbrook Bridges after dark, but caught only schoolie-sized bass. I was amazed at the number and size of the fish we caught, and shortly thereafter received an autographed copy of Al's book, *Bait Tail Fishing.* This lead-head soft-plastic-tail lure was the forerunner of today's ubiquitous plastic tailed jigs.

16 ft. Starcraft, behind Aunt Carries, Narra.
(*Milt Rosko* photo)

Enter the Nineteen-Foot Aquasport

The following summer of 1967, armed with my USCG charter license, I purchased a nineteen-foot Aquasport sporting a one-hundred-horse Mercury outboard, following which my nighttime charter fishing Rhode Island waters hit stride. It seems I'd developed a unique niche fishing for the heavyweight stripers which no other local skipper cared to pursue. (Galilee was, in those years, strictly a meat-fishing town, and cod was the name of the game.) Over the next few seasons, the number of fifty-plus-pound stripers slid into my cockpit rose to near double-digit numbers. That sixty-three-pound striper, taken off the Anawan Cliffs area in northern Narragansett, is still my best. Every one of those monsters succumbed to live eels.

Night fishing the area known as Scarborough Beach, League and Little League Rock, and behind Aunt Carries in Narragansett, I quickly learned that spinner-and-worm rigs caught more than just "schoolies." Slow-trolling live eels in those same areas were another go-to method of the time, and although we caught numbers of impressive stripers, I felt jinxed: I suddenly could not find a fish over fifty. The following year, I fished a few daytime ventures, then some night trips, to Block Island.

I became involved with my first tournament as a director, thanks to Bill Mancini, of the Narragansett Beer *Hi-Neighbor* Point Judith Bass and Bluefish Tournament, held in Galilee over the V-J Day weekend in August. Among many other duties, I was tasked with, just prior to the event, tagging ten striped bass; if recaptured during the tournament, these fish would earn a lucky angler $100. I even managed to persuade Bob Pond to assist in the endeavor. We figured (correctly) that school-size fish were probably safe from tourney-time recapture, since large-for-their-size bass were the event's primary targets.

Pt. Judith Bass & Blue Tournament

Photo by STAFF CARROLL

PJB&B Tourney

By the event's fourth year (1970), the prize for catching the first tagged striped bass or bluefish had risen to $1,000. The following summer the Narragansett Brewery decided to end its sponsorship of the tournament, and that brought the event to a close.

One Record-Breaking Night

Other members of my club (the Scituate Saltwater Anglers), among them Slim Borsay and Jim Paterson, fished every summertime as weather allowed, held a number of internal records. King of them all was a sixty-eight-pound bass taken by Wilfred Fountain from Green Hill Beach in South Kingstown, Rhode Island. To set the record straight, Wilfred spent many late night hours in his own boat, but only when weather allowed. If the weather was poor, he didn't risk it, such as the time I met up with Wilfred on a "wicked-lousy" nor'east night on River Rock in Narragansett. Conditions were "stinko," so we decided to get out of the wind and fish the remaining dropping tide at the "Hill" (Green Hill Beach). Soon after arriving he had a sizeable fish on, hooked only yards from his feet in the wash of a building surf. According to Wilfred, that fish spun his reel spool, loaded with twenty-pound-test Ashaway mono, down to the knot three times, but he eventually beached it yards away to the west about thirty-five minutes later. Wilfred was intent on weighing the fish as soon as possible, and although I had an open box carrier on the roof of my battered Chevy sedan, we thought it best he place it in his car trunk. Late at night, Hap Cane's Top of the Dock Bait and Tackle shop was closed, as were other local shops. Suspecting this, I went home, as did Wilfred. The next morning, he called Rose Tatorie, and she persuaded Staff Carroll, the *Providence Journal Bulletin Newspaper* photojournalist, to come down to Narragansett and take a photo of him with his fish.

Prior to this time, Jack Ryan's (1963) surf-caught sixty-seven-pounder taken at Sandy Point (aka North Bar), held the record, but Wilfred's fish surpassed this Block Island fish by a pound. Wally Brown, in Massachusetts, mounted Wilfred's bass; it now adorns the store-front wall at Snug Harbor Marina. It wasn't until the fall (November) of 1988 that Joe Szabo's 70.5-pound Block Island striper (boat) unseated Fountaine's fish.

Getting back to the Aquasport, early on I realized I had more than a few disadvantages: lack of LORAN, loss of visual ranges once darkness settled in, with island lights a second-rate backup. My fishfinder and compass were a bonus, but limited fish storage; secondary tools like neck-lights, rags for handling eels, gaffs, and a current *Eldridge's*, were occasionally left behind. Later that summer, I purchased a Chevy pickup truck. That problem diminished but didn't disappear.

One late August night in particular, over at the island, the wind came up out of the southeast and intensified, and the North Rip ebbing tide started building; we stubbornly stayed much longer than we should have. The ride back to Point Judith was not only hideous, it was also downright slow and ugly, and only because we could quarter the wind, building waves and driving rain, was it possible. I had to pull the deck drain plug and leave it open, as spray, green water, and rain keep the deck ankle-deep in water. Soaked to the skin and cold, it was a night I have never forgotten—for just a couple of fish. We chased the shivering cold away with a stop at Milt's Dockside Bar and Grille before heading back to Kenport Marina.

19 ft. Aquasport, Lou Fusco & bass

Twenty-six-Foot Bonito Open Bass Boat

Three years later, in 1970, I purchased one of the first of Dick Lema's twenty-six-foot Bonito bass boats, an I-O Mercruiser-powered, forward-casting-platform model. This boat cleared most of my hesitation about fishing island waters at night, which unfortunately I'd only wanted to do under ideal conditions with the Aquasport. I spent eleven seasons in the Bonito, clocking thousands of hours, replacing five V-8 Mercruiser gas engines along with several I-O lower units, all the while employed as a teacher at Westerly High School, Rhode Island.

My early to midseventies island night fishing was good for two reasons: loads of heavyweight bass and almost no competition. Night after night—typically, on moon tides—I'd be the only boat fishing either the North Rip or the Southwest Ledge area. Casting large swimming plugs into the whitewater "suds" of current-swept shoals, trolling multihook plugs deep in turbulent rips, live-lining eels on time-and-again drifts, contributed to many outstanding catches. Only few photos by the late Staff Carroll documented our catches of large stripers. To this day, several of these shots still decorate the walls of our Legal Seafood Restaurant in Warwick, Rhode Island.

Bonito Bass Boat

Living only minutes away from the marina, come dawn I'd leave my pickup truck and its fish at home in the driveway (my wife would later drop them off the Fisherman's Co-op). After a quick shower and breakfast, I'd head off to the classroom in her vehicle. It's safe to say I put in a lot of time, learning things other skippers never would, and experienced some of the best striper fishing New England had to offer. About this time several unsuspected events occurred; I began receiving calls from Tim Coleman, editor of *The Fisherman* magazine, New England edition, wanting information about my island fishing for publication, and my wife began hearing comments while in our supermarket about some unknown gal who was daily dropping off jumbo-sized stripers at the co-op. I even had to put up with Harold Thornton, then-owner of Snug Harbor Marina, who would daily inspect my bass boat for fish scales, so he could pass along estimates of our prior night's fishing success. On several occasions, he showed me scales of forty—and fifty-pound bass I'd missed at cleanup—evidence of my routine exhaustion. Most parties collected a pre-arranged weight of fish and quickly departed, leaving me to the time-consuming cleanup and disposal of all evidence—including fish scales. At the time, I didn't want any publicity about our success, for fear it would impact my business. Only a few photographs exist of our success, and any mention of it was out of the question. That ploy was somewhat successful, for few in my industry knew anything about our Block Island exploits. What mattered were clients who quietly passed information along to friends!

At the time, during the months of June '74 and again in June '75, my log noted we boated a total of sixteen striped bass estimated to be in the fifty-pound class (fifty-three inches or greater, total length), over eight hundred bass in the forty-pound class, and I never bothered to count hundreds of lesser-sized fish. Truth be known, much of it was due to Texas Instruments, maker of a compact-sized LORAN-C receiver that was undercover, but readily visible (but not easily accessible) in the center console. Night after night, whether clear or foggy, I used that equipment to put me right back into my heavyweight drifts. Whether trolling large plugs or drifting eels for nighttime stripers, or gently jigging squid-strips for fluke, or trolling lures offshore for tuna or bonito, that TI LORAN receiver was key to success. Relatively new to that game, the biggest mistake I made was not recording all offshore LORAN number's down, so as to mark action-spot locations, which were later recorded in my log.

Not that I wasn't familiar with LORAN; earlier in the sixties I had the opportunity to occasionally mate for Bob Linton aboard his *Mako II* when cod fishing. Among other things, I was in charge of his LORAN-A receiver, taken from a WWII B-17 bomber. Back then, LORAN-A signals could put you precisely over the target, give or take a nautical mile. Despite fog, it was his fathometer that helped locate the fish that created his success. I remember him frequently stating, "There's so many codfish they'll never be fished out." He wasn't wrong about many things, but that was certainly one of them.

Back then, I used a pencil and notebook-sized piece of white Formica, for fear of writing them on the console (where anyone who came aboard could read them). There were times when I paid dearly for that mistake. I do the same today, but also include fuel-trip gallons used, as I don't trust fuel-tank gauges.

I ran that Bonito single-handed for nearly a decade using LORAN (GPS was not available—no satellites), which carried over to my next boat, but more about that shortly . . .

When I think back on the after-dark success I could have had with earlier boats, were today's equipment available, I could have done even more serious damage to our striper resource. Not too much later, regretting my shameful waste of what was becoming a drastically diminished resource, my conscience forced me to take up a new challenge: marking (tagging) more striped bass for science. At the time, I knew tagging was a good way to produce valid resource information and was confident it could be used to create better management decisions. Little did I realize politics would soon cloud those ethical horizons.

Since the late 1960s and up through today, I've tagged loads of school and giant bluefin tuna, starting with Frank Mather's bluefin tuna research at Woods Hole Oceanographic Institute (WHOI), now under the auspices of the NMFS Cooperative Tagging Center in Miami. A few years later I began tagging sharks for Jack Casey's Apex Predator Shark Tagging Program, now also under NMFS. The number marked presently hovers around 5,500 tuna, sharks, and billfish.

Thirty-five-Foot Legnos Single Diesel

In 1981, I launched a new thirty-five-foot boat and decided to retire from my vocation (teaching) to pursue my avocation (charter fishing). With over twenty years in the classroom and conducting research at both college and high school levels, I set out to develop my charter business to a point I felt I could cover all our bills. For all the financial uncertainty during my transition, thirty-two years later, I can safely say charter fishing was one of the best decisions I've ever made. My move into full-time chartering overlapped with the early years of the "striper moratorium," when minimum striper size limits were mandated. This allowed sexually mature stripers at least one chance to spawn, while offering opportunity for tagging any "short" fish that didn't measure up. It was during this period—with some encouragement from my wife—that I began keeping track of fish tagged, authoring articles for several fishing magazines, and slowly developing what few photographic skills I possessed.

35ft. Legnos

The key to my nineteen-year success with this next boat, built by Peter Legnos in Groton, Connecticut, was heeding some advice about diesel power. Unlike outboards that can be idled down with small propellers, offering slow trolling speeds that stripers liked, diesels spun large propellers that typically resulted in excessive speed, and diminished catch success. For that reason, at the time of construction, thanks to Barry Gallup, I chose a two-cycle 6-71 Detroit Diesel coupled to a Twin Disk Reverse gear with a troll valve. This valve could be controlled from the helm, allowing me to slow-troll more effectively by reducing prop-shaft speed, while watching my fishfinder. Unlike my competition, that had to take their engine in and out of gear to reduce speed or put their boat into a turn, I could easily slow-troll for cod, pollock, stripers, and tuna successfully.

Time and again, when marking a school of stripers beneath the boat, all I had to do was decrease boat speed, allowing our lures to probe deeper, passing through the fish, ensuring multiple hookups.

Outdoor writers like George Heinhold, Al Ristori, Chuck Meyer, Milt Rosko, Vlad Evanoff, and others, who authored stories for *Outdoor Life, Field and Stream, Sports Afield, Saltwater Sportsman, Sport Fishing,* and *The Fisherman,* among others, profiling my striper exploits, greatly enhancing my reputation.

Stemming into a rip on an after-dark foggy tide with two or three undulating swimming plugs close astern was something a hungry bucket-mouthed striper holding station couldn't resist. Knowing when and where tidal rips started to makeup were keys to my trolling success, so I developed a systematic plan of attack rooted in tidal-flow schedules—and on the weather conditions, of course.

Once rip-surface waters began to boil or "heavy" whitewater erupted, it was time to leave one rip and move to another, based on tidal-current timing. Stripers obey laws of nature; they will quickly leave a rip if they have to expend more energy than they can acquire. To be honest, I learned that move and others early in my career after watching several Montauk skippers—some of the best there ever were. During this period, few Rhode Island skippers fished the North Rip or Southwest Ledge for stripers. Most were targeting then-abundant codfish. If I was to learn the finer points of striper fishing, I'd have to fish Montauk waters. If it weren't for skippers like Wrathbun (Connecticut), Potts (New York), Malinson (New York), Holzman (New York), Herlehy (New York), Kohlus (New York), Etzel (New York), and others I could emulate, I would only be a mediocre skipper.

There were countless nights when pea-soup fog prevented us from seeing either the island, it's lights, traffic (tugs and tows), or an occasional skiff—only the rip's unique flow patterns, from the time we left in the late afternoon until we returned to the dock early the next morning.

My thirty-five Legnos was set up as a center console version, with an enclosed marlin tower for protection. I ran that vessel single-handed on many trips for the first eight seasons. Following neurosurgery for removal of a benign brain tumor, one that was causing memory loss, my wife firmly put her foot down (on the side of my neck), demanding that I conduct future trips with an occasional mate. I was, after all, approaching fifty-one years of age.

I installed two different models of 6-71 Detroit diesels in that boat; the first was rated at 260 horse power, with eighty millimeter injectors, and made an easy thirteen-knot cruise. The second Detroit was installed in 1997, a 6-71 TIB, rated at 420 horse power, which I ran for four more years before I sold it. Yes, the reverse gear and troll valve were replaced with newer models. Following some winter-time hull modifications, cruising speed jumped from thirteen to seventeen knots, and top-end increased from nineteen to twenty-two knots—same rpms—due in part to an additional two inches of pitch into the four-bladed prop. Reason for the performance increase was to take advantage of our rapidly developing offshore school bluefin tuna fishing, usually requiring some distant traveling.

Forty-two-foot North Carolina Express Sportfisherman

In the late 1990s, our economy was roaring and I visited several North Carolina boat shops regarding possible construction of a forty-two-foot hull for charter. The reason for change was my wintertime giant bluefin tuna fishing off Cape Hatteras—in weather that would keep me at the dock here in Rhode Island. I simply couldn't believe how well these Carolina hulls performed under adverse conditions. I vowed I'd own one before I met our Lord and Savior.

PROWLER; Bow-on - coming in the gap at Pt. Judith, RI

I quickly discovered that what I wanted was not only cost-prohibitive, but required at least a two——or three-year waiting time, so I hired a boat broker to "beat the bushes" in search of a bare North Carolina hull I could finish off myself (with a bit of help, of course). Fourteen months later, I had a forty-two-foot

ISLAND STRIPERS

North Carolina Express style sportfisherman, with marlin tower, powered by twin 450 horse power Cummins, carrying four hundred gallons of fuel, and with an easy twenty-knot cruise speed. And of course, both Twin Disc reverse gears were fitted with troll valves, since in-gear-at-idle speed was nearly four knots. Presently, with nearly ten thousand hours of operating time on engines, gears and valves, it's been the best-performing sea boat I've ever owned. I should mention that I invested three thousand hours of my own labor into it. This made my wife happy: She hardly saw me for those fourteen months.

In the end, my fishing career and the boats that made it possible underwent a transformation. What started as a primal need to see how many sizeable bass I could catch, progressed to one in which a few were tagged and released, followed by my present day effort (involving three vessels) to mark as many as possible. Following the moratorium, my conservation ethic through striper tagging grew, reflected in part by my involvement with the IGFA. What I grossly underestimated was the tremendous clientele support that ethic generated.

The progression of boats mirrored my desire to learn from others fishing nearby striper waters, as well as other fish such as white marlin and bluefin tuna.

There are many who understand my love and respect for Block Island and its waters, and although its fisheries resources have diminished, my infatuation with the place and its fish has held strong. I hope your experiences on her waters send you home with the satisfaction they've given me. Fair winds, and good luck in all the fishing you do.

Stripers Forever

Stripers Forever, a nonprofit, Internet-based conservation organization, seeks game fish status for wild striped bass on the Atlantic Coast in order to significantly reduce striper mortality, to provide optimum and sustainable public fishing opportunities for anglers from Maine to North Carolina, and to secure the greatest socio-economic value possible from the fishery.

Under this conservative management approach, the commercial harvest and sale of wild striped bass would be strictly prohibited everywhere on the Atlantic Coast. To further reduce striper mortality, the coastal recreational harvest would be carefully regulated to protect the population of large breeder fish and to promote and enforce the use of angling gear and techniques that do not unnecessarily damage stripers that are caught and then released.

The allowable catch of wild striped bass should always be subordinated to conservation measures necessary to maintain a healthy population. To achieve these conservation and policy goals, Stripers Forever will pursue the following specific management goals:

— The adoption of statutes or regulations that will end the commercial taking of striped bass everywhere on the eastern seaboard.
— Improve natural age and size distribution to reflect an unfished striper population as closely as possible.
— Further define and overcome the impact of *Mycobacteriosis* on stripers and humans, as part of the fisheries management process.
— End the overharvesting of striped bass forage species and protect the essential ecosystem for striper survival.
— Reduce the by-catch mortality of striped bass occurring in commercial fisheries directed at other species.

SF History

Brad Burns, president of Stripers Forever, was kind enough to supply the following historical perspective on the group's initial formation and future ambitions:

Brad Burns

"I began fly fishing seriously in 1985 or so," he begins, "and in 1995 I wrote the L. L. Bean *Fly Fishing for Striped Bass* book. For many years until his death in 2003, John Cole, whose book *Striper*, helped save striped bass from their crash of the 1970's. John was my close friend and very frequent fishing companion. Together we helped end commercial fishing for striped bass in Maine, and encouraged the State of Maine to reintroduce striped bass into the Kennebec River, and then raised funds to help with that effort. I was one of the founders in New England of the Coastal Conservation Association (CCA) and it's the State Chairman in Maine, both on the board in Massachusetts, and the National Executive Committee. The late Walter Fondren, Chairman of CCA National, became a friend, and we fished with each other a number of times in Maine for stripers and in Texas for redfish.

"For whatever reasons the very successful CCA model had a hard time making it in the North East. In early 2003 a number of us, including Rip Cunningham of Saltwater Sportsman, Captain Dave Preble and author, Duncan Barnes, past editor of Field and Stream Magazine, David Ross, PhD of Wood's Hole Oceanographic Institute, (WHOI) and Ed Mitchell, fly fishing expert and author, along with several other dedicated individuals, decided to form Stripers Forever. Rip came up with that name. Our thinking was, and still is, that conventional fishery management values would eventually drag the fabulous striped bass fishery that we were experiencing, back down to the low ebb of virtually every other fish population that is managed with commercial fishing as its focus. It is clear now that our fears were well founded. We felt that only by making striped bass a game fish and taking the price off its head, would stripers be managed to sustain a high quality recreational fishery that everyone knew. One that created more jobs and financial activity than the relatively small commercial fishery that stripers could support. Many of us who had been involved with the CCA had seen the success of game fish management in Texas on reds and specs, and in FL on a number of species. We believed and still believe that if we managed striped bass in this way it would provide the greatest value to the greatest number of people.

"We also recognized that building a national organization in the conventional manner of chapters, dinners, monthly meetings etc. would require a lot of time, money, and dedicated volunteers. We felt that the conservation arena was already filled with groups vying for members and funds. In 2001 or so commercial interests in RI had tried to get extra striped bass quota by putting a closed season on recreational anglers during April and May. Even though these were relatively early days in the Internet-world, we were able generate more than enough political pressure to get this stopped. The local, feet-on-the-ground recreational advocates had already given up. The president of one organization told me that the commercials were just too strong, and if we didn't give them this quota then they would take even more. I told him that we couldn't accept that and preferred to go down swinging. We generated tons of letters to the governor—who turned out to agree with us—and so much attendance at the public hearing that the commercials in attendance were simply overwhelmed by the recreational presence. We had only a few days notice to get this done, and the Internet was the only way to do it. Our success was so complete that the Internet-based concept became the model for Stripers Forever.

"My greatest disappointment so far at SF is how difficult it has been to get many in the recreational angling community to see the wisdom and inherent fairness in the concept of making striped bass a game fish. Yes, we have signed up over 20,000 people in SF, but in reality it's only a drop in the bucket. There are many recreational anglers who simply don't recognize that the problems with commercial fishing for striped bass go well beyond the amount of the catch, though the commercial catch including legal, illegal, and by-catch, is large and not to be ignored. The greatest effect is the one that commercial fishing has on the management plan. One of the best examples that exist is the Atlantic States Marine Fisheries Council (ASMFC) vote that took place in November 2011. After a number of years of poor spawning success and continued heavy fishing pressure, it was apparent that the bloom was off the rose with striped bass. Some of the concerned State Fishery directors wanted to reduce fishing mortality for the 2012 season. This vote was rejected on a nearly commercial-versus-non-commercial States party-line vote. The biggest exception was New Jersey, a staunch recreational fishing state that voted against the quota reduction because they felt the recreational community would not be treated fairly in the catch reductions. If striped bass were a game fish, I am firmly convinced that, first, we would never have made the increases in fishing mortality that have contributed to the turn down in the striped bass population, and second, if the number of small fish in the population had declined as it has in recent years, we would already have made great adjustments in the management plan. This tendency to do nothing, or at best too little too late, is symptomatic of why so many of our ocean fisheries exist in a constantly depressed state. The most important, recreational saltwater species in North America should not suffer this same fate."

GLOSSARY

Amphidromous: Migration of fishes from fresh to salt water or from salt to fresh water at some stage of the life cycle for purposes other than breeding.

Anadromous: Animals that migrate from the sea to freshwater to spawn; salmon and striped bass are examples.

Appalachian Mountains: A mountain system of eastern North America, that extends about 2574 km (1600 mi) southwest from Newfoundland to central Alabama.

Apogee: The point in the orbit of the moon or of an artificial satellite most distant from the earth.

Archean: The geologic eon characterized by the development of the first igneous and metamorphic rocks and the first marine microorganisms.

Archeology: The systematic study of past human life and culture by the recovery and examination of remaining material evidence, such as graves, buildings, tools, and pottery.

Bathymetric: The measurement of the depth of bodies of water.

Bolide: Geologists use the term "bolide" more often than astronomers do; in geology it indicates a very large impactor. For example, the USGS uses the term to mean a generic large crater-forming projectile "to imply that we do not know the precise nature of the impacting body . . . whether it is a rocky or metallic asteroid, or an icy comet, for example".

Facultative Anadromy: Animals that move from saltwater into freshwater for purposes of spawning in an attempt to avoid predation while securing forage as juveniles.

Catadromy: Animals that migrate from freshwater to the sea for purposes of breeding; eels are an example.

Continental Drift: The concept that continents can drift or move about on the surface of the earth.

Continental Crust: That part of the crust underlying the continents and composed of granitic rocks, generally 35 km (22 miles) thick.

Contingent: Term used to describe a group of fish that engage in a common pattern of seasonal migration between feeding areas, wintering areas, and spawning areas.

Cretaceous Era: Occurred 135 million to 63 million years ago; end of the age of reptiles; appearance of modern insects and flowering plants.

Ebb Tide: That portion of the tidal cycle when seawater is flowing from high levels to lower levels, such as when the water level will fall in a Sound, Bay, estuary or marsh.

EEZ: Federal waters known as the Exclusive Economic Zone.

Escarpment: A more or less continuous cliff formed by erosion or faulting.

Estuary: A body of water formed where freshwater from rivers and streams flows into the ocean, mixing with the seawater.

Euryhaline: Term for fishes that are able to osmoregulate (regulate body salt concentrations) in marine or freshwaters.

Eutrophication: Term 'eutrophic' means well-nourished; thus, 'eutrophication' refers to natural or artificial addition of nutrients to bodies of water and to the effects of the added nutrients . . . . When the effects are undesirable, eutrophication may be considered a form of pollution."

Detritus: Term for undissolved material from the decomposition of organic remains (e.g., the decomposition of dead marine organisms, or materials from decaying algae). It often settles on the estuarine bottom, where it provides an important food source for scavengers such as zooplankton.

DNA: A complex biological molecule (deoxyribonucleic acid) responsible for carrying genetic information (genes).

Facultative Anadromy: Term for the migration of fish that take advantage of freshwater over saltwater for purposes of spawning and feeding

Flood Tide: That portion of the tidal cycle when seawater is flowing from low levels to high levels, such as when the water level will rise in a Sound, Bay, estuary or marsh

Geology: The study of the Earth, the materials of which it is made, the structure of those materials, and the processes acting upon them.

Glacial Erratics: These can range in size from cobbles to boulders transported by glacial ice from their source areas into regions of dissimilar material.

Holocene: The current geologic epoch, dating from 10,000 years ago; also called the Recent Epoch.

Ice Front: The face or down-ice extremity of a glacier.

Hydrophone: An electrical instrument for detecting or monitoring sound under water.

Hz: one thousand (wave frequency) cycles per second.

Jurassic Period: The span of geologic time stretching from 208 to 144 million years ago. The Jurassic Period was when dinosaurs began to dominate the earth.

Kettle: A depression formed in glacial drift by the melting of a remnant block of glacial ice.

Lactic acidosis: A physiological condition characterized by low pH in body tissues and blood. This condition typically occurs when cells receive too little oxygen (hypoxia), due to vigorous activity.

Laurentide Ice Sheet: A major recurring glacier that at its maximum completely covered northern regions of North America east of the Rockies.

Laurasia: The northern hemisphere super-continent of the early Paleozoic: involving continental sections ancestral to North America, Europe and Asia.

Lymphocystis: A chronic waterborne viral disease of marine and freshwater fish affecting the skin & fins.

Markers (DNA): A unique pattern of nucleic acids responsible for specific genetic information, including memory.

Manisseans: Name given to native Block Island Indians.

Mesocosm: Any system larger than a microcosm, but smaller than a macrocosm.

Mesozoic Era: The major division of geologic time between the Paleozoic and Cenozoic eras; represented by three periods, the Triassic, Jurassic, and Cretaceous.

Metamorphosis: If you slept through grammar school, you missed the class about how some insect's larval stages give rise to the pupal stage before miraculously changing into a moth or butterfly.

Moronidae: A taxonomic family of Perciformes (meaning perch like): approx. 400 species of sea bass and grouper; the family Moronidae, of which the striped bass is a member.

Moraine: A linear ridge of sediments deposited by a glacier.

Mycobacteriosis: An infectious disease caused by bacteria and referred to as a "wasting disease" (loss of body mass & weight); such that inflammation, scaring and destruction of vital organs (spleen & kidney) is signaled by reddened skin ulcers.

Nocturnal: Animals that are active at night.

Osmoregulation: The process of regulating water potential in order to keep fluid and electrolyte balance within a cell or organism relative to the surrounding.

Paleozoic: Period of time from 544 million to about 230 million years ago.

Paleo-Indians: Ancestors of the American Indians.

Palisades: Line of cliffs 15 miles (24 kilometers) long of SE New York & NE New Jersey, on the west bank of the Hudson River.

Pangaea: The ultimate super-continent of the late Paleozoic and early Mesozoic eras, composed of all known land masses joined during the Paleozoic. Pangaea began to separate at the end of Triassic Period; the fragments comprise present day continents.

Perigee: The point in a satellite's elliptical path around the earth at which it is closest to the center of the earth.

Phantom Loran numbers: Converted GPS position locations based on discontinued Loran (LOP's) lines of position.

Phylogenetic: Relating to or based on the evolutionary development or history of an organism.

Phytoplankton: Term given to minute, free-floating aquatic plants.

Piscavorous: A fish eating animal.

Plate Tectonics: The processes associated with the interaction of the earth's crustal plates. The processes involve plate collisions, mountain building, subduction of oceanic plates, rifting, development of island arcs and depositional basins.

Pleistocence Epoch: A period of cyclical glacial and interglacial stages; the older of two epochs of the Quarternary Period, 10,000 to 2 million years ago (Holocene) and the younger epoch 0-10,000 years ago.

Proterozoic: The geologic eon characterized by the development of sedimentary rock, shallow seas, and the first soft-bodied, marine invertebrates.

Purse Seine: A net that encircles a school of fish, enclosing it on all sides, top and bottom.

Radiocarbon Dating: A means of determining the absolute age (up to 40,000 years ago) of earth's materials bearing radioactive carbon (carbon 14) measuring decay rate of this isotope.

Recessional Moraine: Moraine formed during a temporary stage of an ice front in the overall process of glacial retreat.

Rift: A crustal fault (cracks) running parallel to the regional structure, such as a plate boundary.

Sandstone: Sedimentary rock composed of layers of sand deposited on flat or a gently sloping surface, compacted and cemented typically by silica, iron oxide, or calcium carbonate.

Stochastic: Situations or models containing a random element, hence unpredictable and without a stable pattern or order.

Stemming: Maintaining the position in a tidal rip by matching the current velocity with the speed and direction of a vessel.

Squiding: Retrieving a lure such as a diamond jig while drifting or stemming in a tidal rip.

Subduction Zone: The crustal region of plate collision whereby heavier crust, like oceanic crust, descend into the earth's interior, while lighter crust, like continental, overrides the descending plate.

Taxonomy: The classification of organisms in an ordered system that indicates natural relationships.

Taxonomic Affinities: Biological characteristic that link groups of organisms together into a distinct category.

Terminal Moraine: The moraine created at the farthest advance of the ice during a glacial stage.

Tertiary Period: Division of geologic time spanning the interval between about 65.5 and 2.6 million years ago.

Tombolo: A sand bar connecting a large island to a smaller one or to a mainland.

Topography: Graphic description of the surface features of a place or region, indicating relative positions and elevations.

Torpor: Term for a condition in which saltwater "wedge" temps begin to drop below 40 degrees Fahrenheit, causing sub-adult stripers to gradually go into a state of hibernation. While in torpor, fish metabolism slows and fish school-up in tight groups that do not feed.

Troll Valve: A mechanical device that controls the hydraulic pressure on the transmission gear's plates, allowing them to slip much like a clutch, reducing shaft rpm.

Watchung Mountains: The Watchung Mountains (once called the Blue Hills) are a group of three long low ridges of volcanic origin, between 400 ft. (122 m) and 500 ft. (152 m) high, located in Union County, NJ.

Wisconsinan Glacial Era: The most recent glacial stages of the Pleistocene Epoch.

Zooplankton: Term given to tiny, free-floating animal organisms in aquatic systems. Unlike phytoplankton, zooplankton cannot produce their own food, and so are consumers. Unlike phyto-plankton, zooplankton cannot produce their own food, and so are consumers.

INDEX

A

Abbott, Gerald, 38
Adamski, Arthur, 272
Allen, Hank, 173–74, 180
Allen, Nelma, 173
Alosa aestivilis, 167
Altson, John, 270
American eel, 91, 93–95, 97–98
American Fisheries Society Symposium 1, 95
American Littoral Society (ALS), 245, 257, 270
American Museum of Natural History, 337
Ammodytes dubius, 131, 166–67, 387
Anderson, Al, 11, 326–28
    fishing adventures, 348–49, 351
    tagging awards and records, 330–31
    vessels owned, 353, 355, 359, 362
    Game Fish Tag and Release, 251, 257, 266, 327
    Over-Winter Striper Secrets, 35, 91
    "What, You Here Again?," 210
Anderson, Royal, 326
angling, 11, 60, 67, 125, 156, 245, 258, 279, 325–26, 332, 334, 336–38, 364, 368
Anguilla rostrata, 93, 95

apogee, 153, 157, 220, 369
Appalachian Mountains, 26, 369
approach, 203
Atlantic Migratory Striped Bass Stock, 85, 88
Atlantic Multidecadal Oscillation (AMO), 87
Atlantic Ocean, 26
Atlantic States Marine Fisheries Commission (ASMFC), 260–61, 332
Atlantic Striped Bass Act of 1984, *9, 12*

B

Babcock, Elmer, 102–3
Baby Beach, 52, 185
Bait Tail Fishing (Reinfelder), 352
Ballard's Beach, 52–53, 186
Ball's, 190
Barley, George, 331
Barlow's, 188
Barnes, Duncan, 366
Barnes Ice Cap, 29
Beacon Hill, 24, 173
Beane Point, 190
Bellantoni, Nicholas, 38
bell buoy, 238
Benson, Frederick J., 47–48

375

Research, Reflections and Recollections of Block Island, 47
Bernau, Harry, 326
Bird, The. *See* Fidreich, Mark
Black Rock Beach, 53, 188–89, 230, 239–41, 316
Blackstone, William, 44
Block, Adrian, 43, 45
Block Channel, 24
Block Island, 23–24, 26, 28–33
   climate of, 52
   and East Coast American Indians, 36–37
   genesis of, 24, 26, 28–29, 31–32, 38
   geographic position, 149
   tides and currents, 149
   timeline of, 54–56
Block Island Conservancy, 52, 56
Block Island Geology: History, Processes and Field Excursions (Sirkin), 26
Block Island Historical Society Museum, 54
Block Island National Wildlife Refuge, 54
Block Island Race Week, 47
blueback herring, 167
Bluff Head, 189
Bluffs Beach, 53
Borsay, Slim, 355
Boyd, Avis, 12
break, 110, 119–20, 182, 202
Broatch, Kierran, 318
Brown, Wally, 355
Browning, George, 352
Burke, Tom, 328
Burns, Brad, 15, 365

C

Caligus elongatus, 81, 341, 344–47, 385, 388, 390
Calvert Cliffs, 28
Carlsen, Pam, 258, 263, 276
Carole Jaworski, 37–38
Carroll, Staff, 355, 357
Casas, Maria, 15, 345
Castonnguay, Martin, 95
catadromy, 93, 369
Cat Rock Cove, 187
Chaffee, John, 9
Charlestown Beach, 189
Charlestown Moraine, 31
charter fishing, 18, 92, 156, 194, 216, 334, 348, 353, 359
Chase, Brad, 246
Chesapeake Bay, 33
Church, Isaac, 44
Clay Head, 23, 26, 30, 53, 131, 158, 161
Coastal Conservation Association (CCA), 247, 365–66
Coast Guard Beach, 53
Cole, John, 365
Coleman, Tim, 150–51, 210, 358
Conflans, Antoine de, 42
Connecticut River, 24, 30, 43, 54, 100, 168
Conti, Matt, 317
Cooneymus, 189
Cooperative Tagging Program, 285
Corte-Real, Miguel, 41
Cow Cove, 53, 183
Crescent Beach, 52, 185
crust, 25
Cunningham, Rip, 366

D

Dacron, 109–11, 113, 139
Dead Man's Cove, 189
Dement, Jeff, 15, 261, 277–79, 296, 299, 307, 309
diamond jigs, 141, 143, 145
Dickens Point, 189
Dighton Rock, 41

Dodge, Trustrum, 51
Dorie's Cove, 189
double hump, 156, 199, 202, 209, 215, 237
Double Hump, 145, 162, 194, 204, 213, 215
Douton, Kerry, 138
Downie, Robert M., 52
downriggers, 107, 112, 119
Dump, The, 190
Durbin, Ted, 15, 345

E

Earhart, Amelia, 56
Earle, Sylvia, 331
East End, 199
easterly winds, 161
Eaton, Lloyd, 30
   "Prehistoric Fauna of Block Island, The," 36
ebb tide, 126, 152, 154–56, 161, 196, 202, 207, 216, 292, 370
ectoparasites, 340
Eldridge Tide and Pilot Book, 150, 153, 159, 203, 238
elvers, 97
Emergency Striped Bass Study, 12, 285
Endeavor Shoals, 30
Endicott, John, 43
Enquist, Swede, 102
environmental sex determination (ESD), 93
European sea bass, 65
Evanoff, Vlad, 329, 360
Exclusive Economic Zone (EEZ), 122, 222

F

Facultative Anadromy, 65, 369–70
Fidreich, Mark, 237
fishfinder, 153, 204, 213, 215, 217–18, 225, 227, 232, 240, 355, 360

fish lice, 17, 80, 82–83, 273, 304–5, 309, 340–44, 346–47
Fitzgerald, Paul, 349
flat dark water, 179
flood tide, 125, 152, 155–56, 194, 199, 211, 215, 223, 237, 239, 349
fly fishing, 182, 190, 272, 365–66
Fondren, Walter, 365
Fountaine, Wilfred, 355
Franklin, H. Bruce, 73
   Most Important Fish in the Sea: Menhaden and America, The, 13
Fred Benson Town Beach, 52
Furman, Scott, 331

G

gaff, 176, 351
Gail Frances, 352
Gallup, Barry, 360
Gamakatsu, 217, 231, 317
Game Fish Tag and Release (Anderson), 251, 257, 266, 327
"Geology of Block Island, The" (Marsh), 36
Gigging, 91
Gilchrest, Wayne T., 331
glacial erratics, 29, 50, 370
glomeruli, 66
Gorilla Braid, 320, 323
Grace's Cove, 189
Graves, John, 246
Great Point, 188
Greene, Marshall, 138
Green Hill Cove, 186, 240
Greenspan, Ruth, 39
Groves Point, 183
Guthry, Margaret, 55

H

Hall, Rick, 181
Harborside Inn, 53
Hardy, Thomas, 55
Harry, E. K., 330
Harvey, Zach, 118, 150, 161, 314, 319, 322
haywire twist, 110
header, 116
Heinold, George, 329–30
Homo sapiens sapiens, 37
Hooter Buoy, 238
Hudson, 33
Hudson River Foundation (HRF), 84, 259, 263, 280–81
Hummock, 198, 212

I

Inner Rip, 195, 241
internal anchor tag, 259, 263, 281, 283
International Commission on Zoological Nomenclature (ICZN), 67
International Game Fish Association (IGFA), 94, 98, 190, 318, 324, 330–31, 336–39, 363
Isaiahs Gully, 184
Island Free Library, 51, 56

J

J & B Tackle, 138
Japanese sea bass, 65
Jimmis, Frank, 329, 350–51
Jones, Phil, 74
June Bug, 209

K

Karas, Nick, 66

keel sinkers, 119
kettle ponds, 32
kettles, 32, 53, 371
Kidd, William, 55
King, Matt, 316
kink, 107, 110, 120
Kleckner, Robert C., 95
Krueger, W. H., 92–93

L

lactic acidosis, 246, 259, 371
Lacy, Richard, 328
La Dauphine, 42
La Normande, 42
Laurentide Ice Sheet, 28–29, 371
Legnos, Peter, 360
Lema, Dick, 208, 356
Lenape Indians, 42
Lepeophtheirus salmonis, 344, 385, 388
leptocephali, 94, 96
Lewis Point, 189, 223, 238
Lighthouse Cove, 187
Linton, Bob, 358
Little Shooters, 137, 139–40
Lockwood Gorge, 326
Logwood Cove, 161, 190, 237, 241
Loligo pealeii, 169
longfin inshore squid, 169
Long Island Sound, 41, 54–55, 60, 138, 149–50, 156, 202, 291, 318
Lowe, J., 72
Luhr-Jensen J-Plugs, 139
lymphocystis, 71–73, 371, 386

M

Macmillan, Graham, 268
Magnuson-Stevens Fishery Conservation Act, 257
Mancini, Bill, 353

Manisseans, 35–37, 41, 44, 54–55, 371
Mansion Beach, 52–53, 184–85
Marsh, Othniel, 29
  "Geology of Block Island, The," 36
Martha's Vineyard, 24, 26, 38–39, 84
Mashantucket Pequots, 35
Massachusetts Striped Bass Association, 10
Mather, Frank, 330, 359
McBride, Kevin, 37, 39
McCleave, James D., 95
McReynolds, Albert, 313–14, 324
Meltzoff, Stanley, 331
menhaden, 73, 239
Meyer, Chuck, 328, 360
middens, 36
Middle Rip, 125, 196
Minchillo, Vincent, 15, 271
Mitchell, Ed, 366
Mohegan Bluffs, 53–54, 187
Mohegan Bluff Stairway, 188
Mohegan Sun Casino, 35
Mola, Ricky, 144
moon tides, 126, 150–51, 153–54, 156–57, 162, 206, 216, 220, 349, 357
Morone saxatilis, 33, 39, 59, 65, 292, 329, 342, 345, 384, 388
Most Important Fish in the Sea: Menhaden and America, The (Franklin), 73
Mr. Striped Bass. *See* Pond, Robert A.
Murphy, Ron, 15, 205
Mustad Limerick, 134
mycobacteriosis, 73–80, 88, 289, 364, 371, 387
Myerson, Greg, 313, 318–19, 322–24

N

nail knot, 108–9, 139
Narragansett, 36

Neoprene, 174
"Neurobehavioral Nature of Fishes and the Question of Awareness and Pain, The" (Rose), 249
New England Fisheries Management Council (NEFMC), 254
New Shoreham, 38, 45–47, 51, 55, 197
nociception, 248
North American striper, 65
North Bar, 200–202, 205, 236, 241, 355
Northeast Fishery Science Center (NEFSC), 260
North Light, 47
North Rip, 125–26, 155–56, 195–96, 199–200, 202, 208
Northwest Passage, 43

O

offshore sand lance, 166–67, 169, 195
Oldham, John, 43–44
Old Harbor, 49, 52, 56, 156, 180, 186, 190, 240–41
Old Harbor Point, 186, 240–41
Old Whale Rock, 240
Oliveira, Ken, 93
Onrust, 54
Osprey Tackle, 133, 136
otoliths, 64
Over-Winter Striper Secrets (Anderson), 35, 91, 288, 290, 383

P

Paleo-Indians, 40, 371
Palma, Lou, 352
Pangaea, 25–26, 372
panmictic, 93
Paterson, Jim, 355
Peanut, 221, 225, 238, 316
Pebbly Beach, 186

People for the Ethical Treatment of Animals (PETA), 247
Pequot War, 44
perigee tides, 153
Phantom, 181
Plate Tectonics, 26
plugs, 178
Point Judith, Battle of, 51
pollution, 71
Poly, William, 15, 341–42, 345
Pond, Robert A., 9–13, 328, 353
Poop Chute, 186
Pots and Kettles, 53
Pounders, 190
Preble, Dave, 366
"Prehistoric Fauna of Block Island, The" (Eaton), 36
Price, Jim, 73
Princess Augusta, 55
Putnam, Ken, 352

Q

Quantum Reels, 323

R

Raymond, Joshua, 55
Raymond, Mercy (née Sands), 55
recessional moraines, 31, 124
Reiger, George, 69
  Striped Bass Chronicles, The, 69
Reinfelder, Al, 352
  Bait Tail Fishing, 352
Research, Reflections and Recollections of Block Island (Benson), 47
Rhode Island, 40
Rhode Island Saltwater Anglers Association (RISAA), 331
rip
  casting, 128

drifting, 129
fishing, 59, 122, 200
Ristori, Al, 98, 360
Ritchie, E. C., 197
R. J. Schaefer Salt Water Fishing Contest, 101
Roadside Geology of Connecticut and Rhode Island (Skehan), 31
rockfish, 73–74, 76, 79
Rodman's Hollow, 54
Rose, James D., 248–49
  "Neurobehavioral Nature of Fishes and the Question of Awareness and Pain, The," 249
Rosko, Milt, 330, 352, 360
  Secrets of Striped Bass Fishing, 330
Ross, David, 366
Ryan, Jack, 355

S

Sabatowski, Frank, 209
Sabo, Dennis, 327
Sachem Pond, 53
Samson, Jack, 331
sand eels, 86, 125, 130–32, 134, 141, 145, 152, 165–66, 183, 189–90, 196, 200, 238
sand launce, 131
Sands, James, 55
Sandy Point, 53–54, 56, 183, 190–91, 197, 199, 201–2, 236, 355
Sargasso Sea, 93, 95–96
Schooner Point, 189
Scituate Saltwater Anglers, 349, 355
Scotch Beach, 52, 185
sea lice, 82, 344–45, 383–84
Secrets of Striped Bass Fishing (Rosko), 330
Sekora, John, 195
Settler's Rock, 53

Shepard, Gary, 278
Sirkin, Leslie, 26, 29
   Block Island Geology: History, Processes and Field Excursions, 26
Skehan, James, 31
   Roadside Geology of Connecticut and Rhode Island, 31
Skomal, Greg, 246
Smith, Don, 226, 314
Smith, John, 43, 51
Smith's Isle, 43
Snake Hole, 188
Snappy Cab, 173
southeast light, 47, 49, 239, 241
Southeast Point, 187
Southwest Ledge, 30, 155, 158, 165, 208, 221–22, 226, 231, 236–38, 241, 313, 357, 361
Southwest Point, 189
spools, 113
Starcraft Mariner, 352
State Beach, 52
Steve's Cove, 189
Stone, John, 43
Stone, Livingston, 69–70
Stonington, Battle of, 56
strike zone, 205, 207, 213
striped bass, 9, 60, 63–64
   adaptive capabilities, 67–68
   biological history of, 64–66
   freshwater, 68
   great outposts for, 164
   landlocked, 67
   life cycle of, 60, 62–63
   migratory behavior of, 63
   transcontinental, 69
Striped Bass Chronicles, The (Reiger), 69
striper fish lice, 274, 306, 344
Stripers Forever, 76, 364–67
Sub Buoy, 30
sweet spot, 141

Swordfish II, 352
Sylvester, Jerry, 124, 329
Szabo, Joe, 314, 355

T

tagging, 245, 251–53, 263, 282–83, 325
Tatorie, Rose, 355
terminal moraine, 32, 46
Tessier, Larry, 329
Thomson, Betty, 29
Thornton, Harold, 358
Throckmorton, S. R., 69
tidal rips, 125, 129, 158, 361
tides, 151–55, 157, 220
Tiger, 54
Tilson Cove, 187
Tom's Cove, 188
Town Beach, 52, 92, 99, 185
troll valves, 127, 200, 213, 363
Tucker, Clifford, 92, 99–102

U

U-853, 54
umbrella rig, 125, 131, 135, 166, 195, 230
Underhill, John, 45
Underwater Naturalist, 260–61, 269, 276
U.S. Fish and Wildlife Service (USFWS), 245, 247, 259, 265, 270, 285–87

V

Vail Beach, 188
Vane, Henry, 43
Verrazano, Giovanni da, 41–42, 54
Vican, Peter, 227, 313–14
Vikings, 41

Virginia Institute of Marine Science
(VIMS), 74, 246

W

Waldman, John, 15, 33, 84, 329
Wampanoag Indians, 42
Washington, George, 49
wasting disease, 74, 76
West Beach, 190
Whale Rock, 187, 240–41
"What, You Here Again?" (Anderson), 210
Willi, Christopher, 190–91
Williams, Roger, 39, 45, 384
winder, 113–14
wire line, 107–8, 111
wire lining, 118–21
Wire Sources, 117
Woods Hole Oceanographic Institute (WHOI), 330, 359

SELECTED REFERENCES

Ahrenholz, D. W. 1991. Population biology and life history of the North American menhadens (*Brevoortia spp.*) *Mar Fish Rev* 53:3–19.

Anderson, A. 2009. *Over-winter Striper Secrets.* Xlibris Inc.

Beitch, I. 1963. A histomorphological comparison of the urinary systems in the serranid fishes, *Roccus saxatilis* and *Roccus americanus*. *Chesapeake Science* 4:75–83.

Bellantoni, N., 1987. Faunal resource availability and prehistoric cultural selection on Block Island, Rhode Island. Unpublished PhD diss., Univ. of Connecticut.

Benson, F. J. 1977. *Research, reflection, and recollections of Block Island.* The Utter Co., Westerly, RI.

Bigelow and Schroder. 2002. Fishes of the Gulf or Maine. Eds. Bruce B. Collette and Grace Klein-MacPhee. 3rd ed. Smithsonian Institution Press, Washington and London.

Boreman, J., and R. Klauda. 1988. Distributions of early life stages of striped bass in the Hudson estuary, 1974–1979. *Amer. Fish. Soc. Mono.* 4:53–8.

Boxaspen, K. 2006. A review of the biology and genetics of sea lice. *ICES Journal of Marine Science* 63:1304–1316.

Boxshall, G. 1974. Infections with parasitic copepods in North Sea marine fishes. *Jour. Marine Biol. Assoc. of the UK* 54:355–372.

Brodziak, J. K. T., and W. K. Macy III. 1996. Growth of long-finned squid, *Loligo pealei*, in the northwest Atlantic. *Fish. Bull.* (U.S.) 94:212–236.

Bruno, D. W., and J. Stone. 1990. The role of saithe, *Pollachius virens* L., as host for the sea lice, *Lepeophtherius salmonis* and *Caligus elongatus* Nordmann. *Aquaculture* 89:201–207.

Carson, R. L. 1941. *Under the Sea-wind*. Oxford University Press, NY.

Caulkins, F. M. *History of Norwich, CT: From its settlement in 1660 to 1845*. Pequot Press, Chester, CT.

Costello, M. 2006. Ecology of sea lice parasitic on farmed and wild fish. *Trends in Parasit.* 22(10): 475–483.

Daoust, D. 2011. From ROARING BESSIE to SCRIMSHAW. *Wooden Boat*. July/August, 83.

Diodoti, P. J. 1996. Mortality of striped bass hooked and released in salt water. Trans. *Amer. Fish. Soc.* 125:300–307.

Dunning, D. J., J. R. Waldman, et al. 2006. Dispersal of age 2+ striped bass out of the Hudson River. *Amer. Fish. Soc. Symp.* 51:287–294.

Eaton, G. F. 1898. The prehistoric fauna of Block Island—shell heaps. *Amer. Jour. of Science*. 4th ser. Ed. S. Dana.

Ernst, J. 1932. *Roger Williams, New England Firebrand*. Macmillan Co., NY.

Franklin, H. B. 2007. *The most important fish in the sea*. Island Books.

Gauthier, D., et al. 2008. Mycobacteriosis-associated mortality in wild striped bass (*Morone saxatilis*) from Chesapeake Bay, USA. *Ecological Applications* 18:1718–1727.

Gross, M. 1987. Evolution of diadromy in fishes. *Amer. Fish. Soc. Symp.* 1:14–25.

Gross, M., R. Coleman, and R. McDowall. 1988. Aquatic productivity and evolution of diadromous fish migration. *Science* (AAAS) Mar. 11, 1291–1293.

Heinle, D. R., et al. 1977. Contribution of tidal marshlands to mid-Atlantic estuarine food chains. *Estuarine Processes*, Vol. ???????

Hogans, W. E., and D. J. Trudeau 1989. Preliminary studies of the biology of sea lice *Caligus elongatus* and **Lepeophtherius salmonis (Copepoda; Caligoida) on cage cultured salmonids in the lower Bay of Fundy. Canadian Tech. Report of Fish. and Aqua. Sci.** 1715.

Hogans, W. 1994. Communications: Cage cultured striped bass in marine waters of the lower Bay of Fundy. *The Progressive Fish-Culturist* 56:255–257.

Hurst, T., and D. Conover. 2001. Diet and consumption rates of overwintering YOY striped bass, *Moronone saxatilis*, in the Hudson River. *Fish. Bull.* 99:545–553.

Jacobsen, J., and E. Gaard. 1997. Open-ocean infestation by salmon lice (*Lepeophtheirus salmonis*): Comparison of wild and escaped farmed salmon (*Salmo salar* L). *ICES J. Mar. Sci.* 54:1113–1119.

Jackson, D., S. Deady, D. Hasset, and Y. Leahy. 2000. *Caligus elongatus* as parasites of farmed salmonids in Ireland. *Contributions to Zoology* 69:65–70.

Jaworski, C. 1990. Discovery on Block Island; 2,500-year-old village predates agriculture. *Nor'easter*, Magazine of the Northeast Sea Grant Programs 2(2): 32–37.

Jennings, S., and M. G. Pawson. 1992. The origin and recruitment of bass *Dicentrarchus labrax* to nursery areas. *Jour. Mar. Biol. Assn. UK* 72:199–212.

Jones, H. 1968. *Fish migration*. Edward Arnold Ltd., London.

Jordan, D. S., and B. W. Evermann. 1903. *American food and game fishes*. Doubleday, NY.

Kabata, Z. 1979. *Parasitic Copepoda of British fishes*. The Ray Society, London.

Karas, N., 2000. *The complete book of striped bass fishing*. Lyons Press, CT.

Keller, A. A., P. H. Doering, S. P. Kelly, and B. K. Sullivan. 1990. Growth of juvenile Atlantic memhaden, *Brevootia tyrannus* (Pisces: Clupeidae) in MERI. Mesocosms: Effects of eutrophication. *Limnol. Oceanog.* 35:109–122.

Kier, W. M. 1982. The functional morphology of the musculature of squid (Loliginidae). Arms and tentacles. *J. Morph.* 172:179–192.

Krantz, G. E. 1970. Lymphocystis in striped bass, *Roccus saxatilis*, in Chesapeake Bay. *Chesapeake Sci.* 11:137–139.

Krueger, W., and K. Oliviera. 1999. Evidence for environmental sex determination in the American eel, *Anguila rostrata*. *Environ. Biol. of Fishes* 55:381–389.

Lange, A. M. T. 1982. Long-finned squid, *Loligo pealei*. In: Grosslein, M. D., and T. R. Azarovitz, eds. *Fish distribution. MESA New York Bight Atlas Monograph 15*. Albany, NY: NY Sea Grant Institute, 133–135.

Langton, R. W., and R. E. Bowman. 1977. An abridged account of predator-prey interactions for some northwest Atlantic species of fish and squid. *U.S. Natl. Mar. Fish. Serv. Northeast Fish. Cent.* Woods Hole Lab. Ref. Doc. 77-17.

Leach, D. 1958. *Flintlock and Tomahawk; New England in King Philips War.* Norton & Co., NY.

Livermore, S. T. 1876. *A history of Block Island from its discovery to the present.* Hartford, CT: Case, Lockwood & Brainard.

Marsh, O. C. 1896. The geology of Block Island. Trans. *New York Acad. Sci.* 4th ser., 2, 295–298, 375–377.

Mansueti, R. J. 1961. Age, growth, and movements of the striped bass, *Roccus saxatilis*, taken in size selective fishing gear in Maryland. *Ches. Sci.* 2:9–36.

McCleave, J. D., R. C. Kleckner, and M. Castonnguay. 1987. Reproductive sympatry of American and European eels and implications for migrations and taxonomy. American Fisheries Society Symposium 1.

Meade, T. 1988. Sportfishing: $100 million RI industry. *The Providence Journal Bulletin*, Feb. 2, Business Section.

Miner, R. 1950. *Field book of seashore life*. Van Rees Press, NY.

Morison, S. E. 1971. *The European discovery of America: The northern voyages*. New York: Oxford University Press, 283. ISBN 0192159410.

Nelson, G. A., and M. R. Ross. 1991. Biology and population changes of northern sand lance (*Ammodytes dubius*) from the Gulf of Maine to the Middle Atlantic BBight. *J. Northw. Atl. Fish. Sci.* 11:11–27.

Nicholson, W. R. 1978. Movements and population structures of Atlantic menhaden indicated by tag returns. *Estuaries* 1:141–150.

Nigrelli, R. F., and G. D. Ruggieri. 1965. Studies on the viral diseases of fishes. Spontaneous and experimentally induced cellular hypertrophy (lymphocystis disease) in fishes of the New York Aquarium, with a report of new cases and an annotated bibliography (1874–1965). *Zoologica* (NY) 50:83–96.

Nolf, D., and G. L. Stringer. 1996. *Cretaceous fish otoliths: A synthesis of the North American record. Mesozoic fishes: Systematics and paleoecology*, 433–459.

Oines, O., and P. A. Heuch. 2007. *Caligus elongatus* Nordmann genotypes on wild and farmed fish. *Jour. of Fish Diseases* 30:81–91.

_____. 2005. Identification of sea louse species of the genus *Caligus* using mtDNA. *Jour. of Marine Biology of the UK* 85:73–70.

Oines, O., J. H. Simonsen, J. A. Knutsen, and P. A. Heuch. 2006. Host preferences of *Caligus elongatus* Nordmann in the laboratory and its implications for Atlantic cod aquaculture. *Jour. of Fish. Diseases* 29:167–174.

Panek, F. M., and T. Bobo. 2006. Striped bass mycobacteriosis: A zoonotic disease of concern in Chesapeake Bay. In: Ottinger, C., and J.M. Jacobs, eds. Proceedings of the USGS/NOAA workshop on mycobacteriosis in striped bass, May 7–10, 2006, Annapolis, Maryland. USGS scientific investigations report 2006-52416/NOAA technical memorandum NOS NCCOS41.

Piasecki, W. 1996. The developmental stages of *Caligus elongatus* von Nordmann, 1832 (Copepoda; Caligidae). *Canadian Jour. of Zool.* 74:1459–1478.

Prosek, J. 2010. *Eels*. HarperCollins, NY.

Reiger, G. 1997. The striped bass chronicles. Lyons and Burford.

Revie, C. W., G. Gettingby, J. W. Treasurer, and G. Race. 2002. The epidemiology of the sea lice *Caligus elongatus* Nordmann in marine aquaculture of the Atlantic salmon *Salmo salar* L. Scotland. *Jour. Fish Diseases* 25:39–399.

Rhodes, M., H. Kator, I. Kaattari, D. Gauthier, W. Vogelbein, and C. A. Ottinger. 2004. Isolation and characterization of mycobacteria from striped bass (*Morone saxatilis*) from the Chesapeake Bay. *Dis Aquat Organ.* 61:41–51.

Ristori, A. 2010. Would you release a fifty? *The Fisherman*, NE Edit., 21, 2010.

—— 2011. American eel considered for endangered species. *The Fisherman*, NE Edit., 41, 2011.

Ritchie, E. C. 1975. *Block Island: Lore and legends*. Oxford Press, RI.

Ritchie, G. 1997. The host transfer ability of *Lepeophtheirus salmonis* (Copepoda: Caligidae) from farmed Atlantic salmon, *Salmo salar*. *Jour. of Fish Diseases* 20:153–157.

Sampson, J. 2011. The role of neuromasts in non-visual feeding of larval striped bass (*Morone saxatilis*). Master's thesis, Nova Scotia Agricultural College.

Scott, W. B., and M. G. Scott. 1988. Atlantic fishes of Canada. *Can. Bull. Fish. Aqua. Sci.* 219, 731 pp.

Secor, D. H. 2002. Estuarine dependency and life history evolution in temperate sea basses. *Proc. 70th Ann. Internat. Symp. Jap. Sci. Fish. Soc.*

Setzler, E., et al. 1980. Synopsis of biological data on striped bass, *Morone saxatilis* (Walbaum). NOAA Tech. Rept. NMFS Circ. No. 433, 69 pp.

Sheffield, W. 1876. *Historical sketch of Block Island*. Sanborn and Co., Newport, RI.

Sindermann, C. J., 1990. *Principal diseases of marine fish and shellfish*. Vol. 1, 521 pp., Academic Press, NY.

Sirkin, L. A., 1994. *Block Island geology: History, processes, and field excursions*. Book and Tackle Shop, RI.

Stine C., A. Baya, J. Salierno, M. Kollner, and A. Kane. 2005. Mycobacterial infection in laboratory-maintained menhaden (*Brevoortia tyrannus*). *Jour. Aqua. Animal Health.* 17:380–5.

Summers, W. C. 1971. Age and growth of *Loligo pealei*, a population study of the common Atlantic coast squid. *Biol. Bull.* (Woods Hole) 141:189–201. Thomson, B. F. 1977. *The changing face of New England*. Houghton Mifflin.

Tsukamoto, K., and J. Aoyama. 1998. Evolution of freshwater eels of the genus *Anguilla*: A probable scenario. *Environ. Biol. Fishes* 52:139–148.

Tveskov, M. 1997. Maritime settlement and subsistence along the southern New England coast: Evidence from Block Island. *North American Archeologist* 18(4): 343–361.

Waldman, John, 1999. *Heartbeats in the Muck*. Lyons Press, NY.

Walters, Keith. 1990. *Chesapeake stripers*. Aerie House.

White, R. E., Jr., and L. F. White. 2012. *Eldridge tide and pilot book*. Medfield, MA.

Winters, G. H. 1989. Life history parameters of sand lances (*Ammodytes spp.*) from the coastal waters of eastern Newfoundland. *J. Northw. Atl. Fish. Sci.* 9:5–11.

Woodworth, J. B., and E. Wigglesworth. 1934. Geography and geology of the region including Cape Cod, the Elizabeth Islands, Nantucket, Martha's Vineyard, No Man's Land, and Block Island. *Memoirs of the Museum of Comparative Zoölogy at Harvard College.* v. 52, Museum of Comparative Zoology.

Wootten, R., J. W. Smith, and E. A. Needham. 1982. Aspects of the biology of the parasitic copepods *Lepeophtheirus salmonis* and *Caligus elongatus* on farmed salmonids, and their treatment. *Proc. Royal Soc. of Edinburgh* 81B, 185–197.